English Mercuries

EMBLEME 13.

WHat coward *Stoicke*, or blunt captaine will
Dif-like this *Vnion*, or not labour ſtill
To reconcile the *Arts* and *victory*?
Since in themſelues Arts haue this quality,
To vanquiſh errours traine: what other than
Should loue the Arts, if not a valiant man?
Or, how can he reſolue to execute,
That hath not firſt learn'd to be reſolute?
If any ſhall oppoſe this, or diſpute,
Your great example ſhall their ſpite confute.

E 2

English Mercuries
Soldier Poets
in *the Age of Shakespeare*

Adam N. McKeown

Vanderbilt University Press
Nashville

© 2009 by Vanderbilt University Press
Nashville, Tennessee 37235
All rights reserved
First printing 2009

Frontispiece: Emblem 13 from H.G. [Henry Goodyere?], *The Mirrour of Maiestie, or The Badges of Honor Conceitedly Emblazoned* (London: 1618). Reproduced with the permission of Rare Books and Manuscripts, Special Collections Library, Pennsylvania State University Libraries.

Designed by Dariel Mayer

Library of Congress Cataloging-in-Publication Data

McKeown, Adam (Adam N.)
English mercuries : soldier poets in the age
of Shakespeare / Adam N. McKeown.
p. cm.
Includes bibliographical references and index.
ISBN 978-0-8265-1662-6 (cloth : alk. paper)
ISBN 978-0-8265-1663-3 (pbk. : alk. paper)
1. English poetry—Early modern, 1500–1700—History
and criticism. 2. War in literature. 3. Soldiers' writings,
English—History and criticism. 4. Churchyard, Thomas,
1520?–1604—Criticism and interpretation. 5. Donne, John,
1572–1631—Criticism and interpretation. 6. Gascoigne, George,
d. 1577—Criticism and interpretation. 7. Harington, John,
Sir, 1560–1612—Criticism and interpretation. 8. Jonson, Ben,
1573?–1637—Criticism and interpretation. I. Title.
PR535.W3M35 2009
821'.3093581—dc22
2008045732

*To the memory of 1st Lt. Brandon R. Dronet
and the marines of Heavy Helicopter Squadron 464,
for whom it will always be Christmas Eve 2005*

Contents

List of Illustrations ix

Preface xi

Ecole Lemonier: An Introduction 1

1. English Mercuries 21
2. Men, Money, Iron, and Bread 43
3. Thomas Churchyard's "Valiant Soldiers" and the "Public State" 63
4. A Tale of Two Cities: George Gascoigne's Antwerp and *Alarum for London* 83
5. John Donne's Emblem of War 102
6. John Harington's Journey Home 125
7. Remembering Soldiers: Ben Jonson 144

Notes 165

Works Cited 181

Index 195

Illustrations

Figure 1: The door of the Ecole Lemonier, the schoolhouse aboard Camp Lemonier, a forward antiterrorism base in Djibouti (2006)   3

Figure 2: First page of *The English Mercurie*, an apocryphal Elizabethan newspaper fabricated by Philip Yorke, second Earl of Hardwicke, in the eighteenth century   22

Figure 3: Engraving of Adlington Hall, Cheshire, from Joseph Nash's *The Mansions of England in the Olden Time* (1869–1872)   26

Figure 4: Engraving of a fireplace in a gatehouse in Kenilworth, Warwickshire, from Joseph Nash's *The Mansions of England in the Olden Time* (1869–1872)   27

Figure 5: Sketch of the Swan theater by contemporary observer Johannes de Witt (1596)   29

Figure 6: Nineteenth-century woodcut, after the lost original, of George Gascoigne with the motto "Tam Marti quam Mercurio"   33

Figure 7: Engraving of Walter Raleigh with the motto "Tam Marti quam Mercurio," by Robert Vaughn after Simon de Passe (1614)   33

Figure 8: "The Plat for Incamping," from Thomas Styward's *The Pathway to Martial Discipline* (1582)   55

Figure 9: Engraving by William Marshall of John Donne in military garb, dated 1591. Frontispiece to the 1635 edition of *The Poems*.   103

Figure 10: "Ex Bello, pax," an emblem from Geoffrey Whitney's *Choice of Emblems* (1586)   109

Figure 11: "The watchers of peace and war," an emblem from Claude Paradin's *Heroical Devices of M. Claudius Paradin* (1591)   111

Figure 12: Engraving from book 1 of John Harington's *Orlando Furioso in English Heroical* Verse (1591)   128

Figure 13: Engraving from book 15 of John Harington's *Orlando Furioso in English Heroical* Verse (1591)   129

Figure 14: Engraving by William Hole of Prince Henry at the lance, from Michael Drayton's *Poly-Olbion* (1612)   149

Figure 15: Portrait of Prince Henry in battledress by Isaac Oliver (ca. 1612)   150

Preface

THROUGHOUT THIS BOOK I have modernized the spellings in the early texts I have quoted because I want them to be as alive and as familiar to modern readers as possible. I have, however, left the titles in their original form in the bibliography and notes. I have not altered the grammar, nor have I substituted modern words for their early modern forms. Since the names of many of the writers who appear in this book are spelled variously, I deferred to the author headings in the Folger Shakespeare Library catalogue for guidance on which spellings to use.

I would not have been able to write this book without the advice and guidance of the scholars who taught me along the way, Elizabeth Hageman, Rachel Trubowitz, Brigitte Bailey, Leonard Barkan, Ernest Gilman, Arthur Kinney, Karen Ordahl Kupperman, Evelyn Tribble, Nigel Smith, to name a few. The collections and staff of the British Library have been invaluable, and the Folger Shakespeare Library has been a second home. Many of the readers I met there over the years have lent their time, their eyes, and their wisdom to this project. In particular I would like to acknowledge the help of Wayne Lee, Will West, Todd Butler, Diana Solomon, and Jackson Boswell. I would also like to acknowledge Thomas Heffernan and Michael Ames, who were instrumental in stewarding this project through to its current form.

I would especially like to thank Margit Longbrake, Jennifer Fleischner, and Judith Baumel for their unwavering intellectual and personal support.

Lastly, I would like to recognize the service members who took my Shakespeare class at Camp Lemonier, Djibouti, in 2005. Were it not for that distraction and their questions, I would never have recognized that this book needed to be written in the first place.

English Mercuries

Ecole Lemonier
An Introduction

THIS BOOK BEGAN in the small African nation of Djibouti, a stretch of barren and yet strangely beautiful desert on the shores of the Gulf of Aden north of Somalia. Djibouti's claims to fame are few, resources for Shakespeare scholarship not among them. It is said to be the hottest continuously inhabited place on the planet and one of the poorest, but the Djiboutian people are proud of their country and its fragile independence, which owes much to the willingness of its two major ethnic groups to cooperate in building (or rebuilding) their part of the postcolonial Horn of Africa. For the past several years Djibouti has hosted a forward antiterrorism base quietly vital to the war in the Middle East that is ongoing as I write. It was because of that war that I came to be in Djibouti at all. I was one of the thousands of what I like to think Shakespeare would have called "warriors for the working-day," recalled to military service in support of a war without borders and scarcely a name.[1] I began writing this book there in that ancient desert.

To pass the time of my deployment more constructively I offered to teach a Shakespeare class to anyone aboard the camp who wished to take it. Because so many junior enlisted reservists are college students for whom deployment wipes out an academic year, I had no trouble filling the tent that served as our classroom, and my home institution was happy to offer each of the students credit for the class free of charge. Mine—ours—is one of the nicer stories to come out of a war that was up to that point so filled with bad news.

One of the most surprising things about the class was how it was more like any other Shakespeare survey course than not.[2] The younger students were preoccupied with what they might do after class and with what other young people were doing while they were stuck *in* class, even though there was almost nothing else to do. The older students were grateful for a reason to put their professional responsibilities aside for an hour and chip away at bachelor's degrees that had become lifelong projects. Most tried hard to read the plays but entered the Ecole Lemonier, as our tent was called (figure 1), with only a basic understanding of the plot. They were happy enough, most nights, to sit back and listen to me explain it all to them. It could have been any night class in the United States.

A "little academe / Still and contemplative in living art" it was not, however.[3] The relentless thumping of heavy helicopters and transport planes was our constant companion. Other differences announced themselves—alerts on the public address system, a runner excusing his interruption to call one of the officers back to the operations center, an empty chair whose wonted occupant was "downrange" in support of various activities in the troubled and lawless regions abutting Somalia. This book emerged from one of those articulations of difference, a subtle one. One night we were discussing *Henry V*. I was asked if Shakespeare ever fought in a war. The question is familiar to anyone who has taught *Henry V* to people reading it for the first time, and it is informed by Shakespeare's sensitive and searching representations of war in that play, from the anxious campfire gossip to the glorious Saint Crispian's Day speech in which Henry addresses his outnumbered men as "we happy few, we band of brothers" (4.3.60). So strongly does this speech continue to resonate among soldiers that the camp sergeant major had it posted on his office door.

The answer I gave will be no less familiar to Shakespeare scholars than the question itself. Fictions succeed when they speak to our cultural realities. The players, as Hamlet says, "are the abstract and brief chronicles of the / time" (2.2.524–25). The stories we read or see performed on stage appeal to us because they comment on the world we live in, sometimes in surprising ways. Shakespeare was good at synthesizing the discourses at large in his society, the conversations through which early modern English people understood the beliefs, practices, and objects that comprised their reality. In short, the answer to the question was no: as far as we know Shakespeare did not take part in any of the wars that marred the

Figure 1: The door of the Ecole Lemonier, the schoolhouse aboard Camp Lemonier, a forward antiterrorism base in Djibouti (2006)

latter half of Elizabeth's reign, but we should not allow this fact to cheapen his representations of military campaigning. Shakespeare was and is the undisputed master of representing other people's experiences to themselves, perhaps better than they could.

But this old reliable answer was, under the circumstances, insufficient, at least to me. The question was motivated less by an academic concern for the relations between fictions and realities than by a wish for a personal connection to an iconic work of literature and its equally iconic representation of military service abroad. The answer was not unproductive, pedagogically speaking, because it allowed us to marvel at Shakespeare's talent for apparently knowing so much about things he probably didn't know much about firsthand. For some, these are the moments that spark the authorship debate, but for most others these moments lend Shakespeare that aura in which he lives on as the secular prophet of the English-speaking world. For literary scholars, such moments are less mystifying. Plato told us long ago that poets excel at passing off superficial knowledge as expertise.[4] These moments, however, confirm the theories by which literary scholars live. They remind us that what we call personal experience is a product of exchanges between our own thoughts and the discourses at large in the social worlds we occupy, that our personal experiences and, indeed, our identities are bound up in representations, and that the difference between the representation of an authentic experience and an out-and-out fiction is slight, if there is a difference at all.

Or so we say. I am not dissatisfied with the rationale for marginalizing biographical criticism or anything like the pursuit of authors' intents, especially with regard to early modern authors about whom so little can ever be known. A soldier's question about whether Shakespeare had been to war reminded me, however, that human beings undergo definitive experiences to which they are always returning, which they are always trying to sort out and are likely to understand differently as their lives go on. Talking about those experiences and listening to what others have to say are chief among the ways we attempt to make sense of them. The young man who asked about Shakespeare's military service was able to grasp why my theoretical approach to fiction was valid and necessary (at least as an intellectual habit) and why we cannot bog down on biographical facts when considering an author's representation of war or of anything else. Yet he was not at that moment hoping to discover authors' intents but, as it were, authors in tents: he was interested not in theories of reading but in somebody else's reflections on military service. He wanted to know that the author of the book in his hand had borne witness to events not unlike those that were, at that moment, foremost on his mind and upon the landscape of his reality.

And is that not why we read fiction? Is that not the function of art? To give meaning to our experiences or, at least, to serve as a nexus point between our experiences and the possible meanings they might have? Are not more complicated theories of fiction variations on this basic theme? Do not the personal histories of authors (as constructed as they may be) contribute to this function of art? Shouldn't a person sitting in the middle of a war be able to ask if Shakespeare ever served in a war and anticipate a meaningful answer?

As it turned out, I was undergoing a definitive moment in my own life around that same time, an experience that would transform the question posed by the young soldier into a different question that is the starting place for this book. My colleagues had sent me an autographed copy of James Shapiro's *A Year in the Life of William Shakespeare*, and for the first time since my deployment began I was eager to pick up a book and read at the end of the day. I had brought books with me, but my mind was too engaged with the business of the war to do much with them. Shapiro's book was different. Although it is informed by all the appropriate scholarship, it is written as a story rather than a study, which is what I needed there in the desert. At one point in the story, describing the massive troop buildup in London in the months surrounding the "Invisible Armada" scare in 1599, Shapiro asks:

> And what about Shakespeare? As a servant of the lord chamberlain, did he join up with those who wore the privy counsellor's livery and attend upon the queen herself at Nonsuch? And, if so, did his new status as a gentleman lead him to acquire a horse? Or did he decide instead to ride out of town against the sea of defenders heading south, heading back home to Stratford-upon-Avon, convincing himself that at this time of crisis it was best to be by his family's side and out of immediate harm's way? The answer to this would tell us a great deal about what kind of person Shakespeare was. But we don't have a clue what he did.[5]

What did Shakespeare do while his country, already stretched to financial and emotional rupture by a decade of foreign war, was mobilizing its citizens to defend against an invasion by the most dreadful power in Western Europe? What did any of the writers responsible for the great English literary outpouring of the 1590s do with the threat of war, the machinery of war, and the idea of war closing ever more tightly around them?

The young soldier's question was not so different from those Shapiro asks, and the question at which I arrived in contemplating theirs in the solitude of the shipping container I called home was an extension of them. War was everywhere in the English 1590s. There was nothing and nobody it did not affect every day. What did war mean to the writers to whom I had dedicated my professional life? How did it shape their art?

And why didn't I know?

Part of the answer is that war has not been all that relevant to literary criticism since the 1980s. The implication of Elizabethan and Jacobean literature in the consolidation (as well as the subversion) of state power has been relevant, and the militarization of the Elizabethan state and the construction of the Elizabethan soldier often come up in discussions of power and politics. The specific question of how early modern literature and early modern war shed light on each other was not, however, one I had ever been taught to ask. Or perhaps I should say it is a question that has not been revitalized by the poststructural histories that have generated the most influential studies of early modern literature during my professional lifetime.

Not uncommon in the days of the old historicism, epitomized in the works of postwar critics like Paul Jorgensen and Henry J. Webb, studies of the relations between war and early modern literature now live out their retirement in an antechamber to military history (itself an annex to humanities scholarship) rather than to literary criticism. Even Michael Murrin's recent book, *History and Warfare in Renaissance Epic*, is by the author's own admission the product of an "Old Historicist."[6] If I did not know what Shakespeare and his fellow writers were up to during the height of Elizabeth's war years or how those wars shaped the literature of the Elizabethan age, the reason is in part that the critical upbringing I received looked at military history, for the most part, as a "barren field," as one critic has recently put it.[7] This split between military history and literary criticism is unfortunate, because war, more than anything else we like to study, dominated the culture, politics, and economy of England during the decades that created Shakespeare.

This book does not intend, however, to reintroduce military history to early modern literature studies. This book rather goes forward under the assumption that because war and military escalation were conditions of Elizabethan culture, they exerted pressure on all the products of that culture, to include its literature. On Shakespeare's stage and in the booksellers' shops of London we find touching, inspiring, and even infuriating representations of war. Crowding Shakespeare's theaters and the London streets outside were people who had been deployed or were about to be deployed, people who had lost loved ones or would, people who carried in their hearts the memory of war or the fear of war. Across the Channel, across the Irish Sea, and across the River Tweed wars raged or had been raging, and the bones of Englishmen by the tens of thousands burned and rotted as the coffers at home dwindled. What was the effect of these conditions on the literary sensibilities of the era?

A FEW CRITICS in recent years have taken up this question, despite the rift between military history and literary studies. In his influential essay "Shakespeare's Pacifism," Steven Marx argues that "Renaissance pacifism is neither an anachronistic construct nor an ephemeral aberration" but central to the humanist tradition that influenced the attitudes of the Elizabethan literary milieu and its constituent representations of war.[8] Marx's argument, which focuses on *Henry V*, takes aim at a common view of Elizabethan literature as a mouthpiece for a militant patriotism steeped in England's image of itself as a bastion of freedom and true faith besieged by the forces of an evil Catholic empire. The great Victorian historiographer John Richard Green describes this literature as the product of an

> impulse which sprang from national triumph, from the victory over the Armada, the deliverance from Spain, the rolling away of the Catholic terror which had hung like a cloud over the hopes of the people. With its new sense of security, of national energy and national power, the whole aspect of England suddenly changed. As yet the interest of Elizabeth's reign had been political and material; the stage had been crowded with statesmen and warriors, with Cecils and Walsinghams and Drakes. Literature had hardly found a place in the glories of the time. But from the moment when the Armada drifted back broken to Ferrol, the figures of warriors and statesmen were dwarfed by the grander figures of poets and philosophers.[9]

For Green, the victory over the Armada of 1588 translates into a flourishing of literary production. Dread is replaced by optimism, practical exigency by aesthetic aspiration. The battle won clears a space for artistic pursuits spirited by the country's martial achievements and the new pride they usher in. The problem with this vision of the Elizabethan literary renaissance is that the "terror" of foreign threat did not come or go with the Armada but lingered throughout Elizabeth's reign. England was driven from Calais just before Elizabeth's accession in 1558. Her controversial campaigns in Scotland started soon after. Revolts by Desmond in Ireland and by the Northern Earls shook the kingdom in the 1560s and 1570s. Cold war with Spain burdened the decades leading to England's formal entry into the Dutch Revolt in 1585, initiating nearly twenty years of open if sporadic war that did not end until Elizabeth died.

Marx is not the first to point out that the martial concerns of Elizabethan literature might not be viewed as extensions of an Armada victory parade. From his vantage in the weary aftermath of the Great War, Lewis Einstein also argues that Elizabethan literature is imbued with a sense of humanistic pacifism, but he notices too that this literature is nevertheless shaped by a "patriotic ideal" that "grew by a reaction from whatever was foreign."[10] A. F. Pollard, writing between Green and Einstein, connects the outpouring of literature in late sixteenth-century England to "an awakening of national consciousness," a claim that is part of his larger point that in the formulation of the modern English nation, which he identifies with the Tudors, "[language] and literature, too, become nationalised."[11]

Marx and Einstein may be correct that the literature of this period is neither as bellicose nor as intoxicated by the great victory at sea as is often supposed, but there is little debate that it is influenced by a patriotic or a proto-nationalistic idealism related to England's foreign policy and military posture, an idealism that is, as Liah Greenfeld has argued, "striking in its omnipresence and intensity."[12] The question is what to make of the presence of this idealism. Most modern scholars see the literature as contending with it and revising it, not merely rehearsing it. Richard Helgerson's seminal work *Forms of Nationhood: The Elizabethan Writing of England* recognizes that patriotic ideals were developed through institutions that included a "national theater," but that these institutions were also "discursive communities" in which different and often divergent conceptions of nationhood competed.[13] This argument has been developed further by Claire McEachern, Andrew Hadfield, and Krishan Kumar.

Not without good reason, then, literary representations of war have been studied (among the few scholars that have studied them at all) within the context of patriotic or nationalistic idealism, and often as a subversive force within that context. Patricia A. Cahill's *Unto the Breech: Martial Formations, Historical Trauma, and the Early Modern Stage* also challenges the notion that the martial drama that abounds in this era reflects a "national war fever in the wake of the Armada victory." By introducing trauma theory and by paying particular attention to the imagery of the wounded body, she argues convincingly that the proliferation of war on the early modern stage represents "a far messier effort to come to terms with the culture's unequivocal turn toward warfare."[14] For Alan Shepard in *Marlowe's Soldiers: Rhetorics of Masculinity in the Age of the Armada*, the stage deconstructs ideals of soldiership and reveals their complicity in promoting a concept of masculinity that both supports and requires the martial posture of the state. Shepard's work extends an argument made by Jonathan Dollimore apropos of *Coriolanus* that virtue (*virtus*) is not an "essence" but a "political strategy," that the identity of the idealized soldier is not independent from but located within the social networks comprising the state.[15] Nina Taunton's *1590s Drama and Militarism: Portrayals of War in Marlowe, Chapman, and Shakespeare's "Henry V"* shows how drama contends with the rhetoric and philosophy of military leadership expressed in the abundant military writings of the era. Nick de Somogyi, in *Shakespeare's Theatre of War*, traces a circulation of influence between literature and war and argues for a fluid relation in which war is not just reflected on the stage but inflected through the stage, resulting in theater that activates but also intercedes in the public's understanding of the wars that raged beyond England's borders. De Somogyi's book owes a great debt to Paul Fussell's monumental work *The Great War and Modern Memory*, which argues that literary tastes (e.g., irony) influenced the way the First World War was reported and thus experienced, a relation that, in turn, inscribes war into subsequent literary production in general. The image of dawn, Fussell claims, for example, "has never recovered from what the Great War did to it."[16]

My concern with these recent critical efforts is their focus on literature's engagement with war as a discursive phenomenon (and, by extension, on the ideologies that are implicated in discourse) rather than war as something early modern English people really had to deal with every day of their lives. I do not mean, by this statement, to separate reality from discourses or to draw a line against further encroachment of ideology into literary criticism. On the contrary, if, as Louis Althusser says, ideology is a "'representation' of the imaginary relationship of individuals to the real conditions of their existence," the real conditions of existence are just as important as representation to the question of ideology.[17] To understand the full range of war literature's ideological tensions, we need to understand war as a discursive phenomenon, but we also need to pay more attention than we have of late to war as a real condition of existence, something that really hit English people in their bodies, souls, and purses every day.

Fussell, writing in the aftermath of America's "living room" war in Vietnam, said of the First World War, "Sometimes it is really hard to shake off the conviction that this war has been written by someone."[18] As much as we can all probably relate to this idea, we should also ask to what extent our reading of the Great War is informed by our literary sensibilities—and what in those records we are not seeing because of this bias. Alan Shepard wrote in an earlier article on Marlowe's soldiers that the "dissenting voice" (embodied not only in certain of Marlowe's characters but also, by inference, in Marlowe and the enlightened reader of Marlowe) is "the most effective tool by which civilians may resist martial law."[19] Statements like this validate our preferred image of literature as a voice in the wilderness and the reader as a politically engaged actor. In *Faultlines: Cultural Materialism and the Politics of Dissident Reading*, Alan Sinfield makes a related point in his repudiation of the use of Shakespeare "to underwrite state bellicosity."[20] Sinfield reimagines *Julius Caesar*, a play often read as a study in state violence and the nature of political actors, as a reminder that "cultural producers" (figured in Cinna, the poet) play an important role in the political forum, that "dramatists, copywriters, and literary critics" possess "a certain distinctive power ... to write some of the scripts."[21]

But while the scripts are written, the realities are staged, and the dissenting opinions are voiced, wars go on, heeding a logic and consisting of objects and practices that only sometimes percolate up into literary discourse. There are, in other words, many aspects of war and living with war that do not fit into a war that seems to have "been written by someone." We need to find a way around our own literary preoccupations to better understand how the literature itself is engaging with war. One feature of the recent scholarship on war and Elizabethan literature will make this need obvious: none of it focuses on the writings of people who served in war.

SOME CRITICAL OBSERVATIONS on Elizabethan war literature in general provide insights on this glaring omission. Murrin notes that the overall lack of military experience among English writers contributes to their tendency to represent romanticized individual combat more than military campaigns and, just as often, to avoid representations of battle altogether.[22] To be fair, Murrin is concerned with the epic tradition, and so we can accept his observation without quibbling too much, and we can even go so far as to agree that among the most famous Elizabethan writers in all genres, we do not find the veteran presence that we find among their counterparts of the Spanish Golden Age. Not surprisingly, contemporary war plays a much more important role in the works of the latter. A comment by A. D. Harvey, however, is more indicative of the problem. He proposes that the "first attempt in England to write a serious work of literature about a contemporary war was probably Edmund Waller's 'Of a War with Spain, and a Fight at Sea,' published as a broadsheet in 1658."[23]

There were, in fact, *many* serious works of literature about contemporary war written in Elizabethan England. Even if we disallow the great mass of military memoirs, treatises, and pamphlets and count only those writings that might normally be included in an undergraduate literature class (verse, drama, and prose fiction), the writings on contemporary war, soldiers, and military affairs by veteran poets such as Thomas Churchyard, Barnabe Rich, George Gascoigne, John Harington, and John Donne are considerable.[24] Harvey cannot be unaware of these writings, and thus he cannot be saying that there is no "literature about a contemporary war" in Elizabethan England. Rather, he is saying that none of these writings constitutes "a serious work of literature." We cannot dismiss Harvey's comment outright because even literary critics interested in war in Elizabethan England have more or less neglected the numerous available literary writings about contemporary wars and have looked instead to works that historicize, romanticize, or allegorize war such as those that round out the opuses of Marlowe, Shakespeare, Spenser, and Sidney. Harvey is not alone in filtering the war literature of this period through preconceptions of what serious literature about war looks like, and we should ask why this is.

I digress for a moment back to Africa.

THE SHAKESPEARE CLASS I was teaching in Djibouti generated some interest among visiting reporters. I learned during interviews and correspondences, however, that the story posed certain challenges. The first was how to describe what was going on in Africa. The mission in the Horn of Africa was part of Operation Enduring Freedom, which also includes the war in Afghanistan, and along with Operation Iraqi Freedom comprises the Global War on Terrorism. But the story of the war, as it had taken shape at that point for three years, was the story of Iraq. The story of a Shakespeare class taking place in the middle of the war but not in the middle of Iraq would be confusing, I was told. Would it be a war story or just a story about soldiers? What war? What does it look like? Are you waiting to go to Iraq? "It's too bad you're not in Iraq," one person said. Not from my perspective.

Another problem was the narrative arc. Most mainstream journalists wanted me to make the Shakespeare class the story of one sensitive intellectual's attempt to create a meaningful experience in a war otherwise without meaning. One right-leaning journalist thought the story would read well as that of a patriot who risked the censure of an elitist and hypocritical academy to serve his country and give Shakespeare back to the regular guys fighting the war. The problem with either of these narratives is that I have read too much Shakespeare to imagine that literary works and armed forces are not in the same business of extending power, and I have read too much late twentieth-century criticism to imagine that the university and the military are not both parts of some larger cultural mechanism that conceals itself in the apparent antagonism between two of its more recognizable avatars. In short, I did not then and do not now regard serving in a war and teaching Shakespeare as incongruous, considering that so much of both industries involves teaching and leading young adults as they try to make their entrance in a world that prefers they do so through one institution or another. Nobody wanted to hear that.

None of this is to suggest that anyone should have been obliged to find my story interesting just because. The point, rather, is that a real war story by a real soldier about other real soldiers fighting in a real war did not make for a serviceable war story because it lacked certain key elements of setting, plot, character, and theme. It did not matter that those key elements belonged to the established fictions rather than to my or perhaps any other real soldier's experiences; in order for the story to register as a war story it had to assume a certain shape, even if that shape would have rendered the war unrecognizable to me. This problem is not unique to war stories but is part of the larger problem of life imitating art, or hyperreality, or any of the terms by which this phenomenon is known to postmodernity. War stories make the problem more visible because they are always *about* the most violent and terrifying form of political rupture known to our world, and thus they can scarcely take shape in the imagination in a context that is not already formed by the political concerns of our world. Indeed, sometimes this expected context is scrupulously formed by institutional pressures. In any case, the concept of *the war* precedes narratives of war and shapes those narratives.

Those who write about war from firsthand experience are not, as Fussell shows us, freed from these narrative and psychological constraints any more than their stories are freed from the narrative and political structures in which all war stories are bound, for their experiences with the war are also preceded by a complex of discourses and images by which they measure and evaluate their own experiences; however, for those who do experience war firsthand, the war also exists outside those structures. It exists as a real event separate from the ideas that precede it but also as a text, figuratively speaking, informed by ideas that have no proper place among the discourses and images that form a coherent narrative of the war as the folks at home have come to expect it. This tension between narratives and the breakdown of the expected order of the expected story is going to be, in some part, the organizing force of veterans' war stories, the aspect of the literature that makes it serious even while compromising much of what we expect serious literature to do.

For this reason I believe it is imperative to examine the war literature by Elizabethan veterans, not to privilege them as observers of war and not to suggest they were the only ones who struggled with the costs of war (for everyone in Elizabethan England had to bear those costs in his or her own way). Rather, because in their case the tortured process of negotiating a set of conflicted and deeply personal relations to war through another set of conflicted discourses about war in order to arrive at a meaningful narrative is especially pronounced. If we do not recognize these literary efforts as "serious"—or recognize them at all—we need to revise our assumptions about war and its place in the culture of Elizabethan England.

THE FIRST CHAPTER in this book, "English Mercuries," initiates this revision. It examines a document called *The English Mercurie*, a contemporary account of the Armada defeat long supposed to have been England's first newspaper and a possible source for Shakespeare's use of this term "English Mercuries" to describe the soldiers heading off to France in the choral prologue to the second act of *Henry V*. The document thus seems to emerge from a proudly patriotic society whose greatest writer's greatest war story derives in some part from a popular report of the greatest military victory of the age. *The English Mercurie*, however, is a hoax produced in the eighteenth century amidst other efforts to invent for England a national identity and a historical mythology to support its imperial project. In this first chapter I attempt to strip away the fictions that have allowed *The English Mercurie* to pass as current and arrive at a different understanding of what war meant to the writers of the Elizabethan period. In the process I show that Shakespeare's use of the term "English Mercuries" does have a contemporary resonance but not in any report of the Armada victory. Soldier poets of the time, the veterans who came home to develop literary careers, often presented themselves as servants of Mars and Mercury (the gods of war and writing). Shakespeare's "English Mercuries" who follow Henry to war in France call attention to the play's concern not just with war but with war stories, how and by whom they are told and also read, how the voices of soldiers relate to the production and politics of those stories.

The rest of the book brings to light the stories of those English Mercuries long buried under assumptions and preconceptions about war literature and the cultural location of war in the Elizabethan period. In the second chapter, "Men, Money, Iron, and Bread," I create a context in which the stories of soldiers might be more clearly heard. It is not a review of battles, commanders and their tactics, new military technologies, or theories of war but a sketch of what a military expedition might have been like for Tudor soldiers. In writing this chapter I draw to the greatest extent possible on firsthand narratives, and I filter these narratives through my own experiences as a military officer and veteran of foreign war. In many respects, the process of deploying soldiers and the conditions of their lives in an expeditionary camp have not changed that much in four hundred years, and thus in constructing my narrative of mobilization and deployment I draw on my own knowledge to give shape and context to the stories but also to question and qualify them constructively.

Deciding whom and what kinds of writings to include in this book proved challenging. Many veterans wrote about war in Elizabethan England, but most did not think of themselves as poets, nor would we think of what they wrote as *literature*. The first century of print witnessed a flood of military manuals and memoirs. Many were written and also consumed by the new breed of professional soldiers who were taking over the business of war from gentleman amateurs, but the popularity of these writings also owes much to courtesy books that advocated sound knowledge of the theory and practice of war as aspects of the complete gentleman. Any polished Elizabethan male preferred to think of himself as a man of both letters and arms. Philip Sidney fashioned himself so successfully in these terms we often forget that he wrote all he would ever write before he served abroad in Elizabeth's armed forces. Thomas Digges embodies another version of this problem. Prior to his peripheral military service, he published an influential "arithmetical military treatise" called *Stratioticos* (1579), begun by his father, which develops an approach to warfighting grounded in classical erudition. The Elizabethan era is, overall, awash with military men who wrote books and with writers who imagined themselves men of arms. I focus this book on the few who actually were soldiers and who actually did go on to carve out careers as poets afterward. Some explanation of these definitions is in order.

The reason I am separating memoirs and treatises from more "literary" Elizabethan war literature is complex, vexed, but, I think, necessary. It is not enough to say that a study that began with a question about Shakespeare and that seeks to illuminate the literature of the Elizabethan era ought to focus on literary writings rather than on military handbooks, because to separate these two categories would require a distinction of "literature" from other kinds of written material that is becoming less and less useful to critics. Less useful, but not perhaps without some historical basis.

For Sidney, poetry (by which he meant all categories of what we might call belles lettres) is in the business of idealizing reality.[25] Sidney may have known as well as anyone that reporting and storytelling are not so different, but, nevertheless, the aesthetics of Neoplatonism from which Sidney's theory of poetry in large part derives recognizes that art is successful when it looks beyond observable reality to another world of scintillating essences. Publishers of military treatises and memoirs, on the other hand, stressed that their products were in the closest possible contact with real events. For Sidney, adherence to the facts is characteristic of the "meaner sort" of art.[26] Additionally, early modern writers and readers would have placed memoirs and treatises in the category of forensic or deliberative rhetoric, in that they seek to explain past events and provide advice for undertaking future ones; they would have viewed war poetry, on the other hand, as a type of epideictic rhetoric in that it seeks out in a given subject what is worthy of praise or blame. These distinctions are always blurry, but they are nevertheless ones early modern writers and consumers of books were trained to observe. So even while in terms of twentieth-century literary theory the difference between a poetic representation and a true report is tenuous, and even while true reports of the Elizabethan era recycle the language of poetic representation and vice versa, the writing industry of the late sixteenth century understood that poetry was not memoir or treatise and appealed to different audiences for different reasons or, at least, understood that people wrote and consumed the two products under different pretenses. For this reason, this book focuses on works that were written within the category of poetry by people who sought the "title of poet," to borrow a line from Sidney and for audiences who brought to those works expectations appropriate to that category.[27]

Who are the English Mercuries on whom I focus in this book? They are Thomas Churchyard, John Donne, George Gascoigne, John Harington, and Ben Jonson, and to each I have dedicated a chapter. Another prolific soldier poet, Barnabe Rich, has entrances and exits throughout. Each to some extent foregrounds his wartime experiences in the fashioning of his literary persona. Each positions his identity as a "Martialist" alongside his identity as a "Mercurist."[28] Thomas Churchyard, the most prolific of the Elizabethan soldier poets, and to a lesser extent George Gascoigne built their literary fame upon their military careers. John Harington earned his literary fame prior to his deployment to Ireland, but his experiences on that disastrous campaign dominated his writings afterward. John Donne returns to his experiences during the Cadiz and Islands expeditions throughout his literary career, both as a poet and a minister. Jonson will remind his audiences that he was a soldier to give authority to his criticisms of the military profession early in his career, but he will also assert his military experience toward the end of his life when he developed nostalgia for the martial spirit of the old queen's reign. With Harington, Donne, and Jonson I deal with literature written in the Jacobean and even Caroline periods, because their memories of serving in war belong to Elizabethan England and shed light on its literature, culture, and politics.

There are other Elizabethans famous for both their military and literary endeavors whom I have not included for various reasons. I exclude George Chapman and Michael Drayton because their military experiences are too conjectural, and I exclude Philip Sidney because his literary career ended when he went to war in the Low Countries—and died there. Another omission is Walter Raleigh. Although his military and literary careers overlapped, as a celebrity commander and ranking courtier he does not offer much of a vantage on the significance of war to those Elizabethans who bore its costs most personally. Edmund Spenser and Christopher Marlowe might have been included in this book, but, then as now, diplomatic service and espionage are not the same as military service. Spenser witnessed Ireland at its worst, and who knows what Marlowe might have witnessed or in what he might have participated, but neither, as far as we know, was a soldier.

Soldiers are the focus of the third chapter of this book, "Thomas Churchyard's 'Valiant Soldiers' and the 'Public State.'" Churchyard learned the art of poetry as a boy in the service of Henry Howard, Earl of Surrey, and he learned the art of war as a mercenary during the last years of Henry VIII's reign. He would continue going to war and writing poetry throughout the long decades of Elizabeth's reign, and he would outlive her. His writings are, on the surface, humble accounts of military campaigning designed to honor "valiant soldiers" as well as "prince and public state." These writings, however, reflect a sensitive and critical appreciation of how war stories create a relationship between soldiers and the state they serve. I focus on Churchyard's account of the Scottish campaign of 1560, which he memorialized in 1575 as "The Siege of Leith." In that poem Churchyard takes aim at the preferred memory of the campaign, in which the statesmanship of William Cecil, Lord Burghley, resolved the conflict when military leadership failed. By praising the soldiers who were supposed to have failed at Leith, Churchyard does not merely tell a war story but challenges another story in which the Elizabethan government, rather than its soldiers, is the hero of the war. In the process, Churchyard raises the question of how the state defines itself through acts of remembering and forgetting wars as well as the even larger question of how the praise or censure of individual subjects forces us to reconsider the relationship of those subjects to the state they serve. This latter problem informs Churchyard's most admired work, "Shore's Wife," which he wrote in the 1560s but revised and republished during the military escalation of the 1590s.

The next chapter, "A Tale of Two Cities: George Gascoigne's Antwerp and *Alarum for London*," compares Gascoigne's eyewitness account of the "Spanish Fury" in *The Spoil of Antwerp* (1576) with *Alarum for London*, a play of debated authorship based on Gascoigne's work published amidst a storm of anti-Spanish propaganda in 1602. Gascoigne's work is a war story from a soldier's perspective, and while it criticizes the ferocity of the Spanish assault, it is circumspect and concerned with the complexity of the political situation, with the logistics of the military action, and with larger philosophical questions about war. The play based on his work is a more straightforward condemnation of Spanish cruelty, steeped in a burgeoning tradition that has come to be known as the Black Legend, in which Spain was labeled a conqueror so barbaric as to be intolerable even to Spaniards. By considering the adoption and modification of Gascoigne's work during this outpouring of anti-Spanish sentiment, we gain a vantage on how Elizabethan wartime propaganda exploited soldiers' narratives of war but also how those narratives crosscut the propaganda to reveal anxieties and tensions constituent to it. Through analysis of the hero of *Alarum for London*, an ambivalent old soldier called

Stump, I suggest the play imports into an England whose foreign and military policies were becoming dangerously simplified a more complicated and mature attitude toward war, its causes, and its costs.

The fifth chapter, "John Donne's Emblem of War" reconsiders one of the most acclaimed poets of the era in terms of his military career. Too rarely do we think about Donne as a soldier, but he was a veteran of the Cadiz and Islands voyages who wrote about those campaigns in his poetry and developed images of war throughout his career, most famously in his sonnet "Batter My Heart." I suggest that Donne's writings on war draw on the conventions of sixteenth- and seventeenth-century meditative verse, and specifically the emblematic tradition, to create images of war that resist moral or political simplification and instead challenge the reader to confront the contradictions not only in war but also in peace. The "emblem" or "icon," terms Donne often uses in conjunction with war in his sermons, was not a static image that conveyed a fixed idea in a visual form; it was more a visual puzzle that served as a site for contemplation through which the viewer was expected to negotiate paradoxes. Donne's emblems of war ask their readers to see war as both a testing ground for personal and national valor and a destructive force that ravages human pride and renders whole countries bare, peace both an Eden on earth and a state of gnawing restlessness and internal anxiety. The chapter considers a broad swath of Donne's poetry, as well as his sermons, before concluding with a discussion of "The Storm" and "The Calm," which he wrote just after the conclusion of his adventures in Spain and the Azores.

In Chapter 6, "John Harington's Journey Home," I study the writings of Harington following his unceremonious return to England after Essex's debacle in Ireland. Harington established his literary fame by translating one of the most heroic and patriotic works of the sixteenth century, Ariosto's *Orlando Furioso*. When his literary career failed to blossom, and having alienated himself from Elizabeth's court with his biting, scatological satire *The Metamorphosis of Ajax*, Harington went with Essex to Ireland in 1599 as an infantry captain and returned humiliated less than a year later. Out of favor and scarred by the wars, Harington dedicated himself to his books in the last decade of his life, and through his letters and poems from this period we get some of the most harrowing accounts of a veteran's attempt to come to terms with the war in which he volunteered and with the country that scorned him when he came home.

The final chapter is "Remembering Soldiers: Ben Jonson." It examines Jonson's nostalgia, which developed late in his life, for the old fighting spirit of the Elizabethan age. Jonson had no love for the patriotism and martialism of the Elizabethan court, and he did not trade on his experiences as a soldier in shaping his literary career. And yet we find him reinventing the Elizabethan soldier as a hero in his Caroline plays *The New Inn* and *The Magnetic Lady*, as well as in other poems from the same period. I suggest Jonson's change of heart is a response to England's changing attitude toward war in the reign of Charles, who dispensed with his father's pacifist policies and plunged England once again into foreign conflicts. Jonson's reinvention of the Elizabethan soldier during this period of military escalation does not, I suggest, attempt to connect Caroline foreign policy to the myths of Elizabethan England, although such efforts were afoot in the England of the 1620s. Jonson draws rather on the myths of Elizabethan England to create soldiers who are moral exemplars who function to warn Caroline England of its moral and physical unfitness to get involved in foreign war.

My hope is that through these readings I provide an answer to a soldier's question posed in a coyote brown tent in the middle of a war and, in the process, help us rethink the writings that continue to shape our own cultural reality. Shakespeare never did fight in a war, and that fact does not matter, really. What matters is that we understand the wars he was speaking to in his writings, the wars that shaped the literature of his age and the people for whom he wrote. I believe the writings of Elizabethan veterans will help us understand.

1
English Mercuries

ONE OF THE most compelling contemporary accounts of an Elizabethan military operation comes from a pamphlet from Whitehall called *The English Mercurie* (figure 2), which is dated 23 July 1588. Published on the direction of Elizabeth's chief minister, William Cecil, Lord Burghley, "for the prevention of false reports" while the Spanish Armada was still at large in the English Channel, the pamphlet seems typical of the era's attitudes toward war. It rings with all the expected patriotic idealism and martial hyperbole, speaking of Spanish warships "of a size never seen before in our seas," of English sailors "far from being daunted by the number and strength of the enemy," of "Her Majesty's wisdom and foresight for defense of the kingdom." It names many of the brightest stars of Elizabeth's military machine, including George Clifford, Francis Walsingham, Charles Howard, and those venerable sea dogs Francis Drake, John Hawkins, and Martin Frobisher. The story it tells is the now familiar one of how the courage of these worthies along with the "Grace of God [prevented] from landing one man on English ground."

The trouble with *The English Mercurie* is that it is not an Elizabethan document at all but a hoax perpetrated in the eighteenth century by Philip Yorke, second Earl of Hardwicke. So successful a hoax it was, however, that George Chalmers celebrated it in a 1794 *Gentleman's Magazine* article as the first example of an English newspaper, a distinction to which it clung throughout the nineteenth century despite numerous efforts to discredit it.[1] The hoax has often eluded the inveterate skepticism of researchers, and despite a thorough debunking by Alexander Andrews in *The History of British Journalism* in 1859, Charles Dudley Warner cites it as authentic in his famous 1897 essay, *The People for Whom Shakespeare Wrote*.[2] We find it identified as a 1588 publication in a 1931 Huntington Library checklist that elsewhere calls it "fictitious," and at the moment I am writing this book it is referenced

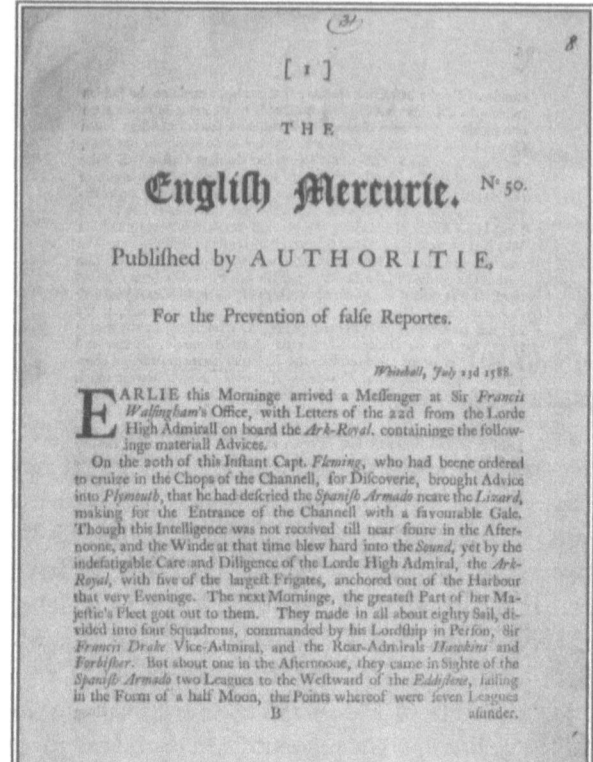

Figure 2: First page of *The English Mercurie*, an apocryphal Elizabethan newspaper fabricated by Philip Yorke, second Earl of Hardwicke, in the eighteenth century. © British Library Board. All Rights Reserved. Shelfmark Add.4106(29).

without any mention of its provenance on several university Web pages dedicated to Elizabethan history and its source documents.[3]

I point out the success of this hoax not to throw stones at anyone unaware of the provenance of this strange document, but because it points to the much larger problem of how we understand the attitudes of Elizabethan England toward its military culture and the forms those attitudes take in written artifacts. The enticing credibility of *The English Mercurie* might be viewed as an expression of what Michel Foucault calls in *The Archeology of Knowledge* "these pre-existing forms of continuity, these syntheses that are accepted without question."[4] Our trust in the document tells us less about Elizabethan attitudes toward military commitments than about our attitudes toward Elizabethan England.

BY THE TIME the second Earl of Hardwicke perpetrated the hoax (and it is not clear what he meant to accomplish with the document, which was not made public until after his death), the association of the title "Mercury" with news pamphlets was well established. The term was used by a French newspaper, the *Mercure François*, which began circulating in the first decade of the seventeenth century, and at about the same time a satire appeared, *Mundus alter et idem*, attributed to Joseph Hall and concerned with news from North America, the fictional author of which was a "Mercurius Britanicus." A few decades later an antiroyalist newspaper appeared by this same name. Many "Mercuries" emerged in print from the middle of the seventeenth century; in the late 1600s, for example, the *Athenian Mercury* appeared in English coffeehouses and continued to circulate for many years. The origin of the association of this term with English newspapers is not certain but is in many ways obvious. As the god of writing and the divine messenger, Mercury is the perfect masthead. *The English Mercurie* would seem to do what all successful literary hoaxes do: give informed readers something that has all the indicia of authenticity, starting with the title. That these "Mercuries" were especially interested in war and other calamities of global politics also lends credibility to the hoax. It would make perfect sense that a newspaper printed from Whitehall in 1588 would be called *The English Mercurie*, and it would also make sense that the occasion of its appearance would be the signal military campaign of the era.

Beyond the esoteric history of early modern English news pamphlets, the term "English Mercury" resonates with modern readers because it appears in the choral prologue to the second act of *Henry V*, in which Shakespeare describes the young men of England rallying around their king and following him to the wars in France:

> Now all the youth of England are on fire,
> And silken dalliance in the wardrobe lies:
> Now thrive the armorers, and honor's thought
> Reigns solely in the breast of every man:
> They sell the pasture now to buy the horse,
> Following the mirror of all Christian kings,
> With winged heels, as English Mercuries.
>   (act 2, prologue, lns. 1–7)

By invoking Shakespeare *The English Mercurie* alters the historical record. The hoax pushes the origin of the English newspaper back beyond the sticky internal politics of the English seventeenth century and connects it to the defining moment of the Elizabethan age. It also recreates a Shakespeare whose most patriotic play is in conversation with a published account of the Armada victory. The result is a fiction of Elizabethan England in which literature, popular reporting, political crisis, and patriotism cooperate to form the idea of a proud and coherent nation.

The second Earl of Hardwicke was not alone in creating this fiction in the late eighteenth century. Benedict Anderson has suggested that the idea of nations as imagined communities has much to do with the emergence of "print-capitalism" in the eighteenth century, which effected a merger of the real conditions of the nation (to include its history) with printed representations of those conditions.[5] The creation of this imagined community was vital to the English imperial project, which required the distribution of ideas of national identity, shared beliefs and manners, and common goals and values across an increasingly dispersed and diverse population.[6] Theaters as well as newspapers were understood as "bulwarks of the national character and fomenters of those manly, civilized, and patriotic manners necessary to English success abroad and stability at home."[7] Shakespeare and the Elizabethan age had long been vital to this project.

By the late eighteenth century the age of "Shakespeare idolatry" had been underway for more than a generation, and it was to a great extent around the notion of Elizabethan patriotic virility that this idolatry centered.[8] The suggestion that Shakespeare would help early eighteenth-century England understand its present in terms of its glorious past was implied in *The Tatler* by Richard Steele, who likened John Churchill, Duke of Marlborough and hero of the War of the Spanish Succession, to "that noble figure which Shakespeare gives Harry V upon his expedition against France."[9] In the decades that followed, Shakespeare and other Elizabethan writers would be invoked again and again in what Abigail Williams has called "Poetic Warfare," an unofficial and yet comprehensive effort to rally English people around the works of the pre–Civil War writers.[10] By the 1730s Shakespeare was well on his way to becoming a "national poet," having been reedited and republished several times, most famously by Alexander Pope, who brought out his edition of Shakespeare in 1725 after translating the *Iliad*.[11] The connection between the works of Shakespeare and the heroic works of classical antiquity was not lost on Joseph Warton, who said in 1756 that Shakespeare gratifies "the spectator, who loves to see and hear our own Harrys and Edwards, better than all the Achilleses or Caesars."[12] In 1779, Tom King wrote a pageant called *The Prophecy or Queen Elizabeth at Tilbury* in the face of growing concerns of a French invasion. Twenty years later William-Henry Ireland brought forth an apocryphal last work of Shakespeare called *Vortigern*, which in its enactment of the ancient fall of Briton to the Saxons cooperates with the era's "search for the national origin of the English."[13] As we might predict, Shakespeare was during these years the most popular playwright in the American colonies, where his plays were performed hundreds of times between 1750 and the Revolution.[14]

So while we may never know why Hardwicke created *The English Mercurie*, we can be sure that at the time of its creation the theaters and popular print were insinuating Shakespeare and his age into a nationalistic ideal that involved patriotism and martial virility. The conflation enacted by the hoax, of Shakespeare's most resonant war story and England's, feeds into the production of nationhood taking place in the late eighteenth century and stands on the idea of a racially and politically unified England whose military and foreign policies were extensions of this national coherence.

The history that stands between the creation of the hoax and ourselves is as important to this story as the history that stands between it and Shakespeare, because our capacity to evaluate the relations implied in the hoax depends on ideas about Shakespeare that were solidified in the nineteenth century. As the Victorian and Edwardian treatment of Shakespeare has been well documented, it can be captured here in a few cogent examples.[15] Joseph Nash's *The Mansions of England in the Olden Time* (published in four volumes during the 1830s and 1840s) peoples its drawings of Elizabethan and Jacobean architecture with ladies and gentlemen frozen in vignettes of intrigue, swordplay, and sundry ruffed-collared antics reminiscent of pre–Civil War theater (figures 3 and 4). These histrionic images, many celebrating the martial feistiness of the era, lend authenticity to the notion of England in the "olden time" by presenting readers with activities assumed to be characteristic of the era. The 1906 edition of this popular book went a step further by rearranging Nash's images by subject, providing not just images

Figure 3: Engraving of Adlington Hall, Cheshire, from Joseph Nash's *The Mansions of England in the Olden Time* (1869–1872). By permission of the Folger Shakespeare Library.

English Mercuries 27

Figure 4: Engraving of a fireplace in a gatehouse in Kenilworth, Warwickshire, from Joseph Nash's *The Mansions of England in the Olden Time* (1869–1872). By permission of the Folger Shakespeare Library.

of a fantastical old England but a more coherent visual narrative of it.[16]

While Nash and his editors were drawing on images of early theater to authenticate their images of extant buildings, others were at work trying to authenticate early theater itself. William Poel, who started a reading club called the Elizabethans in 1879 and had directed the Shakespeare Reading Society of University College London, founded the Elizabethan Stage Society in 1895.[17] With no background in theater, Poel nevertheless went on to spearhead a movement to reintroduce Elizabethan stage conventions to Shakespeare productions. The discovery of the document we now know as Johannes de Witt's sketch of the Swan theater (figure 5) contributed to this effort. Until 1888, the sketch had been seen by no one other than Arend van Buchel of Leyden, the man who received and copied the drawing from his friend de Witt in 1596. The discovery of the drawing in 1888 was, like the unearthing of Laocoön in 1506, a case of the world stumbling upon just the sort of thing many would seem to have been desperately seeking. The de Witt sketch along with some critical comments and other contemporary documents were printed in Karl Theodore Gaedertz's *Towards an Understanding of the Old English Theatre* and became central to Elizabethan stage reconstructions from then on.[18]

The notion of "Elizabethan stage conventions," as with everything else constituent to the Elizabethan revival from the Restoration forward, says as much about the present as the past. To reinvent Elizabethan England, one must decide which of the numberless and contradicting artifacts reflect the character of the age as the present prefers to imagine it. Such was the case in the late nineteenth century when Poel and others separated Shakespeare from the popular theaters and cloistered him in "municipal, university, or inn halls" where reenactments of Elizabethan stage conventions were less likely to bore the audience.[19] The desire to put Shakespeare and the Elizabethan era in an authentic environment might be viewed as an innocent enough (or naive enough) antiquarian fantasy, but given the evolution of Shakespeare and the Elizabethan age as icons of a preferred notion of Britishness, it must also be viewed as an effort to fix the Elizabethan era to a certain ideology, to limit its possible significance, to disallow the possibility that it can be invoked in a variety of contexts for a variety of reasons.

The utility of having an ideologically stable construct of Elizabethan England ready to deploy would prove invaluable in the first half of the twentieth century. With war looming on the continent, the "Shakespeare's England" exhibition appeared at Earls Court in 1912, and it included a replica of an Elizabethan village and Drake's ship as well as the performance of a number of plays.[20] When England was hip deep in the bloodiest war the world had ever endured, Shakespeare was called upon again to stir patriotic zeal by reminding English people of their glorious past. A celebration planned by Lord Bryce on the tercentenary of Shakespeare's death in 1916 endeavored to create "some fitting memorial to symbolize the intellectual fraternity of mankind in the universal homage accorded to the genius of the greatest Englishman."[21] For this occasion Israel Gollancz included his "Notes on Shakespeare the Patriot" in the program, drawing extensively on *Henry V* to make his case.[22]

Given the extent to which England has recruited Shakespeare

English Mercuries 29

Figure 5: Sketch of the Swan theater by contemporary observer Johannes de Witt (1596). Foto Marburg / Art Resource, NY.

for its patriotic causes, *The English Mercurie* might be viewed less as a hoax than as a supplement that adds something to the documentary record of Elizabethan England that English speakers from Hardwicke's time to our own seem to wish were there. Like all supplements, however, it also calls attention to deficiency.

For all the encomiums to England and Gloriana and the warlike spirit of both, we do not find a celebratory replica of Drake's ship, even a verbal one, in Elizabethan England (although a replica of Drake's ship *The Golden Hinde* still sits at anchor next to a replica of Shakespeare's Globe in modern London). While John Stow mentions that many "books, pictures & ballads were published in [Drake's] praise," there is little account of Drake's victory beyond this ephemera; indeed, Henry Roberts justifies his poem in honor of Drake by saying, "I did expect some Ovid's pen to paint his worthy praise, But none have writ."[23] The only work from the period that incorporates Drake into a narrative worthy of Ovid's pen was written not by any Englishman but by Lope de Vega.[24]

Overall, we find little Elizabethan literature that celebrates the wars that have, for succeeding generations, become central to the mythology of the era. Although Shakespeare invites the audience to connect Henry V to the Earl of Essex—the "general of our gracious Empress" (act 5, prologue, ln. 30)—*Henry V* is not about a contemporary war. Nor is the First Tetralogy, although we might view it as a comment on Henri IV's abortive wars against the Catholic League.[25] Neither is anything written by Sidney nor, unless we overdetermine the significance of allegory, is anything written by Spenser.[26] Aside from *Massacre at Paris*, neither is anything written by Marlowe. War abounds in the works of these writers, but that war is historicized or romanticized, and no writer commits himself to an unambiguous or even direct representation of the military engagements in which England was embroiled and which have come down to us as definitive of the period. I suspect the second Earl of Hardwicke wished they had, as I am sure have all those who have read *The English Mercurie* and have let themselves be thrilled by its possible authenticity. But none of these great Elizabethan authors wrote such a thing. To a person, these patriotic writers in this patriotic age more or less avoided the subject of contemporary war altogether.

One is tempted to attribute this avoidance to Elizabethan censorship, but censorship, as Mark Matheson has put it, is "a force difficult to assess."[27] Elizabethan censors were concerned more with heresy and sedition, the latter of which could include "critical comments on the policies or conduct of the government" and "unfavorable presentations of *friendly* foreign powers."[28] The representation of any living monarch or any other political personage was also discouraged. Within a government that was sensitive as to what constituted criticism, what kinds of representations of friendly powers were favorable, or what powers were even friendly, there was a certain wisdom in steering clear of contemporary political matters, to include war, as subjects of literature.[29] That said, Elizabethan censorship was not systematic, nor was it organized under a single authority.[30] The record of the period's licensed publications resists any generalizations about censorship beyond those I have made here, and even those are tenuous. The military manuals, memoirs, and pamphlets do not shy away from discussing contemporary war and other political issues or from referring to living monarchs and military leaders, nor does George Whetstone avoid such references in his verse remembrance of Philip Sidney.[31] John Wolfe, whose press produced no less than sixteen different books on the Armada victory in the years following, suffered little from constraints on discussions of contemporary politics and war.[32] As late as 1587, two years after Elizabeth sent the Earl of Leicester to the Low Countries at the head of a large expeditionary force, the Warwickshire Protestant firebrand Job Throckmorton was jailed for writing a sermon urging war in the Netherlands.[33] At the same time, the clergy of the English Church were instructed to preach a message of national unity to rally the kingdom against the pending Spanish invasion.[34] In sum, it is difficult to argue with Cyndia Susan Clegg's conclusion that "press censorship was less a part of the routine machinery of an authoritarian state than an *ad hoc* response—albeit authoritarian—to *particular* texts."[35] Whatever we decide censorship's influence to be in any specific case, it can be only part of the answer to the question of why the great literary figures of the Elizabethan age dealt so indirectly, if at all, with the wars that dominated the lives of the English people.

    I suggest the root of the deficiency supplemented by *The English Mercurie* is revealed in the title that contributes so much to its hold on our imaginations. We can, as I have suggested, pose a reasonable explanation for why "Mercury" might be an appropriate title for an Elizabethan newspaper—had there been any—and there is every good reason (from a hoaxmonger's perspective) to ask the "greatest Englishman" to supply a resonant title for this fanciful newspaper. But the question of why Shakespeare called Henry's soldiers "English Mercuries" becomes urgent, given that this phrase would seem to be the glue that holds together the idea of Elizabethan England on which the hoax depends. In the context of the speech, Mercury is invoked to describe the speed at which the young Englishmen prepare themselves for war and rush to it, but Mercury was in Shakespeare's time as well known for his function as a messenger and writer as for his speed. Moreover, were it not for the reference to "winged heels" we should expect Shakespeare's chorus to liken the heroic English soldiers not to Mercury here but to Mars (to whom Henry is compared in the first choral prologue). There is thus a tension between the gods of war and writing implied in the substitution.

This tension has an identifiable Elizabethan locus in the self-fashioning of a number of Elizabethan war veterans who came home to England and sought literary careers. George Gascoigne, for example, uses the phrase "Tam Marti quam Mercurio"—a servant of both Mars and Mercury—as a motto during his brief career as a soldier poet (figure 6). Walter Raleigh would later adopt this motto for himself (figure 7), and it was evidently well known enough that Ben Jonson invokes it ironically in *The Poetaster*.[36] Gascoigne's friend and former comrade George Whetstone used in his praise of Sidney the phrase "a perfect mirror for the followers of *Mars* and *Mercury*," later echoed by Robert Naunton.[37] Another of Gascoigne's friends and former comrades, Barnabe Rich, drew on the opposition of the two gods in his *Right Excellent and Pleasant Dialogue Between Mercury and an English Soldier*, the longest and most revealing Elizabethan work exploring this theme.

In Rich's dialogue, the speaker is led by Mercury to the court of Mars to learn about the art of war from the mouths of fallen soldiers. The speaker is at first delighted by the court of Mars, where the heroes of antiquity and England pass their time in martial exercise to the music of trumpets and drums. Soon after, however, the speaker is led to War himself, carrying famine, sword, and fire in his grip and seated in a chariot driven by Envy and drawn by Malice, Strife, Contention, and Discord. Seeing the ugliness of war face to face, the speaker all but forgets his initial infatuation with the glorious court of Mars: "This irksome sight did so much abhor me and thoroughly discourage me, that where before I had a kind of Martial desire to serve as a soldier, as occasion did permit, I now protested to myself not only to leave the exercise of so vile a profession but also to dissever myself from the fellowship of any such as were followers of so filthy and hateful a service." Disillu-

Figure 6: Nineteenth-century woodcut, after the lost original, of George Gascoigne with the motto "Tam Marti quam Mercurio." © National Portrait Gallery, London.

Figure 7: Engraving of Walter Raleigh with the motto "Tam Marti quam Mercurio," by Robert Vaughn after Simon de Passe (1614). Courtesy of Smithsonian Institution Libraries, Washington, D.C.

sioned and horrified, the speaker asks Mercury to lead him back to the place where he began his journey. Mercury instead subdues the speaker's resistance with an oration on the history of soldiers and soldiering before disappearing and leaving the speaker alone in the court of Mars.[38]

For Rich, Mercury serves as a messenger between soldiers and the world at large and a spokesman for them, since nobody, by the soldiers' own admission, "will look for eloquence to come from soldiers."[39] With Mercury's disappearance at the court of Mars, the speaker is transformed into both a soldier and Mercury. He is left alone to cope with war both as a subject of art and history and as a facet of his personal reality. He is also put in a position to complete the narrative without the benefit of a divine interlocutor. He takes the place of soldiers; he also takes the place of Mercury. The *Dialogue Between Mercury and an English Soldier* is an internal dialogue (a dream sequence) between one who is both Mercury *and* an English soldier, a spokesman and envoy for the soldiers and one of them, a man of letters and of arms. Shakespeare's invocation of Mercury where we might expect Mars in the choral prologue to the second act of *Henry V* is, in this light, a complicated substitution that invokes a tradition of self-representation among Elizabethan soldier poets like Gascoigne and Rich, who defined themselves in the opposition between Mercury and Mars.

But how does *Henry V* address that tradition? What about the play's engagement with it is illuminating to students of this period? I ask these questions because it is Shakespeare's relation to Elizabethan war that influences our sense of the attitudes of this period. One is tempted to say that by calling his soldiers "English Mercuries," Shakespeare implies that they are literary creatures created by a poet and not by a *soldier* poet like Gascoigne or Rich, whose representations of war are informed by their own service in the court of Mars. This possibility is compelling with regard to a play in which the opening choral prologue asks for a "Muse of fire" so that the "wooden O" of the theater—as well as the "flat, unraised spirits" who populate the stage—can "hold the vasty fields of France" and "bring forth so great an object" as war (prologue, lns. 1–25). Gascoigne and Rich had that fiery muse in the form of their own memories of war. Shakespeare did not. He served only Mercury, and his soldiers are thus only Mercuries in the same spirit in which Naunton describes the bookish and militarily ineffectual Leicester as having "more of Mercury, than he had of Mars."[40]

Another possibility is that the identification of soldiers with "Mercuries" calls attention to the role of soldiers as intermediaries between England's foreign wars and the idea of those wars in the popular imagination. News of the world was, as John Florio observed in 1591, the "first question of an Englishman."[41] The chief medium for news was word of mouth, and its chief distributors were those who made their livings traveling, which meant the distinction between news and rumor was a fragile one that grieved Elizabethan government officials at all levels.[42] Soldiers, as world travelers and witnesses to the most exciting events taking place in Europe, would have held a privileged place in the Elizabethan news culture, and thus they are often represented in fictions as distributors of (often self-aggrandizing) tall tales and lies. The hero of Nash's "unfortunate traveler," Jack Wilton, for instance, brings home a passel of ridiculous stories from his service in France, many gathered secondhand from the drunk and swaggering captains he encountered. This critique of soldiers' credibility in Elizabethan literature is evident in the figure of the braggart soldier, a fixture on the Elizabethan stage borrowed from classical comedy via Italian popular theater and developed by Shakespeare throughout his career. We cannot know exactly how news of the wars in the Low Countries, Spain, Scotland, or Ireland passed by word of mouth in Elizabethan society, but we know that the image of soldiers as "unscarr'd braggarts of the war" resonated with English audiences.[43] Even the high-ranking soldiers and mariners who participated in the Cadiz expedition of 1596 flooded England with conflicting reports of what took place during that campaign.[44] We also know that so many different accounts of the Armada invasion circulated throughout Europe that for a time it was not clear on the continent that the Spanish had been defeated at all.[45]

Elizabethan war stories emerged in a climate characterized on the one hand by a passion for news, especially news of foreign wars, and on the other hand by uncertainty regarding the reliability of any such reports. This climate was altered in ways both subtle and overt by propaganda and censorship. This dimension of Elizabethan war reporting feeds the credibility of *The English Mercurie*, which pretends to be a state-generated document promising to prevent "false reports." Shakespeare's chorus in *Henry V* would also seem to have a connection to false reporting. It takes the place of Rumor, who introduces the second part of *Henry IV* with a promise to "noise abroad that Harry Monmouth fell" (prologue, ln. 29). Indeed, the news source employing the name Mercury that Shakespeare might have known when he wrote the choral prologue to *Henry V* is *Mercurius Gallobelgicus*, published in Cologne and distributed across Europe from 1588 into the seventeenth century, which prompted John Donne in an epigram of the same name to declare that this Mercury "liest like a Greek."[46] By 1641, "trotting mercuries" are named among "temporizing poets, unlicensed printers, upstart booksellers, . . . and bawling hawkers" as purveyors of suspect news in an anonymous publication.[47] And even if soldiers are not liars, in an environment where wars overseas are bound up in stories, the status of soldiers as soldiers could be activated only through the telling of stories. The most resonant speech in *Henry V* appeals to the weary English soldiers' image of themselves as reporters of their own experiences who can roll up their sleeves back in England and declare, "These wounds I had on Crispian's day" (4.3.48).

Far from connecting Shakespeare's soldiers and his greatest war story to a clear articulation of Elizabethan patriotism, the term "English Mercuries" applied to soldiers conjures images of unreliable war reporters and also implicates those who claimed to write and fight "Tam Marti quam Mercurio" in this shell game of lived experiences, unreliable reports, out-and-out lies, and popular fancy. The effect is the dismantling of the authenticity—of even the potential authenticity—of war reporting, which clears a space in which the voice of the chorus can assert its equivalency with the experiences of soldiers. If all war stories are fictions, then all soldiers are Mercuries.

THE CHORUS, HOWEVER, is not a trustworthy narrator. Ostensibly, it functions as an orienting device that, like a dumb show, removes some of the burden of plot revelation from the dialogue, but it tends to tell stories that conflict with those the audience sees taking place on stage. It is the chorus who opens the play with glorious descriptions of kings and armies, only to yield the stage to scheming prelates who start war as a means of evading taxes. It is the chorus who tells us, after Henry conquers France and wins his princess, that "his England" bled out not long after (epilogue, 12). It is the chorus who tells us that the men of England, hungry for honor, go to war like "English Mercuries," only to step back and allow the audience to witness an England made up of people who "condole the night" (2.1.127) remembering the life and honoring the death of their dear friend John Falstaff and who "shog" off (2.3.45) to their king's war.

The chorus transforms *Henry V* from a war story to a story

about war stories, the people who tell them, the circumstances in and the media through which they are told, the social relations that are activated through the exchange of war stories, and the relations between war stories and the real conditions of people's lives. *Henry V* is also about the tendency, in the absence of certain authority, for the clearest and most sensuous voice speaking about war to dominate all the others. The chorus tells us to create pictures in our minds that flesh out its vision of war even while other stories are taking shape all around it, contradicting and undermining it. But when no witness to the war can make a greater claim to authenticity than any other (when all soldiers are Mercuries), a pluralistic discourse made up of the many individual voices of the people who carry the burden of war is subsumed by the most prevalent one. The voice of the chorus is nearly the voice of Henry speaking to his troops at Agincourt.

To be clear, I am not proposing here that patriotic war stories stand in the way of the true facts of the Elizabethan world or that the "real conditions of people's lives" (a term I used earlier that I am adapting from Louis Althusser)[48] can be discovered if we look closely enough—as if true facts and real conditions can be separated from the narratives by which people understand them. Nor am I suggesting that there was not a patriotic sentiment informing the Elizabethan literary milieu or that *Henry V* is not capitalizing on its popularity to some extent. What I am suggesting is that the variety and complexity of Elizabethan attitudes toward war get lost if we fail to recognize the ways this sentiment has been either positioned as representative of the era in the centuries that followed or scrutinized and challenged by the literature of the time, even the literature that seems most clearly to express it.

If we recognize that *Henry V* is not just participating in this patriotic chorus but calling attention to its relation to the processes by which a society's attitudes toward war are swallowed up and synthesized by a dominant discourse, we can hear other voices or, at least, question their absence. Leaving aside the hole in the center of the play where Falstaff, that great dissident, should be, we are allowed to witness this subsumption of alternative voices in the fourth act, when Williams, Bates, and Court discuss war with their disguised king. Bates wishes that they were all "quit" in France and home in England (4.1.116). Williams is not sure if the king's cause is "just and his quarrel honorable" and adds that the king "will have a heavy reckoning to make" if he leads men to their deaths in an illegal and immoral war (4.1.128–35). Their half-formed concerns about their own predicament are filibustered rather than answered by Henry, who erects and then knocks down straw-man versions of the soldiers' objections. The men concede half-heartedly to their king's arguments, and they do fight for him, misgivings and all. What thoughts they carried with them onto the field of Agincourt we cannot know. Williams appears briefly at battle's end, but all the rest vanish as the nameless dead are counted.

TO HEAR OTHER voices speaking about war we must disburden ourselves of the "syntheses that are accepted without question."[49] We must ask what any given piece of Elizabethan literature is saying about war without assuming that one answer (the voice of the chorus, the voice of *The English Mercurie*, or the voice of Israel Gollancz) dominates.

In Christopher Marlowe's *Edward II*, for example, we witness what seems another Elizabethan drama dealing with a king whose leadership failure is figured as a deficiency in his martial temperament, a deficiency which is itself conflated with effeminacy. Typical of Marlowe, this deficiency is painted in bold strokes. Unlike Hamlet, whose effeminacy and martial inadequacy are suggested by his being housebound and mother smothered and too morally fastidious to don armor with his father and "take arms against a sea of troubles" (3.1.58), Edward's effeminacy is laid bare in his hysterical fawning upon his homosexual lover Gaveston, for whom he sacrifices the welfare of England. Thus when the younger Mortimer and Lancaster confront Edward with a list of threats to his kingdom about which he has done nothing while dallying with Gaveston, our impulse is to read the scene, steeped in the assumption that a good king must be warrior, as an indictment of Edward's fitness for rule:

> *Mortimer Junior*:
>   The idle triumphs, masques, lascivious shows
>   And prodigal gifts bestowed on Gaveston,
>   Have drawn thy treasure dry, and made thee weak . . .
> *Lancaster*: Thy garrisons are beaten out of France
>   And lame and poor lie groaning at the gates;

> The wild O'Neil, with swarms of Irish kerns,
> Lives uncontrolled within the English pale;
> Unto the walls of York the Scots made road,
> And unresisted drave away rich spoils. (2.2.162–67)[50]

But these words would have had a different resonance among the people in Marlowe's audience, who by 1593 were already wearied by five years of intense military actions abroad. More than thirteen thousand English soldiers were deployed the year *Edward II* was staged, mostly in support of the troop surge in France that began in 1591, and Parliament complained about the crown's increasing demands for war funding, as it had in 1589.[51] The concern enacted in *Edward II* in which a monarch is chided by his restless lords for neglecting the kingdom's military interests is the opposite of the concern that was gripping the English people when the play was first staged. That is, it was not the Scots who were carting off England's "rich spoil" but England's own foreign military commitments, and it was not clear (at least to Parliament) that the attention paid to enemies abroad and the costs of combating them were justifiable. Even within the play, the peril facing England is not the immanent threats listed by Mortimer Junior and Lancaster but Mortimer Junior and Lancaster themselves, who wish to seize power for any plausible reason. The threat to England is domestic unrest and opportunism, a point that also would have resonated in a kingdom that had only a thousand soldiers standing on its own soil to provide a defense.[52]

So what is *Edward II* saying about war? In the figure of the negligent and incontinent young ruler chided by masculine and warlike rival lords, the drama invokes the ideal of the monarch as a military leader in a way characteristic of what we now think of as Elizabethan patriotic literature. We have seen this same arrangement in the relationship between Hotspur and Hal in the first part of *Henry IV*. But these warlike lords are also rebels, and given the serious doubts about the necessity of continuing costly wars abroad in 1593, their militaristic importunities smack of political angling in the spirit of Henry IV's advice to Hal in *2 Henry IV* to "busy giddy minds / With foreign broils" (4.5.213–14) rather than allowing people to think too much about domestic problems. Given the ambiguity of the warnings of Mortimer Junior and Lancaster, even the significance of the figure of a monarch too concerned with his lover and not enough with threats to the kingdom is uncertain. It is easy to imagine that many in the audience, rather than being disgusted with Edward, would have been pleased with a monarch who withdrew from foreign wars to dote on court favorites. That is, after all, what England got in 1603 when James succeeded Elizabeth.

If we consider for a moment that the king has "two bodies" and regard Edward as a man and not a monarch, the scene also enacts a dilemma that was no doubt felt by everyone in England in whose ears buzzed constant reminders of threats abroad while life at home—with all its wants and hopes—went on.[53] *Edward II* is, after all, a domestic drama on many levels. It is about internal politics, about households and marriages, and about people and the other people they love. It is less about state matters than about individuals who live their lives in the shadow of state matters. What do indistinct, unseen, and reported threats to the kingdom have to do with these very personal concerns? Why must we sacrifice the people we love and the things we love to do according to the warnings of fear-mongers? What voice can we trust? Edward declares at one point, "[So] I walk with [Gaveston] about the walls, / What care I though the earls begirt us round?" (2.2.221–22). Why, given that all the warlike earls are condemned at play's end while Edward is sadistically murdered, should we not see him as a kind of hero?

Regardless of how we answer these questions, the point is that *Edward II* does not simply lay out a patriotic ideal of martial kingship and Edward as a counterexample. It stages the relation between the individual and the threats to the kingdom as a complicated, personal, and ambivalent one in which ignoring those threats is as legitimate a response to them as accepting somebody else's self-interested version of what those threats are and what ought to be done about them. In order to see this complexity and consider the different attitudes toward war the play is setting in motion, we need to suspend the assumption that the moral logic around which the play coheres is one that celebrates martial vigor as a badge of true manhood and sound government. The play may be acknowledging the pervasiveness of a patriotic ideal constructed on these terms, but the play is not championing that ideal unequivocally.

Neither is *Henry V*.

HAD WILLIAMS, BATES, and Court not made their brief appearance around the campfire on the eve of the battle of Agincourt, we might regard *Henry V* as a drama that rehearses assumed Elizabethan attitudes toward war and its necessary role in preserving the kingdom and defining the subjects of that kingdom as ready and courageous soldiers. However, when Williams, Bates, and Court *do* appear, they draw attention to and also trouble the play's preoccupation with the representation of soldiers and wars. By the time the soldiers are given a voice, the chorus has already bound them to its literary and ideological project, the one that began three acts earlier in the invocation of a "Muse of fire" (prologue, ln. 1). But just as the "English Mercuries" conjured by the chorus in the second act are challenged by clichés of a corrupt soldiery grudgingly joining Henry on his dodgy war for profit, Williams, Bates, and Court challenge the image of themselves as "horrid ghosts," "sacrifices," wretches plucking "comfort from his looks" (act 4, prologue, lns. 23-42). Far from fearful shadows waiting for "a little touch of Harry in the night" (act 4, prologue, ln. 47), the soldiers have strong opinions about the situation they are in and about the king who put them in it. Henry does not bring comfort to them but—in a thin disguise as an average Englishman (as though his words belonged to popular opinion and not his own private agenda)—chides them, threatens them, and breaks up their discussion. And were it not so, the vexed literary project engineered by the chorus could not continue. The soldiers have to be absorbed within the patriotic discourse or the war story becomes unstable.

And that may be the point. The term "English Mercuries" reminds us that the soldiers crafted by the chorus as a literary and political convenience are also messengers, tellers of their own stories and representers of their own realities. This aspect of soldiers was, as I have suggested, well known to the Elizabethan people, who relied on them for news of wars abroad, and vital to the literary personas veteran poets crafted for themselves. What *Henry V* identifies in the tension embedded in the term "English Mercuries"—the tension between soldiers as courageous servants of the state and soldiers as messengers from foreign battlefields—is the production of a dominant discourse on war through the subordination of individuals and individual stories as well as the cooperation of literature in this process.

Henry V also charts the resistance to this process. In the context of the literary culture of the late Elizabethan period, in which many soldier poets identified themselves as Mercuries, we can scarcely help but see in this patriotic and politically orthodox play an invitation to reconsider how soldiers represent their own experiences in war, how they create fictions out of those experiences, and how those fictions compete with fictions like the one the chorus is trying to tell, which *The English Mercurie* summarizes and projects, and which we have too often allowed to speak for the Elizabethan era and its attitudes toward war. The play is asking us to go back to that moment around the campfire and think hard about what those English Mercuries were trying to say and what happened when they tried to say it.

The remainder of this book is dedicated to what those English Mercuries, the soldier poets of Shakespeare's age, did say, to their experiences, and to the way they negotiated their experiences in war through dominant discourses about war to create literature. Before going forward, however, I spend some time examining the material conditions of their experiences on deployment so we can better understand what they had to endure abroad and what memories they brought home to England and to their writing.

2
Men, Money, Iron, and Bread

D URING A RAID on the Portuguese city of Cascais, Robert Devereux, the dashing and controversial Earl of Essex, challenged any of "his quality" to single combat.[1] There were no takers, and Essex was probably the better for it. William Drury issued a similar challenge to a French lord in Flanders some years earlier. The French lord agreed but decided to shoot Drury instead, and Drury died of the ensuing bullet wound a few days later.[2] With the English clamoring outside the city walls, anyone in Cascais of Essex's "quality" would have been thinking more about secreting cash and valuables than about breaking lances. Although such challenges were not uncommon, personal combat of this kind was no longer part of practical warfighting in the sixteenth century.[3]

Military organization and strategy throughout Europe underwent great changes during the sixteenth century, to which modern scholars have given the term "military revolution." There is considerable controversy as to when, why, where, and even if this revolution took place, but most agree that warfighting in the sixteenth century was beginning to take on modern characteristics that include the emergence of the military professional, new "fire" weapons, new tactics to deploy and counter them, and a reduced role of the aristocracy.[4] Essex's raids on Spain and Portugal, like all the wars that serve as the backdrop for the chapters in this book, will seem familiar to twenty-first-century readers. Artillery pieces and harquebusiers, the forerunners of the modern riflemen, were as important as ladders, pikes, and swords. Battles took place in the open field under streaming banners but also house to house on city streets, with enemy small-arms fire coming from windows and alleyways.[5] The success of any campaign involved both controlling the public confidence at home and controlling objectives abroad. The force itself stood less on the martial courage of its gentleman commanders than on the quality of its administrative, operational, and logistical planning. As Thomas Styward wrote in *The Pathway to Martial Discipline* (1582): "Men, money, iron, and bread is the strength of the wars."[6]

Our vision of war in the Elizabethan era is oriented toward the exploits and the errors of men like Essex rather than toward the quotidian details of life on deployment. One practical reason for this bias is that fewer documents representing the experiences of ordinary soldiers survive. What we do know arrives mostly from the writings of the gentlemen who served as commanders and other educated people (often their friends) who received commissions from them. These writings are understandably concerned with the deeds of noble commanders and represent war from their perspective, but they pose other critical problems as well. As I have mentioned, military handbooks and memoirs were so much in vogue in the sixteenth century that any published account of military campaigning from the Elizabethan era must be viewed to some extent as a literary endeavor undertaken with the goal of appealing to a reading public that had certain expectations of this sort of writing. Typically, these memoirs and manuals blur personal experience with established historical narrative as well as with principles of maneuver and engagement derived from ancient and other early modern sources.[7]

The focus on what men like Essex did or failed to do also reflects the priorities of a generation of scholars (among whom I count myself) who enjoy dark comedy, especially those in which the star performers are hawkish aristocrats, overprivileged young men, and popular media. While chivalry was becoming obsolete in practical terms, stories of the great military leaders of antiquity were flowing from the burgeoning print industry and finding their way into the writings of Machiavelli and Castiglione, whose thoughts on the arts of war deeply influenced sixteenth-century European gentlemen's presentations of themselves.[8] Essex epitomized the idea of the gentleman commander poured in the mold of the Roman generals celebrated in the popular histories and idealized by academic military theorists like Thomas Digges; at the same time, more seasoned and pragmatic tacticians pointed out that the Romans would not have conquered a fortified Europe by their methods and would have abandoned those methods "had they known artillery."[9]

This tension between an elegant and classically grounded

model of military command and control and the demands of modern warfighting created obvious conflicts of priority for Elizabeth's gentleman commanders.[10] By upholding the standard of the noble soldier (however fanciful it may have been) a sixteenth-century gentleman could gain very real positions of power and responsibility, even though fighting according to the precepts of this model might be ineffective on the battlefield. Thus we see a Philip Sidney holding the governorship of Flushing and riding out at the head of a company of horse (itself an increasingly obsolete apparatus) with only his poetic imagination and his court appointments as credentials. Thus we see an Essex throwing down the glove before the walls of Cascais, meeting man to man with the dreadful O'Neill in Ireland, and later abandoning his force there and riding by night to beg the graces of his sovereign lady (even at her toilet). But the bitter ends of Sidney and Essex belong more to the pages of Dante (or perhaps Camus) than to Ariosto. Sidney died by infection from a gunshot wound and Essex was relieved, humiliated, and executed as a traitor. Still, Sidney and Essex were the most celebrated soldiers of the Elizabethan era, and their rewards in life and fame in death were extensions of the behaviors that doomed them as battlefield commanders. Their stories roll a number of sociological, political, and epistemological threads up into one irresistible narrative, and given that so much early modern ink is dedicated to them, it is possible to imagine that the story of noble commanders is *the* story of Elizabethan war—or the most interesting one.

In this chapter, I tell a different story, the story of life on deployment that is central to the representations of war by Elizabethan soldier poets. The actions of the great commanders and the harrowing encounters with enemy forces are a part of that story, but, then as now, a military expedition consists mostly of moving around, sitting around, and waiting to go home. Any attempt to tell this story will run up against the paucity of documentary evidence attesting to what people did when they were not fighting; for someone trained as a literary critic and not as an archivist, this problem is daunting. My solution is to pull details of life on deployment from the military books and other writings that survive and to filter these details through my own experiences as an officer familiar with the processes of mustering, deploying, feeding, paying, redeploying, and reintegrating soldiers. My rationale for drawing on my own experiences in the late twentieth and early twenty-first centuries to illuminate deployments that took place four hundred years earlier is that military campaigning has lately reembraced an entrepreneurial spirit upon which Elizabethan expeditions relied heavily that has been dormant in Western warfighting for most of recent history. Back on the scene is the mercenary, the private supply chain, the reliance on reserve and foreign forces, the cutting of logistical corners, and other practices designed to shift the cost of war away from the national treasury and toward people, units, and privateers who take on the government's mission at the price the government is willing to pay. Many of the challenges warfighters and planners face under these conditions today are similar to the ones Elizabeth's administrators and officers faced, and our solutions are similar. My hope is that, as a literary critic and veteran, I can make a different kind of sense of the materials available and fashion from them something like a coherent narrative about life on an Elizabethan deployment. What I am not attempting to do is revise the history of Elizabethan warfare. That task is undertaken tirelessly by military historians to whom my debt in this chapter and this book is immeasurable.[11] Throughout, I focus on "men, money, iron, and bread," relegating what is known in modern operational parlance as "the big blue arrow"—the larger strategic goals and command structures of military operations—to the background.[12]

Before going forward, I want to make a brief and broad statement about the physical place of war in Elizabethan society. Reconsidering Elizabethan attitudes toward military commitments is, as I have suggested, a purpose of this book, and the chapters that follow approach this issue from the perspective of individual soldiers and writers, with the hope of filling in a larger picture through the accretion of details. Behind those individual perspectives, however, lie some imposing and plain facts. On average, some fifteen thousand Englishmen participated in combat deployments each year from 1585 until the end of Elizabeth's reign.[13] These men consumed, on average, twenty thousand pounds of bread, twenty-five thousand gallons of beer, and thirty to fifty head of cattle every day, all at the expense of taxpayers who faced scarcity and soaring food prices at home.[14] More than once during these years of military escalation, hunger riots broke out in which desperate citizens attempted to stop food stores from being shipped to the wars overseas.[15] Elizabeth's overseas campaigns were, literally and figuratively, eating up the resources of her subjects.

Another source of tension at home was the nature of Elizabeth's wars. Most Elizabethan military operations were expeditionary in nature, which is to say they involved placing forces on foreign soil for the purpose of achieving a strategic objective there. Even the wars in Scotland must be considered expeditionary in that it was more difficult and costly to move troops and supplies through the barren country of the border marches than it was to transport them by sea to the continent.[16] A problem with expeditionary warfare of the kind Elizabeth waged is that its objectives do not have an immediate value to the people who have to pay for it. Elizabeth's expeditions did not acquire new wealth or new territory and did not vanquish enemies outright (except perhaps in the Scottish campaign of 1560, about which I will say more in the next chapter). Their objective was, for the most part, to disrupt the buildup of foreign power near England's borders and navigation routes.[17] The Elizabethan rationale for engaging in this type of expedition was the same as that in the United States today. As Anthony Wingfield contends in his reflection on an earlier expedition to Spain and Portugal, the assault on the Spanish port was preventive; were it not undertaken, he asks, "what should hinder the King of Spain to bring his forces home unto us?" He will later say that war on Spanish soil will "free ourselves from the war at our own walls."[18] Elizabethans had reasons to fear a Spanish invasion—England narrowly escaped one in 1588 and was prepared for a second—but the disruption of foreign military buildups in strategic locations abroad is not as tangible a goal as the repulsion of a foreign invader from one's homeland. Public support for preventive expeditionary campaigning is bound to dwindle when debts and casualties mount, as they did throughout Elizabeth's reign, and the question of why forces should be overseas in the first place haunts even the most stalwart supporters. (As I mentioned in the preceding chapter, Parliament balked at funding Elizabeth's expeditions, even in the year after the Armada invasion of 1588.) Because the value of a preventive expeditionary campaign stands upon conjecture as to what it prevents rather than proof of what it accomplishes, such a campaign creates tension and anxiety in the public conscience that, in turn, spawns both jingoism and dissent, depending on how one prefers to exorcise those tensions and anxieties. It is not overstating the case to suggest that every comment on war written during the military escalations of the latter half of Elizabeth's reign needs to be considered in the context of the tremendous emotional and economic strain military expeditions were exerting on the English people.

WINGFIELD REPORTS THAT of the thirteen thousand soldiers and mariners with whom he served in 1589, six thousand came home. Chillingly, he cites these numbers not to lament the cost of the war in terms of personnel but to suggest that the ravages of disease among the force were not as bad as rumor held: "So as we never being 13,000 in all, and having brought home above 6,000 with us, you may see how the world hath been seduced in believing that we have lost 16,000 by sickness."[19] Today, the loss of half an element the size of a division in one campaign would be catastrophic, but evidence suggests that a 50 percent attrition rate was not unusual for expeditionary warfare in sixteenth-century England. Although major battles could claim hundreds and even thousands of men at once, the horrific attrition rate seems mostly attributable to living conditions en route and in country. In any case, the story of any Elizabethan deployment begins with the likelihood that only one man in two will make it home.

Elizabeth's soldiers were, for the most part, amateurs, called up for five months at a time, although they might be required to serve up to two years at the discretion of the commander.[20] When the kingdom needed to raise an army, each county was assigned a quota based on its overall population, which it was obliged to outfit. Most of those called up would be foot soldiers, who outnumbered horsemen about ten to one, as the cost of outfitting a horseman and transporting horses by sea was considerable and the importance of cavalry in sixteenth-century ground warfare was diminishing. Styward mentions that "it is necessary to retain citizens for horsemen, the country for footmen," which suggests that small rural counties were exempt from having to fit out even one horseman.[21] The task of mustering the soldiers often fell to the muster master, a royal appointee who would ensure that the quota was drawn from all able men between sixteen and sixty in each county. The task of ensuring this list was complete and accurate fell to county officials like the constable and the justices of the peace.

Accusations of justices protecting "the properest and most serviceable men at every muster from the wars" are as ubiquitous as witch lore in the documents of the Elizabethan era and ought to be viewed with like scrutiny.[22] I want to stress that throughout this discussion of the muster process I am talking about mustering troops for expeditionary campaigns, not for the militia. Elizabethan England maintained a militia, as most countries do to this day, consisting of citizens who could be mobilized as need be for homeland defense, but the cost of maintaining a militia is small compared to the cost of outfitting and deploying an expeditionary force.[23] Records of the muster rolls from the Elizabethan era do suggest that about half the men between sixteen and sixty from each county were for various reasons deemed unable to serve.[24] Some were, no doubt, physically unable to serve, but others were excluded because they were abroad, either from the county or the country. Others were not listed at all. There is no record in the muster rolls of Warwickshire, for example, of any man between sixteen and sixty named Shakespeare from the town of Stratford.[25] While this absence may delight Oxfordians and others who are pleased to believe Shakespeare did not exist, it more likely reflects the tendency of the muster system to shelter the more affluent and mobile members of society from involuntary military service. Most Elizabethan writers avoided the draft one way or another. While this fact supports the charges of corruption levied against justices of the peace, I suggest the problem was more complicated, as a comparison of the Elizabethan muster to the modern process of reserve activation will illustrate.

Because the need for new troops today is ever increasing, reserve units, rather than being mobilized en masse, are regularly tasked with providing certain personnel to augment a standing active component unit or a new unit created ad hoc. It is a common practice for a reserve commander, after soliciting volunteers, to claim to have nothing more to give and to push any shortfalls back on higher headquarters. In its turn, higher headquarters will reiterate its demands with greater urgency, but since it relies on the local unit for accurate personnel accountability it has little choice but to look elsewhere for people at the same time. This push and pull will continue until the "gaining force" has its critical personnel in place (although it will almost always be incomplete), which entails compromises on both sides. When activations are ordered, there is thus considerable tension between the local unit and gaining force commands, and higher headquarters ends up accusing the local unit of concealing serviceable assets, which it often does. The reason is a simple conflict of interests. Local unit commanders are evaluated by higher headquarters but stand or fall on the loyalty and good service of their troops. The commanders will protect their interests as far as practicable. If the story of modern reserve activation were written from the perspective of higher headquarters elements, no doubt the reserve commanders would come off about as well as Elizabethan justices of the peace.

Given the deployment tempo during Elizabeth's war years, it is impossible to imagine justices of the peace and the royal government *not* becoming frustrated with each other's excuses and demands. When Elizabethan forces abroad reached their height of twenty-two thousand in 1599, that number represented about one-half of 1 percent of the population of England and about 5 percent of the kingdom's eligible males.[26] The United States has never placed that many people into combat zones without a draft, the most recent iteration of which during the Vietnam era resulted in widespread uprisings. Elizabethan drafts were no less unpopular, but unlike the United States today, the Elizabethan government did not compensate its mustering officials adequately for the tasks they were asked to perform. Elizabethan officials were expected to generate income from their positions, and justices were no exception. Bribery and other forms of corruption influenced the selection of soldiers even in the best of times, and in a period of military escalation justices had to balance the demands of the royal government with the interests of the population on whom their livelihoods depended. Gentleman chroniclers tend to overlook this conflict of interests and pin the problem on the obstinacy, crookedness, and even disloyalty of justices. Wingfield goes so far as to suggest that the reason justices "have sent . . . the scum and dregs of their country" is that they "have always thought unworthily of any war."[27] Henry Knyvett addresses this problem more evenhandedly in *The Defense of the Realm* (1596), suggesting that mustering officials as well as suppliers and operational commanders need to be freed from any financial incentives not to act in the royal government's best interests at all times.[28]

Once mustered, the troops would be formed into companies of one hundred or so commanded by a captain, who was often a gentleman or a person of some means. The muster master was responsible for the soldiers' training, but the training itself would often be conducted by an "ancient"—a trusted veteran of the company and the forerunner of the modern noncommissioned officer. The training was perfunctory. It might last six days and allowed only basic familiarization with the weapons, even if the soldier were training with complicated and dangerous firearms like the musket and harquebus.[29] Most of the people mustered would be trained on the pike, brown-bill, and other polearms.

More troubles ensued with the movement of forces, then as now a burdensome and costly process. Troops and gear have to be staged before they can be deployed, and even in today's era of airplanes, electronic communications, and decent materiel and personnel records keeping, the staging process is a wildcard. One never knows for sure who is going to be at the staging site and what equipment they will have. The days and weeks before the actual movement are spent scrambling to complete training, dividing up the on-hand equipment, and tracking down stragglers. An Elizabethan expeditionary force waiting to deploy would, due to inadequate administrative mechanisms and corruption at all levels, experience shortfalls of key supply items like food stores, carts, and artillery pieces.[30] The force was, as Thomas Gainsford put it in 1619, "smothered between malignant circumstances of time, and ill conditions of men devoted to private ends."[31] One expedition to Spain, for example, sat in Plymouth so long waiting for a favorable wind that it was forced to consume its stores and embark with insufficient food reserves. When it finally sailed, it was missing much of the artillery it was supposed to have. The Essex expedition to Cadiz was unable to conduct follow-on operations because it had exhausted its supplies of food and beer.[32] More food could be purchased in ports of embarkation, but commanders would pay dearly for it, as the self-interestedness of "victualers" was only slightly less notorious than that of justices of the peace.

Commanders could expect to lose men and supplies en route to the area of operations. Shipping ground-combat assets is always a problem, for the obvious reason that ships are designed to carry cargo and accommodate the mariners who must manage that cargo. When the cargo is human, the economy of shipboard space and movement is stretched. Modern amphibious vessels have berthing areas designed to accommodate the hundreds and sometimes thousands of ground-combat personnel and their equipment, but Elizabethan sailing vessels did not. Cargo holds designed to carry crates, spools of cloth, and barrels were retrofitted to carry men and beasts, but in the cramped and unsanitary conditions, disease and discontent spread rapidly. Wingfield notes that "in the seventeen days we continued on board, we had cast many of our men overboard."[33] Keeping a ground-combat element entertained on a sea voyage is still a problem. Even with gyms, movie theaters, and abundant food, fights are common and an alarming percentage of a ship's enlisted females will leave it pregnant. Embarked Elizabethan soldiers were hungry but also drunk, given that beer was far less likely than water to cause parasitic diseases. Accidents were frequent. Loss of men at sea was a normal operational risk and viewed as the "will of God."[34] At night, in fog, or during tactical movements ships were obliged to sail dangerously close to one another, using the sound of drums to maintain distance.[35]

Under these conditions, military justice had to be swift and severe. Death was the accepted recompense for mutiny and for striking an officer but sometimes also for stealing and many other minor crimes.[36] To instill discipline in a recalcitrant unit, Elizabethan commanders might even resort to the barbaric practice of decimation, the killing of one man in ten as punishment for the entire unit's failings.[37]

The greatest danger of all, however, was hunger. It is not by accident that the most vivid experiences recounted by Elizabethan veterans are of starvation in the ships and expeditionary camps. Withholding battle against an enemy force until it had wasted away by hunger and disease was an important tactic of sixteenth-century warfare. As Styward says, "It is better to subdue the enemy through scarcity and want of necessary things than through many assaults."[38] Thomas Churchyard, describing his experiences in Flanders fighting with the Prince of Orange against Fernando Alvarez de Toledo, the "Iron Duke" of Alva, complains that the Spanish would show glimpses of themselves and flirt with battle only to vanish, forcing the Protestant allies to consume their food and supplies: "Our victual weared scant, so garments, horse shoes, and other necessaries could not be gotten for money, that was a misery remediless, and a mischief that neither man nor beast might easily abide."[39] Only when the allies were weakened by hunger and want did Alva force the decisive action by way of ambush.[40] The

English expedition to Ireland in the late 1590s ran into a similar tactic, as Gainsford reports: "For when the Irish found themselves uncapable of such a business [i.e., defeating the English forces] by way of expurgation or assault, they took another course by intercepting the passages to famish them: which when the English understood, they were as resolute to affront all mischances, as the enemy violent in contriving displeasures and so with noble steadfastness bare up a head against the stream of sickness, and wants, eating horses and weeds and if it had been possible, the very dirt and stones."[41] When Don Juan del Águila surrendered to Charles Blount, Lord Mountjoy, after the battle of Kinsale, the beginning of the end of the O'Neill rebellion in Ireland, the terms of the agreement stipulated in three separate articles that the Spanish would not be overcharged for food and supplies during their passage out of Ireland.[42] Withdrawing from Ireland without means of sustenance would have been for the Spanish as hazardous as withdrawing under fire.

Contributing to the effectiveness of this tactic was the possibility that in a war-ravaged countryside all available food and supplies would be consumed. An expedition could not carry much more food than was necessary to reach the area of operations, so once there it had to rely on the resources at hand, which meant buying food from local merchants or commandeering it from the local population.[43] Both created problems. Expeditions were often well furnished with money, but, as Churchyard intimates in an earlier quote, if there is nothing left to buy, all the money in the world is of no use. If there was food for sale, it was often of poor quality. Elis Gruffydd, a veteran of the French campaign during the reign of Henry VIII, describes in nauseating detail an intestinal ailment (probably amebic dysentery) that swept through the camp due to some spoiled grain that was handled and prepared improperly: "Sour bread from wheat which had never been put through a mill but was beaten in a mortar with pestles and slipped the fundaments of the people who ate it like filthy excrement, which with the coldness of the water which was the greatest part of the drink of the common soldiers, and the damp which chilled the bodies and hearts of the people, threw them into the sickness called by physicians Lienttsia."[44] We might suspect that the water, not the wheat, was the larger problem here, but, of course, the beer would have been the first thing to go in any expedition, and if it was available for sale at all it would be pricey. Soldiers in Gruffydd's era were paid about six pence a day, while a barrel of beer might cost eleven shillings.[45] Foraging from the countryside was a common practice, but it also compromised good order and discipline.[46] For this reason it was increasingly discouraged during the sixteenth century (one of the many moves toward professionalism that characterizes the military revolution).[47] But if there was no food to buy or if commanders refused to pay the exorbitant prices, there was no other choice.[48] Given that an expeditionary camp constituted a larger concentration of people than the population of any but the larger sixteenth-century market towns, it could quickly exhaust the resources at hand.

So great was the pressure of hunger on sixteenth-century campaigning that expeditions were typically broken off during the winter months. Gruffydd reports that an official of a besieged French town rebuffed an English commander's threats by reminding him that "by winter according to the old English custom you will go home to your kinsmen."[49] The French official was right. Churchyard, who also served in the French campaign, remarks that in autumn "the camp retired for that year, and broke up at Reims in Champaign, where the king paid his army for five months."[50] If an expedition did winter over, the problem of hunger was made more acute by the difficulty of foraging in the frozen countryside, as an anonymous veteran of the Irish campaign recounts: "On the other [i.e., the English] side, our men in numbers scant equal to them, all almost tired and wearied out with the misery of the long winter's siege, our horses decayed, lean and very weak, our best means of victuals and forage likely to be cut from us, with many other impediments whereof I speak not."[51] Although it is difficult to imagine a campaign succeeding if the enemy knows in advance when the campaign season will end, seasonal campaigning is still practiced today by Talibani forces in Afghanistan, and for the same reason: climate and conditions can and do pose as great a threat as enemy action, and breaking off the fight and starting again in the spring is sometimes sound operational risk management.

Even with ample food and supplies, life in a sixteenth-century expeditionary camp was challenging and dangerous. The perimeter of the camp was established by wide trenches, protected by interlocking fields of fire (figure 8).[52] The camp was crowded and it stunk. Open fires were used for cooking, heating, and forging.

Men, Money, Iron, and Bread 55

Figure 8: "The Plat for Incamping," from Thomas Styward's *The Pathway to Martial Discipline* (1582). By permission of the Folger Shakespeare Library.

Trenches served as sewers. The greatest affront to the air quality aboard the camp would be the shambles, the area designated for the voiding of offal and the slaughtering of animals. Soldiers were billeted in tents, except when commandeered structures were involved, but in both cases bedding was minimal.[53] Reports of men seeking shelter under hedges are common. Soldiers lived in crowded, wet, and often cold environments where they were vulnerable to disease. If the official report from the Irish campaign is typical, one man in ten would die of diseases in camp.[54]

If this number seems hard to accept, it is worth considering that in a modern expeditionary camp—which is also plagued by overcrowding, filth, fatigue, bad air, and the cooperating pollution of human waste and burning fuels—almost everyone gets at least a stubborn cold and a fungus somewhere, and many return from deployments with respiratory and digestive tract ailments that persist for months and even years. All the food, clean water, ibuprofen, and prophylactic drugs imaginable cannot keep diseases from exacting a toll on people who are tired, crowded together, and living around filth, contagion, and vermin. One cold winter in Korea I was billeted for a month with eight others in a small, unheated building without potable running water and with bare floors on which to sleep; all of us came down with the same acute respiratory infection accompanied by headache and fever that made physical activity challenging. Had we no decent food, clean water, or dry sleeping bags, it is easy to imagine how one or more of the nine people in that room would not have lasted another month. Given that the sixteenth century did not have antiseptics and did not understand bacterial infections, we can understand how so many died. Losses of this scale would have to be considered part of the operational cost.

Add to these conditions the lack of medical care. Elizabethan expeditions went out with about two surgeons for every one to two thousand people, whereas a modern expeditionary force of one to two thousand has the equivalent of its own small hospital. Field medicine of the Elizabethan era might have been more effective than we imagine, owing to a revival of the art of surgery in Elizabethan society at large.[55] Field surgeons were clever and resourceful in dealing with trauma. Manuals touching upon military medicine written during this era, the most important of which were William Clowes's *Approved Practise for All Young Chirurgeons* (1588) and Thomas Gale's *Certain Works of Chirurgerie* (1563), deal at length with gunshot wounds. The treatments they prescribe include cleaning and draining the wound, finding the bullet and all fragments, removing any wood and cloth that accompanied the bullet, and then applying various boiling compounds of turpentine and alcohol. Although horribly painful, these techniques for cleaning and disinfecting wounds probably saved a lot of lives, at least among the officers and gentlemen who received such care. Common soldiers did not.

The camp housed the soldiers, their equipment, and also food vendors and other merchants (see areas designated for merchants, artificers, and victualers in figure 8). It may seem strange for a military encampment to allow merchants to come and go or to set up shop aboard the camp, but this arrangement is alive and well today. In modern expeditionary camps, contracted food service workers live alongside soldiers, and local merchants are permitted to set up shops at certain times and in designated places. Most nontactical supplies are acquired not via the military supply chain but through local merchants. These merchants are happy to cooperate, for, like their sixteenth-century counterparts, they make a killing at the expense of the government paying for the expedition. As Gruffydd remarked of one deployment in which he participated: "Everyone who was trafficking in food and drink gained, except the King, which lost on this expedition alone more than a thousand pounds."[56]

The camps were subject to random artillery attacks, as camps are now, but indirect fire weapons are always of limited value when the gunner has no time to observe the impact of the round and adjust fire. The value of random indirect fire is disruption and terror in the enemy rear. Churchyard describes how the French used random indirect fire for just this purpose against the English in Scotland, which "by chance it killed a horse and man."[57] Other enemy actions in the rear area might include covert infiltration for the purposes of sabotaging gear and assassinating personnel.[58] The losses from this sort of attack are negligible in terms of people and equipment, but their effect on morale is pronounced and continues to be a major concern in expeditionary operations today.

IT IS TEMPTING, as I turn the discussion to combat operations, to invoke the image of early modern armies clashing in the great tangled wedges of men and horses so familiar from history books and filmed representations, but it is difficult to find a detailed firsthand account of an action of this scale. An eyewitness is bound to have a more localized perspective, and combat actions take up a small percentage of any deployment. The assault Wingfield describes with which I began this chapter was, in total, an evolution of a few months from start to finish, but the land and sea battles combined took only a day or two.[59] Consistent with this chapter's goal of providing a sketch of life on deployment as those who were there recounted it in their writings, I focus this discussion of combat on the details to which soldiers paid attention. In so saying, I do not wish to suggest that massive combat actions are not a part of Elizabethan soldiers' experiences, but I do suggest that to gain a vantage upon actions so large requires a much broader perspective on battle than any individual soldier is likely to have. For accounts of major battles, their attendant circumstances, and their outcomes, I defer to the many historians, both modern and early modern, who have dedicated their intellectual lives to this subject.

Movement to contact could itself be treacherous and exhausting. A veteran of the 1596 Cadiz expedition notes that the force had to march "three English miles" across deep, dry sand.[60] Cadiz was protected by long-range guns, so while the men were taking two steps forward and one step back in shifting sand, they would also have been taking fire. If a river had to be forded, other problems might arise, as Churchyard recalls in his reflections on an expedition to Flanders: "[The] legs of the horses kept up the water so long a season, that the river rose a yard in height, by which means, many horsemen and footmen were drowned, and all our victual had taken great wet, and was in a manner marred and spoiled quite."[61] Although a thousand horses walking across a shallow river could conceivably act as a dam and raise the water levels upstream, I suspect the problem here is rather that the horses churned up the riverbed, causing the rear half of the column to stumble or sink in the mud. In any case, the tactical movement of personnel always takes a toll on an expeditionary force because it often requires going where maneuver is difficult and visibility is poor. During a movement to contact, moreover, emotions are high and nerves are taut; under these conditions moving things are bound to fall, crash, run into each other, or roll over.

When it came time to engage the enemy, especially in a siege situation, the assault was often led by a small body of light infantrymen called the "forlorn hope" or "*infants perdu*," who were to charge the enemy position, as Styward says, "whatever shall happen."[62] During one battle during the O'Neill rebellion, the forlorn hope received orders "that the shot should not be discharged till [they] presented their pieces to the rebel's breasts in their trenches."[63] For their trouble the forlorn hope received twice the pay of average soldiers.[64] In general, the task of the forlorn hope was to force the enemy into taking action at the time and place of the assaulting commander's choosing. Forcing action on favorable terms is still a tenet of modern warfighting but would have been even more important in the sixteenth century, since, as we have seen, the longer a force on the defense could withhold battle, the better its chances of winning without the hazard of engagement. As Churchyard puts it, drawing on a Roman proverb: "A bridge of gold give him that runs from thee, / The wise man bids."[65] Styward, speaking more as a tactician than a poet, mentions that captains were trained not to fight unless necessary and only if victory was likely to be achieved.[66]

Accounts of skirmishes from sixteenth-century veterans remind us that, indeed, nothing about combat has changed much. When the hurly-burly's done and the battle's lost and won, a lot of shots are fired. Most hit nothing but enough do. Some hit the enemy. Some hit friends. People die. A veteran of one expedition reports that twenty or thirty men were slain when friendly fire brought down a tower, so incensing the soldiers of the affected company that they mutinied.[67] Elsewhere during that battle, people watched one of their beloved captains bleed out when his lower extremities were crushed in the collapse of a wall.[68] In general, captains receive as much criticism as praise in the memoirs of veterans. Gruffydd states that during his deployment to France "more than four hundred were killed and wounded . . . because of the lack of prudent captains experienced in the ways of war."[69] John Harington, for example, had no military experience but was given command of a company in Ireland, a command he would abandon. Absent a concept of building autonomy into the scheme of command and control (and with inexperienced captains and undisciplined, half-starved soldiers), a sixteenth-century skirmish must have resembled a jailbreak more than maneuver warfare.

Under these conditions, the notion of achieving an objective becomes somewhat difficult to define. Modern operational planning is a fluid and iterative process that begins with a sketch of the situation, continues through a statement of mission and subordinate element tasks, and ends with a scheme for dealing with logistics (expressed as "beans, bullets, band-aids, and bad guys"). The scheme of logistics is crucial for capitalizing on an objective once achieved and creates a stable platform for follow-on operations. Elizabethan commanders were not good at this aspect of warfighting, without which an objective can scarcely be said to have been achieved and follow-on operations are all but impossible. Commanders had little choice but to rely on the resources of the captured objective to feed soldiers and provide them with a place to rest and recover. Town officials might assist in this process in hopes of easing the burden on their people, but for the expeditionary force these resources were at best unreliable.[70] Wingfield, reflecting on the 1589 attack on Cascais, cites "the scarcity of surgeons," "the want of carriages for the hurt and the sick," and "the penury of victuals in the camp" as reasons for the ultimate failure of the expedition.[71] Knyvett connects the logistical shortcomings of sixteenth-century operational planning with the quality of service commanders should expect from the common soldier: "what service can be looked for of such soldiers, as for wont of garments and other necessaries ashamed of themselves, perish for cold and hide themselves or mutiny when they should take actions of most moment?"[72]

A grim consequence of the inability of sixteenth-century English expeditions to cope logistically with the aftermath of victory was the execution of enemy prisoners. In 1589 some five hundred soldiers who "found favor to be taken prisoner" were put to death.[73] After the battle of Kinsale, all the Irish prisoners were hanged.[74] In Boulogne all the sick were executed.[75] Enemy prisoners present a tremendous logistical burden, which is a problem even for a modern armed force. For a sixteenth-century expedition that could not feed its own soldiers, tend to its own sick and wounded, or bury its own dead, executing enemy prisoners made practical sense.[76]

Of men, money, iron, and bread, money might have been the least of the expeditionary force's problems (if the greatest of the crown's). The soldiers and mariners who ventured to Spain and Portugal in 1589 were paid after they returned home to England.[77] The soldiers with whom Gruffydd served in France were paid every two weeks without fail.[78] Sometimes soldiers would be paid at the end of the month, after it was determined whether they had served each of the thirty days required to rate a full month's pay. If a battle was won and the soldiers were discharged early, they were paid for a full month anyway.[79] Pioneers (or combat engineers, as we call them today), who as hired laborers rather than trained soldiers were prone to abandoning the force, might be paid at the end of each day to encourage their staying in camp.[80] Lest we get too rosy a picture of the likelihood of soldiers getting paid, George Gascoigne complains of wintering over in Delft without so much as "one penny pay."[81]

That soldiers ought to have received a greater share of the rewards for participating in an expedition was a concern, as was the lack of a reliable pension system. Knyvett points out that these pay-related problems have a direct effect on command and control: "For otherwise how or with what credit or conscience can [a captain] command, work any great effect with, or chasten those whom indeed he doth not truly pay [and] recompense, or at the least so provide for, as they want nothing necessary, and may be in some hope by good husbandry, of a little store to relieve them at the end of the wars?"[82] The complaint that captains lined their own pockets rather than paying soldiers fairly during and after an expedition is oft heard in the military treatises of the Elizabethan era, and many urge captains in various ways "not be covetous or niggardly, never to keep back [from their] soldiers."[83] We must assume there is substance to these complaints, but we must also consider that commanders, like justices of the peace, were given every practical incentive to derive an income from their positions. The incentive for captains to withhold money from their soldiers was that they got to keep it for themselves. A strong incentive. I do not doubt that if battalion commanders today were underpaid *and* given their charges' pay as a lump sum of cash for which they were accountable to no one except the soldiers, the same problem would occur. Captains may have been self-interested, but the larger problem was the administrative superstructure, which, as today, costs more to build and maintain than does putting a combat element on the ground. The Elizabethan government's solution was to shift the problem and the blame to the captains. With Elizabethan veterans, the problem of compensation was more complicated but ultimately caused by a similar refusal on the part of the government to meet the actual costs of its undertakings, coupled with an inefficient system for distributing what it *was* willing to pay.

UPON CONSIDERATION OF what being deployed in support of an Elizabethan expedition entailed—from the disorganized muster, through administrative and tactical movements imperiled by hunger and disease, through the chaotic assaults and withdrawals, and finally to the unceremonious discharge—it would be easy to conclude that the experience was a six-month to two-year dose of hell from which one would be lucky to escape alive. It was, but it was also much more than that.

Young people want adventure and they do not mind taking risks to find it. Those of us entrusted with the care and feeding of young adults, whether in the armed forces or in institutions of higher learning, know this very well, and we spend considerable energy steering the risk-taking inclinations of young people toward constructive ends. When a country goes to war, many young people gravitate toward the war because it is an adventure. Which is not to say that encouraging young people to find adventure in foreign war is not exploitative and in some cases contemptible. Nor do I wish to imply that most Elizabethan soldiers volunteered for service. They didn't. The soldiers on whom this book focuses did volunteer, however, because they wanted adventure, because they wanted money, because they wanted something the war could provide.

In the perversion that is war, the potential for hardship and death, set against the proclivity of young people to seek adventure, becomes its own perverse reward. This is true now and was then. Wingfield, making this point, sneers at critics who "by their experience, not having the knowledge of the ordinary wants of the war, have thought that . . . not to have their meats well dressed, to drink sometimes water, to watch much, or to see men die or be slain was a miserable thing."[84] We might agree with the critics that to endure starvation, fatigue, amebic dysentery, long watches, and grim death is a "miserable thing," but Wingfield's point, which must ever be kept in mind when considering representations of war by Elizabethan soldiers, is that the act of enduring all these hardships is a point of pride, as well as, for many, a life-defining experience. Elizabethan soldiers *were* proud people in a country that was proud of them, but they were also physically and emotionally scarred people in a country that exploited them, disparaged them, and grumbled at having to maintain them.

Indeed, nothing about war changes much.

3
Thomas Churchyard's "Valiant Soldiers" and the "Public State"

IN HIS INTRODUCTION to *Churchyard's Choice*, Thomas Churchyard, one of the most prolific of Elizabethan soldier poets, declares that "before all other things (except the honoring of Prince and public state) a true writer ought of duty, to have in admiration and reverence the valiant soldiers."[1] This statement would seem to be in keeping with Churchyard's reputation today (if he has one at all) as a venerable but dawdling moralist who represented war with a soldier's eye but without much critical shrewdness, or, as one scholar has more graciously put it, as a "politically correct" Tudor writer.[2]

To his contemporaries, Churchyard was not politically correct.[3] He became known as a gadfly of the state early in his career with a short poem called "Davy Dycar's Dream," first published in 1551 after Churchyard returned from the wars in Scotland.[4] "Davy Dycar's Dream" is a lament upon the moral and social decay of modern times presented as a dream, but its flashpoint comes near the end when Davy imagines a day when "Rex doth reign and rule the roost, and weeds out wicked men."[5] The line was understood by many as an attack on certain unpopular ministers who ruled England in the name of the boy king Edward VI. Dozens wrote detractions against Churchyard, Thomas Camel chief among them, while others defended him. So rancorous was the controversy that Churchyard was questioned by Edward's Privy Council, a situation in which Edward Seymour, Earl of Hertford and renowned protector of radical authors, had to intervene.[6] Churchyard never denied the allegations outright but turned the tables on those who made them, imploring them to state whom they thought he was criticizing and why. No one dared take that bait. The storm around Davy

Dycar continued to sell books into the 1580s, and Churchyard continued to earn fame as a literary malcontent until his death in 1604.[7]

The image of Churchyard as a politically correct Tudor writer is not a misreading, however. It derives from Churchyard's stylized persona as a "small soldier" who told his war stories for whatever meager rewards they might bring, an uncomplicated man who, in his own words, "hath used both sword and pen with poet's fortune."[8] The Churchyard I present in this chapter is not the politically correct Tudor writer but a critical observer of the Elizabethan war machine who used his authority as a veteran to question not only the state's rationale for waging war but also the role of war in creating relations between the state and its subjects. Throughout Churchyard's opus, the soldier emerges as a figure at odds not with the enemy but with the apparatuses of his own government, to the extent that Churchyard's war literature seems to play a game of chicken with state authority at the same time it pretends to be a humble memoir of a humble soldier. Churchyard's use of his old soldier persona to mask his biting commentary did not go unnoticed by his contemporaries. Edmund Spenser personifies him in "Colin Clout's Come Home Again" as "*Harpalus* now woxen aged, / In faithful service of fair Cynthia," but also as "old *Palemon*," whose "careful pipe" "may make the hearer rue."[9] Elizabeth herself noted the barbs hidden in Churchyard's war stories: she was angered by some remarks in the *Choice*, and Churchyard was forced to flee the country for a time.

As I am sure Churchyard's life and work are unfamiliar to even the most experienced readers of Elizabethan literature, I stress two things before delving into his poetry and the relations he probes between soldiers and the state. The first point is that Churchyard is not an oddball among Elizabethan writers. His critically honed war stories, usually told in collections of rhyming iambic pentameter, were popular throughout his long career, despite his complaints to the contrary, and even late in life he was hailed as the forebearer of the "grandiloquentest" of English poets by Thomas Nash and as "the most passionate among us" by Francis Meres.[10] I mention this aspect of Churchyard because, as I have argued in the introduction and first chapter, we must get around the centuries that stand between ourselves and the Elizabethan era if we hope to reconsider the place of war in the period. The idea of an Elizabethan England unified around its military posture becomes unstable if Churchyard is placed where I suggest he belongs—at the center of Elizabethan war literature—for the heroes he canonizes are not military leaders or doers of brave deeds but ordinary people who, in the clutches of a powerful and impersonal state, struggle to survive and help each other as they can. This image was a compelling one to Elizabethan readers. Churchyard gave it to them again and again and they continued to buy it, although it did not find its way into the fanciful reconstructions of "Shakespeare's England" at Earls Court in 1912.

The second point I stress is that Churchyard consistently challenges the assumption that has made war literature and critical inquiry into war literature somewhat unpopular in the post-Vietnam era, that is, that a story about valiant soldiers is necessarily one that glorifies state policy. Read rhetorically, Churchyard's declaration that "before all other things (except the honoring of Prince and public state) a true writer ought of duty, to have in admiration and reverence the valiant soldiers" calls attention to the disparity between these two epideictic efforts. Honoring "Prince and public state" is, literally, a parenthetical for Churchyard. It is separable from the imperative to praise "valiant soldiers." Throughout his career, and especially in *Churchyard's Chips* (1575), on which this chapter for the most part focuses, Churchyard challenges his readers to recognize that the valiant soldier is not an extension of the public state but its foil as well as its victim.

CHURCHYARD WAS BORN near Shrewsbury in 1520, the son of a wealthy farmer, and as a teenager he entered the service of Henry Howard, Earl of Surrey, where he learned the poetic skills that would sustain him for the next sixty years. We know little about the reasons he undertook the military service that would supply most of the subject matter for his writings. Surrey went to war in France in 1542, and Churchyard, as a servant of the earl, may have gone with him. However he may have gotten to France in 1542 and however long he may have stayed, Churchyard was there fighting on the side of the Holy Roman Emperor Charles V in the early 1550s. Prior to that, in 1548, he took part in a campaign against the French in Scotland. In 1560 he was fighting again in Scotland, and not long after he was in Ireland fighting under Henry Sidney. Later in that decade he was serving in the Low Countries on the side of the Prince of Orange, and a few years later he was back fighting in Ireland. His last military campaign came in the early 1580s, when he returned to war in the Low Countries at around age sixty. He wrote between deployments throughout the forty years of his military career and was a member of the Middle Temple, where he participated in the bustling literary activity for which the London Inns of Court were famous. He was, as much as any Elizabethan, a servant of Mars and Mercury.[11]

He was almost forty years old when he went to war in Scotland for the second time in March of 1560. He was among some seven thousand soldiers whom he describes as "more raw than ripe, unready, out of use."[12] Their mission was to aid Scottish rebels in their assault on the port town of Leith, where the regent Marie de Guise had holed up her dwindling French forces.[13] It was, for the English, a costly campaign and for Churchyard a frustrating one. Nearly a thousand men perished, many through hunger, during a stalemate that lasted months in the trenches around Leith. As Churchyard describes the situation in "The Siege of Leith" fifteen years later, his fellow soldiers wasted away at their posts while a neglectful country sat on its hands:

> As time consumed, so still our men did waste,
> And needful was for aid or else for peace;
> And to be brief, our country made not haste
> From watch and ward our soldiers to release.
> Great murmurs still among us did increase,
> But duty bade each soldier do his best,
> Till sweet relief should bring poor souls some rest. (p. 11)

What the English soldiers were murmuring about in the no-man's-land between their trenches and the walls of Leith, Churchyard leaves unsaid, but the image of soldiers content to wait for "aid" or for "peace," as if the outcome of the campaign did not matter, recalls the murmurs that were abroad in England when Churchyard wrote his poem.

The Leith campaign is not the kind of war people like to memorialize. The leadership was inexperienced. Not enough resources were committed to it. There was no contingency plan. Casualties were horrible. The military action failed. Worst of all, in retrospect there was no clear reason to have invaded in the first place.

Marie's regency was crumbling. Her husband was dead, her health was failing, and there was not much Scottish left in her daughter Mary, who had been raised in France and had married the Dauphin François II.[14] The tide of Catholic sympathy in Scotland had also turned since the accession of Elizabeth in 1558. Exiled Scots Protestants like John Knox once again found a safe haven in England and began to reassert their influence in Scotland.[15] What strength remained in the regency lay in France, and it was the fear of French reinforcements landing in Scotland that prompted England to act. That fear was unfounded. In his *Annales* of the year 1560, William Camden says that "it came to be known for certain that the French were determined to invade England," but he also admits that the French commanders advising Marie "[knew] the difficulty of the matter [and] refused it."[16] Marie died in the middle of the siege, and, not long after, the unhappy campaign was brought to an end by the Treaty of Edinburgh. It was the first major diplomatic coup for William Cecil, later Lord Burghley, on his way to becoming the most influential statesman in England for the next thirty-eight years. Although an inquiry into the failure of the campaign did not result in any findings of fault, its legacy remained one of military incompetence rescued by diplomatic cunning.[17]

Churchyard's poem is written as a memorial to the Leith campaign, but how does one go about memorializing a war whose memories are so unpleasant? The modern example of the Vietnam Veterans Memorial provides some insight. When the organizers of the memorial fund solicited design concepts in 1979, they emphasized that the memorial should honor the soldiers who fell and not the controversies surrounding the conflict.[18] The rules called for a conciliatory design that would not make a "political statement" but rather honored "the service and memory" of the soldiers.[19] The memorial was to transcend the divisive memories of the war itself and focus on the people who served and died in it, separating them from the political controversies that dogged the war and its aftermath.

Churchyard embarks upon his memorial to those who served at Leith in much the same fashion, stressing at the outset of the poem that he is not out to rekindle unpleasant memories: "And some say, each leader was not skilled: / But what of that? I write not of abuse. / If faults there were, I ought to make excuse" (p. 1). His concern is with remembering those who deserve remembrance.

"Who serveth well at length must needs have fame" (p. 4), he writes, but "all have not fame that worthy are therefore" (p. 3). Like the Vietnam Veterans Memorial Fund officers, Churchyard builds his memorial on the promise that a monument to soldiers can be separated from the politics of the war in which they served, that remembering their actions will not recall the failures and abuses of the war. This assumption is either devious or naive, for to say that in order to honor soldiers we will look past the troubling memories of a particular war, we call attention as much to what we wish to forget as to what we wish to remember.

Jonathan Baldo demonstrates in his article "Wars of Memory in *Henry V*" what everyone who lived through the installation of the Vietnam Veterans Memorial knows well: memories of war are engaged with a "national narrative" that forms from a people's collective "will to forget" as well as its "will to preserve or remember."[20] Baldo focuses on *Henry V*'s relation to contemporary military campaigns in Calais and Ireland and shows how the play questions the processes by which the state creates and enforces certain memories of these wars and engineers the collective forgetting of others. Central to his argument is the work of the chorus in *Henry V* to frame images of war within a preferred narrative.

We need not confine a discussion of these processes to *Henry V* and its oblique and partial references to contemporary wars. We find concrete, real-life instances of this process in the case of the literature involving the battle of Lepanto. *The Lepanto*, written by James VI of Scotland (later James I of England) in 1591, tells of the famous naval victory over the Turks by a coalition of mostly Italian, papal, and Spanish forces led by Don John of Austria in 1571. It was a signal military victory for Catholicism, but in England it was not the attractive subject for artists and writers that it was in Spain and Italy, where it was treated by Lope de Vega, Cervantes, Titian, Tintoretto, and Veronese, among others. James says at the outset of his minor epic that he understands that its hero is a "foreign Papist bastard" but that his reason for dealing with the sensitive subject at all (Don John was also known to the English as a hammer of Protestants in the Low Countries) is that the defiance of the Turks by the Holy League is analogous to the defiance of Catholic persecutors by the forces of Protestantism.[21] The story of the great Catholic victory becomes a suitable subject for English and Scottish readers only when it is fit to the proper political frame, even if that fit is a Procrustean one in which Don John, of all people, becomes a Protestant hero. John Polemon also frames his story of the battle of Lepanto in his *Second Part of the Book of Battles, Fought in Our Age* (1587) with a title that assures its readers that its constituent stories are intended for those who "Practice Arms" or for those "Such as Love to be Harmless Hearers of Bloody Broils."[22] In both cases, a story that energized Catholic Europe could not be retold in England unless its potential significances were circumscribed by assurances of the correct religious and political orientation or neutralized by appeals to practical or frivolous interests. Neither author would have his readers suppose that the story of the battle of Lepanto were simply a record of the event, for the event cannot be recorded without activating its connotations as a rallying cry for Catholic Europe.

When Churchyard declares that the chief aims of poetry should be to praise "valiant soldiers" and honor "Prince and public state," he is acknowledging a connection between the memory of war and the idea of the "public state" to which James and Polemon make concessions and which the Vietnam Veterans Memorial Fund officers were willing to overlook. The winning submission for the memorial's design not only failed to transcend the politics of the war in Vietnam but became, for all intents and purposes, a monument to those politics, as was perhaps its intention all along. There can be little doubt that "The Siege of Leith," too, challenges the political framework in which the memories and lack of memories about the Leith campaign are bound. It is not until after the reader has been alerted to the murmurs about the incompetence of military leadership that Churchyard lists his ho-hum reasons why the soldiers of Leith are not honored for their service—"Some serve so long, their names are clean out wore; / Some have ill friends, ill hap, that is more" (p. 3). The cat is quite out of the bag at this point, however, and we cannot but look for connections between the rumored incompetence of military leadership and the plight of the soldiers. While Churchyard implies that there were problems with military leadership, as soldiers will, his attention turns to the diplomatic conclusion of the campaign.

In one of the poem's several tense instances of preteritio, Churchyard would seem to chide those who harbor criticism about the Treaty of Edinburgh and its implications, but, as with the "abuse" by military leaders, the issues are conspicuously included in the poem, even while they are rejected:

> Because the brute and beetle headed brains
> Can not conceive the deepness of this peace,
> And that some think that we have lost our pains,
> Or that by this may further wars increase,
> For that I would such fond conceits should cease. (p. 12)

The "deepness of this peace" might be read here with a great deal of irony, as might be the idea that the treaty might "further wars increase." When Mary returned to Scotland and refused to ratify the Treaty of Edinburgh, the Protestant faction whom the English had backed at Leith embraced her as their queen, but by the middle of the 1560s these same Protestant Scots rebels were up in arms against her following the bizarre assassinations of her husband and chief minister.[23] Scotland had degenerated into something between a soap opera and a civil war from the time Churchyard served at Leith until the time he wrote these lines praising the "deepness" of the peace. To make matters worse Mary fled Scotland and lingered on as Elizabeth's prisoner as Churchyard wrote his memorial to the campaign, a living symbol of Scotland's dangerous past and uncertain future as well as a reminder that Tudor concepts of justice, laws of succession, and the rights of princes were not absolute at all but could be and were bent to accommodate the shifting interests of the regime.[24]

As for the "brute and beetle headed brains" who believe the English had "lost [their] pains" at Leith, Churchyard can count himself among them. In a risky passage earlier in the poem, he praises the French soldiers as well as his comrades, the former for their skill and the latter for doing their duty to "the queen" with nothing to show for it:

> I spoke before of bickering by the French,
> But here the heat of serving might be seen;
> They bearded us, and made them trench for trench,
> And showed themselves trim soldiers, as I ween.
> But what of that? We came to serve the queen
> Though to our loss. (p. 8)

The poem cannot hold the mounting weight of innuendo at this point. When even the enemy soldiers are worthy of praise while service to the queen comes at a "loss," it becomes clear that the project of praising soldiers is at odds with the imperative to honor prince and public state, that the former challenges the narratives on which the latter in some part depends. In this tension we are forced to ask questions of Leith, or, perhaps, we recognize the questions we should have been asking all along. What really happened at Leith? Who is to blame for what went wrong? Whose version of the story are we accepting as the true one?

Burghley gained more from the Leith campaign than anyone else, for it was through its settlement that he solidified his reputation as a statesman. Fittingly, Churchyard dedicates to Burghley a few lines of his monument to the soldiers of Leith, though it is a strange tribute that begins by calling attention once again to the tension between the praise of soldiers and the praise of the state:

> But or I go too far in soldiers' praise,
> The instruments that ended all this toil,
> I must set forth whose grave and sober ways,
> And stoutness both, did give the French a foil. (p. 11)

It is only in the marginal note "Lord Burghley ended these broils" that we understand just who or what these "instruments" are. The term is vague, as is the grammar surrounding it. At a glance, "the instruments that ended all this toil" would seem to be an appositive renaming "soldiers," which agrees with "instruments" in number. However, the language of the marginal note both parallels and rhymes with "the instruments that ended all this toil," associating Burghley with "instruments," even though the word does not agree in number with "Lord Burghley." One way of accounting for this peculiarity is that there are two poems taking place on the same page, one in which soldiers are the instruments that ended the broils and another in which Burghley is. To see the latter, the reader must stop praising soldiers for a moment and instead praise a great statesman. But the poem goes on to introduce the problems associated with the treaty engineered by that great statesman: the treaty squandered a military advantage and left England vulnerable to more war. The latter problem becomes pressing given that the treaty required the English to abandon their fortress at Eyemouth near Berwick, their strongest foothold on Scotland since the unhappy conclusion of the wars of the Rough Wooing (of which Churchyard was also a veteran) a decade earlier.[25] Indeed, the initial enthusiasm for the treaty dampened when it became clear that a peaceful Scotland would not emerge from the rule of the government set up by Burghley.[26]

It is difficult to accept "The Siege of Leith" as a tribute to Burghley's diplomatic acumen when the moment of his praise is a marginal note amidst more than six hundred lines dedicated to English soldiers who came "to serve the queen" to their "loss" and who would have preferred to be "at home . . . keeping crows" (p. 9). It is, rather, a monument to the suffering of soldiers and to the policies of a government, epitomized in its great instrument Burghley, that made that suffering possible, that did little with any advantage England gained through the sacrifices of soldiers, and that was yet ready to take what credit there was to take.

As a war memorial, "The Siege of Leith" challenges the established narrative of the Leith campaign and questions whose interests are served in the depiction of war and soldiers. The idea that diplomats and not soldiers are the heroes of Leith affirms the importance of Elizabeth's bureaucracy and reinforces the familiar image of soldiers as untrustworthy and but necessary evils. I cite George Gascoigne's description of various types of soldiers from "The Steel Glass" as a representative summary:[27]

> I see not one therein, which seeks to heap
> A world of pence, by pinching of dead pays,
> And so beguiles, the prince in time of need, . . .
> I see not one, within this glass of mine,
> Whose feathers flaunt, and flicker in the wind . . .
> I see not one, (my Lord) I see not one
> Which stands so much, upon his painted sheath
> (Because he hath, perchance at *Boulogne* been
> And loitered, since then in idleness)
> That he accompts, no Soldier but himself,
> Nor one that can, despise the learned brain,
> Which joyneth reading with experience. . . .
> These bloody beasts, appear not in my glass,
> Which cannot rule, their sword in furious rage,
> Nor have respect, to age nor yet to kind:

But down goeth all, where they get upper hand.
Whose greedy harts so hungry are to spoil,
That few regard, the very wrath of God,
Which grieved is, at cries of guiltless blood. (pp. 156–57)

This roll call of negative stereotypes is well known to any student of Elizabethan literature and culture. It includes captains who defraud the country by leaving the names of the dead on the payrolls, soldiers who boast and swagger but who are ineffectual in combat, soldiers who trade on their past glories, soldiers who eschew education, soldiers who scorn everyone but themselves, and soldiers who commit war crimes. So familiar are these stereotypes that a list of the fictional soldiers of this period who embody some or all of them would be a long and tedious one. To what extent these stereotypes have some basis in truth is an important question in its own right but one that belongs perhaps more properly to the work of military historians. More important for this discussion is the question of how these stereotypes contribute to the function of war memorial to create a narrative about "Prince and public state."

Elizabeth was notorious for skimping on military funds and for being no friend of professional soldiers. Burghley, for his part, advised his son that anyone who lives "by that profession can hardly be called an honest man or a good Christian" and that "soldiers in peace are like chimneys in summer."[28] A generation later, the affluent minor official Francis Osborne gives a chilling and unequivocal statement of how a prudent government ought to manage its armed forces:

> Another error may happen, especially where a free state is founded in arms, by conceding too great a power to the soldiery, who like the spirits of conjurers do oftentimes tear their masters and raisers in pieces for want of other employment. Therefore, since it is beyond the plenty of any nation to proportion a reward suitable to the opinion they have of their own merit, it behooves the supreme power to bury the covetousness and ambition in the fields of others by a foreign war, yet as little to their discontent as may be, always giving them the honor of good servants though bad masters, remembering that the cause you raised them for is not so deep buried but it may rise again to the terror of all that withstand it.[29]

Chimneys in summer, indeed. For Osborne, it is also to the state's advantage to let as many soldiers die abroad as possible, provided the state keeps some around and feeds them with token honor in case their services should be needed again.

Nothing is gained by positing here a maudlin or naive idea of how soldiers ought to be treated; the fact is that paying for and also managing soldiers who are not fighting is a problem for all governments. There are many good reasons for taking a dim view of military spending and professional soldiership and as many for urging one's children to stay out of the armed forces. The point is that these attitudes among the power brokers of an Elizabethan regime that was both militaristic and dedicated to its own preservation must be questioned. To what extent does the commonplace image of the Elizabethan soldier as incompetent, greedy, or vainglorious reflect the specific needs of the regime? As "The Siege of Leith" makes clear, the soldiers and Burghley cannot be at the same time "the instruments that ended all this toil." Burghley's act of statecraft requires for its significance the incompetence and failure of the military, an idea that was readily believable due to the proliferation of negative stereotypes. Churchyard upsets this relationship by asserting a different memory of the soldiers at Leith, one in which they and not Burghley defeated the French and in which soldiers on both sides are men of honor and courage. This alternative image of soldiers does not correct the historical record as much as it forces the reader to recognize that in war memorial, an idea of the state and the image of soldiers produce each other. If the soldiers are not to blame for what went wrong in Scotland, then necessarily an exploitative, self-serving, and inept state is.

THIS ASPECT OF the poem becomes clearer when it is set in the context of Churchyard's other writings about veterans' experiences. In "The Unhappy Man's Dear Adieu," Churchyard refers to the present as a "a hungry age, when soldiers starve and pine" and goes on to complain how, worn down by deployments, the soldier must of necessity return to war again:

> Now must I leave the Land I like so well,
> And creep away to foreign country strange,
> Now must stiff joints among strange people dwell,

Now for hard beds I shall soft lodging change;
  Now from sweet peace, in war shall body range.
Now shot and sword, and heavy coat of steel,
In most weak plight, my weary bones shall feel.[30]

The problem with what to do with veterans once their services were no longer required was much on the mind of Elizabethan England. Those who were disabled in war were supposed to receive a yearly stipend, but the thousands who returned in one piece were expected to reintegrate quietly into civilian life. Mixed messages attended this process. On the one hand, soldiers might be allowed to keep the weapons they carried as part of the compensation for their service, but, on the other hand, they were encouraged to lay those arms aside and take up their wonted trades once home. Styward provides the following summary of the instructions given to men upon discharge:

> [Their captains] letting them to understand that the wars being ended; the Prince is not further to use them, exhorting every man, quietly to deport into his country from whence he was pressed, or to the place of his longest abode, not looking to make an art or exercise of arms for that is not to be used, but when the Prince through constraint shall be enforced to the same. And when they are come into their country, require every man to frame himself to such science, occupations, trades, and traffics as they have chiefly been brought up with all.[31]

The concern over discharged soldiers turning feral back in England and making their living as highway robbers is commonplace in Elizabethan writings (epitomized in Shakespeare's Falstaff), but the style of warfare that evolved in the sixteenth century required an unprecedented degree of professionalism from soldiers and officers, and the idea that these newfangled military professionals could just stop being soldiers at the end of the war was in conflict with the warfighting needs of the state. The operational tempo of Elizabethan expeditionary warfare required, as I have discussed in the second chapter, the deployment of about fifteen thousand soldiers annually. This requirement stretched the antiquated muster system to breaking and resulted in the fielding of poorly trained and poorly equipped troops. The Elizabethan "Trained Bands"—a body of select militiamen who could be mobilized rapidly—were too few to solve this problem.[32] An obvious solution was to retain former soldiers in a pay status so that they could be activated as needed, but Elizabeth did not develop this option.[33]

The solution she did employ was to rely on professional soldiers to fight wars but to pay them only when they were fighting. This practice of keeping a class of professional soldiers unemployed until they are needed is a too, too familiar one among U.S. reservists today. For many, deployment or other commitments related to war makes a civilian career or degree program difficult to manage, which makes reservists dependent on the military for employment even while they are not paid unless they are deployed. As a result, many seek deployment for lack of other work, and yet their service is not permitted to continue if they are at all close to accumulating the requisite number of active duty points to rate a pension.

What are the "occupations, trades, and traffics" to which soldiers are supposed to return under these conditions? What were the trades Churchyard and men like him had "chiefly been brought up with all" after years of regular deployment to foreign war? The Elizabethan regime had few places for professional soldiers who were not deployed, and so going back to war became a way of making a living. "A Tragical Discourse of the Unhappy Man's Life" captures this problem as the narrator reflects on the short-lived pleasure of his homecoming:

> Three years, at least, I saw the Emperor's wars,
> Then homeward drew, as was my wanted trade;
> Where sun and moon, and all the seven stars
> Stood on my side, and me great welcome made;
> But whether fair and flowers full soon will fade:
> So people's love is like new besoms oft,
> That sweeps all clean, whiles broom is green and soft.[34]

The phrase "as was my wanted trade" speaks to the expectation that returning soldiers should return to their civilian occupations upon coming home, but the narrator's "wanted trade" here *is* drawing "homeward" after the war and, by implication, going off to war again. There is no other trade or life available, and the image in the final couplet of the broom sweeping the unhappy man away again bodies forth the idea that there is no home for a soldier in peaceful domesticity.

"A Tragical Discourse" thus develops an image of the soldier as a servant to a forgetful and ungrateful state whose only use for him is more war. As in "The Siege of Lieth," the enduring image of the soldier Churchyard creates in this poem is one who is abandoned, exploited, and alone:

> But post alone I stood, alack the while!
> And country clean forgot me: this is true,
> And I might live in sorrow and exile,
> And pine away for anything I knew ...
> Not one at home did seek my grief to heal:
> Thus was I clean cut off from commonweal.[35]

He makes this point in another poem published along with "The Siege of Leith," "The Praises of Our Soldiers":

> And least esteemed of all the men that lives,
> (Like hackney horse cast off when turn is served)
> Yet are you there that greatest honor give
> (If world may judge what soldiers have deserved)
> Unto your prince; for you are pale and park
> To keep the deer, and lanterns in the dark.[36]

And like "The Siege of Leith," the poem stands on the tension between the act of praising soldiers and of honoring the state. It asserts its praises for soldiers as "lanterns in the dark" and celebrates their capacity to give "honor" unto the "prince," at the same time leaving no ambiguity that the fate of soldiers in the Elizabethan state is to be "cast off when turn is served." Once again, Churchyard's praise of soldiers does not praise the state but rather reveals its faults.

HOW HONORING SOLDIERS precipitates a revaluation of the state they serve is a cohesive force in *Churchyard's Chips*, but it also raises questions about the relation of individuals to the state that extend beyond the plight of soldiers. For Churchyard, the soldier as a "hackney horse cast off when turn is served" is a vivid case of a much larger problem of personal exploitation that he developed throughout his career and most notably in his most admired work, "Shore's Wife." First published in 1561 but revised and republished during the military escalations of the early 1590s, the poem tells the story of the haunting figure of Mistress Shore, sometimes called Jane, the quasi-legendary mistress of Edward IV and éminence grise during his tumultuous reign. Elizabethans were fascinated with the figure of Mistress Shore, and her story was told or alluded to in a number of works from this period. It is a complicated tale. Shore was a commoner married to a well-to-do London merchant, but when she attracted the eye of the king she left her husband for the court and remained there until Edward's death. No favorite of Richard III (as readers of Shakespeare's play by that name are well aware), she was implicated in the king's death, only to be spared, as Thomas More says in his *History of Richard III*, by the maneuvering of Lord Hastings.[37] Although she escaped prosecution, her hour upon the political stage was over.

Although the story of Jane Shore has nothing to do with soldiers, it has everything to do with the politics of praise. As I have suggested throughout this chapter, an idea of the state is implicated in whom, what, when, and how a society memorializes. Elizabethan interest in Jane Shore has much to do with the vilification of Richard III, whom the Earl of Richmond supplanted to become Henry VII of England and the founder of the royal house of Tudor.[38] Mistress Shore's shadowy presence in the story of Richard's rise and fall cannot completely account for her popularity with Elizabethan readers, however, for her own story is charged with social and moral problems that under any other circumstances would have affronted Elizabethan convictions about personal and political duty.[39] As a commoner who shared the king's bed as well as his confidence, she crosses the most important political boundary Elizabethans knew. As a woman pulling the strings of government, she undermines conventional beliefs about the social role of women. As a wife who leaves her husband for the fame and luxuries of the court, she violates the primary social and moral obligation of women, to remain faithful servants to their husbands. In the popular fictions Mistress Shore tends to be a solitary figure wracked by the woe, sorrow, and shame appropriate to a woman who has transgressed so many boundaries, and yet she tends also to be represented as a loyal subject put into an impossible situation by the state and wracked on fortune's wheel. As she says in Thomas Deloney's 1593 version of her story, "The king commanded, and I straight obey'd."[40]

Given the concern Churchyard demonstrates in his war poetry for those who serve the state "though to [their] loss," it is not surprising that he would also be interested in Mistress Shore as a literary topic, nor is it surprising that he should revise and republish his representation of her during Elizabeth's war years. Reminiscent of Churchyard's approach to reinventing the battle at Leith, Churchyard's Shore will lay out all the reasons her positions as kept woman, unfaithful wife, and manipulator of the state are morally untenable only to raise the more important question of who is responsible for the situation she finds herself in:[41]

> Yet give me leave to plead my cause at large,
> If that the horse do run beyond his race,
> Or any thing that keepers have in charge
> Do break their course where rulers may take place,
> Or meat be set before the hungry's face,
> Who is at fault? th'offender, yea or no?
> Or they that are the cause of all this woe. (p. 131)[42]

Although couched in an argument that resembles the chestnut about whether it is right or wrong for a starving man to steal a loaf of bread, Shore's question to the reader belongs in the province of political rather than moral philosophy, and it hinges on the relationship between "keepers" or "rulers" and the people who are subjected to their will. She does not give the reader much time to think about the question before answering it herself. Her argument is that those who have near or complete power over others are to blame when the actions on the part of the former lead to transgression on the part of the latter. This is essentially the same argument Williams puts to his disguised king in Shakespeare's *Henry V* before the battle of Agincourt, to which Henry protests that the power to command others to act does not make the commander accountable for the moral failings of those he commands.[43] Henry's argument is a straw man, however; he offers a logical and sound argument against his culpability for the incidental moral failings of the soldiers he has ordered into battle but steers well clear of Williams's central point, which is that those with the power to command are responsible when others who are morally and legally bound to obey are compelled to perform unjust or immoral acts. Churchyard's Shore would seem to agree.

Shore will reiterate that the problems that accumulate around her do not belong to her moral choices but to a political order in which people are obliged at the behest of their rulers to do things they know are wrong. She asks:

> What help is this? the pale once broken down,
> The deer must needs in danger run astray:
> At me therefore why should the world so frown?
> My weakness made my youth a prince's prey.
> Though wisdom should the course of nature stay,
> Yet try my case, who list, and they shall prove
> The ripest wits are soonest thralls to love. (p. 132)

By invoking her susceptibility to falling in love in the final couplet of the stanza, Shore recalls the "amor vincit omnia" theme as well as the pervasive social paranoia about the supposed libidinousness of women, but in this case the line is a red herring that serves to put a damper on the political charge of the stanza.[44] The tone of the language does not belong to a woman in love, and Shore has once again cast the relationship between kings and subjects as analogous to that of keepers and game. This relation has different connotations than the preferred Elizabethan conception of princes as fathers to their subjects. Keepers do not have the interests of their charges at heart but tend to them only so they may be consumed in due course. Shore reinforces this relationship by calling herself a "prince's prey."[45]

Although Churchyard's Mistress Shore appeals to the weakness of her political position as an excuse for her choices, the core of her defense is that she made the best of the situation by serving the commonwealth and striving to win justice for her fellow citizens. Although she confesses she enjoyed the material rewards of her position, she took greater pleasure in protecting the interests of ordinary people, never forgetting where she came from or how easily fortune could cast her down:

> I took delight in doing each man good,
> Not scratting all myself, as all were mine,

> But looked whose life in need and danger stood,
> And those I kept from harm with cunning fine...
>
> I offered aide before they sued to me,
> And promised ought but would perform it straight;
> I shaked down sweet fruit from top of tree,
> Made apples fall in laps of men by sleight.
> I did good turns whiles that I was in height,
> For fear a flaw of wind would make me reel,
> And blow me down when Fortune turned his wheel. (pp. 134-35)

I am not arguing that Churchyard's Shore is entirely altruistic or saintly. She speaks often of the pleasure she takes in the perquisites of her position, and, again, her words recall many pervasive social fears about women's sexuality and their potential to usurp power from men. What I am stressing, rather, is that the aspect of her story that dominates Churchyard's poem is her quiet service to the common people almost against the tendencies of the state, which she must circumvent by "cunning" and "sleight." Sounding like one of Churchyard's old soldiers, Shore claims she served not "to purchase praise and win the peoples zeal" but "to do some good" and to "uphold the common weal" (p. 135).

Despite her good service to the commonwealth, Mistress Shore is discarded when she is no longer of use. Scorned and forsaken, she laments how the good deeds of people are forgotten once they can no longer perform them, and she leaves the reader with a graphic image of an exploitative society in which "we feed on flesh, and fling away the bone" (p. 139). The thematic parallels between Churchyard's Mistress Shore and his soldiers, those quiet servants of the commonwealth who are "cast off when turn is served," are obvious. So too is the problem of a self-serving state. Churchyard's Mistress Shore is a loyal subject whose reward, like that of the men who fought at Leith, is personal loss. The woman ordered into moral turpitude or the man ordered to foreign war to serve a state that throws away the bones when the flesh is gone must each hazard something the state cannot repay. Viewed as complements to one another, Churchyard's soldiers and Mistress Shore are two compelling memorials that we can recognize as praiseworthy only if we also recognize the culpability of the "Prince and public state."

REFLECTING ON HIS own service to the state, Churchyard writes to his friend and benefactor Sir Christopher Hatton: "The last reward of a soldier is death, this do I desire, as a man that have made choice, though unworthy of that profession. I seek no farm, I sue for no pension, nor I love not to live as an almsman. I covet to die like a soldier and a true subject, as loath to live any longer in misery, when I see the world waxeth weary of my well doing."[46] Like everything else Churchyard wrote, the letter is as much a performance of a literary persona as a statement of fact, and as such it is as important for what it tells us about Churchyard's audiences as for what it tells us about his life. What it tells us, I suggest, is that the figure of the soldier in the Elizabethan imagination is informed by the idea of a state that is exploitative and self-interested, enough so that Churchyard could invoke this politically loaded image of the soldier and find an audience for it until the day he died. The image of the forgotten, exploited, and abused soldiers cannot be memorialized unless we acknowledge, even tacitly, the forces that forget, exploit, and abuse them. It is the image of those destructive forces at work in the Elizabethan regime, more than of its soldiers, that takes shape in Churchyard's writings.

4
A Tale of Two Cities
George Gascoigne's Antwerp and *Alarum for London*

GEORGE GASCOIGNE WENT to war for the time-honored reason of having burned the bridges to just about every personal relationship and professional opportunity he had. The clever, well-educated, but self-consciously feckless son of a well-to-do farmer, Gascoigne had by his early thirties landed once in debtor's prison, been sued by his own brothers, and been barred from a career in politics on the grounds of his being "a notorious ruffian, an atheist, and godless person."[1] In the early 1570s, he went to war in the Low Countries in the service of William of Orange, returning to write most of the poetry, prose, and drama for which he is remembered today. He later went back to the Low Countries as an employee of the state (perhaps as a spy) and came home again in 1576. He died soon after. He was not yet forty. The motto under which he labored in his short happy life as a military man of letters in the 1570s was "Tam Marti quam Mercurio" (see figure 6)—as much a soldier as a poet—which might be read as a tongue-in-cheek comment on the quality and quantity of his contributions to either profession.[2]

It was after returning from the Low Countries the second time that Gascoigne wrote a short prose work called *The Spoil of Antwerp*, which is best known today as the source document for a propagandistic drama called *Alarum for London*, usually attributed to Thomas Lodge, registered in 1600 and published in 1602. So tightly is this play bound to Gascoigne's prose work that its most recent publication (1970) lists both Lodge and Gascoigne as the authors, extending the logic of the 1872 London edition that published the two works together.[3] Connecting Gascoigne to the 1602 work gives the play some historical weight as well as eyewitness credibility, locating its acerbic anti-Spanish flavor within the tradition of military memoir, in this case one by a famous soldier poet from the early days of Elizabeth's reign.

The relations between the two works are complicated. Gascoigne's is more circumspect and ambivalent in its attitudes toward the Spanish, more philosophical about war and soldiers in general. The play transforms Gascoigne's account into what seems to be a militant attack on Spain characteristic of the propaganda of the war years. A comparison of the two works gives us insights into the structure of anti-Spanish propaganda and the different ways it adopts and modifies other narratives. This comparison also reveals uncertainty in the propaganda. By drawing on Gascoigne's narrative, *Alarum for London* imports the ambiguities that attended England's attitudes toward the Spanish, its Protestant allies in the Low Countries, and its commitments to war in general that inform Gascoigne's *Spoil* and the literary milieu in which it was written. As a result, the comparison allows us to question not only the central claims of anti-Spanish propaganda but also the extent to which this propaganda represented the attitudes of English people during the war years.

THE SPOIL OF *Antwerp* tells the now familiar story of the destruction of one of the richest cities in the Netherlands by the Spanish in 1576, an action that has come to be known as the "Spanish Fury." It is not a work of propaganda, however, nor was Gascoigne a propagandist. Like Thomas Churchyard, Gascoigne spent much of his literary career dodging Elizabethan censors and had to revise many of his works under the threat of punishment.[4] Although Gascoigne describes the actions of the Spanish as "barbarous and cruel," he also calls out the moral failings of the city and its inhabitants. Thus the story seems less a political attack on any one country than a *de casibus* tragedy that cooperates with the Tudor predilection for turning "all political ends to divine actions":[5]

> And therewithall, if the wickedness used in the said town, do seem unto the well disposed Reader, a sufficient cause of God's so just a scourge and plague: and yet the fury of the vanquishers do also seem more barbarous and cruel, than may become a good Christian conqueror: let these my few words become a forewarning to both hands, and let them stand as a lantern of

light between two perilous rocks: that both attending the one, and detesting the other we may gather fire out of the flint, and honey out of the thistle.[6]

The lesson Gascoigne tells his readers they will find in the story of the sack of Antwerp is rooted in the Old Testament. English observers would have easily connected "the wickedness used in that said town" to the story of Sodom and Gomorrah and viewed Antwerp's destruction, as Gascoigne suggests, as a form of divine justice.

English notions about Antwerp are crucial to Gascoigne's moral lesson. Antwerp was England's most important trading partner in the 1570s and hosted a large community of English merchants, but it was also notorious for its moneylending. Antwerp financiers owned the majority of England's foreign debt, and many of these moneylenders were part of Antwerp's significant Jewish community, which did not help English people reconcile the business of the city to their religious and moral convictions.[7] For Londoners, Antwerp was a city of bottomless moneybags and all the material excesses and moral failings that went along with them. In his general description of Holland from his *Alarum to England*, for example, Gascoigne's friend and fellow soldier Barnabe Rich describes the people of the Low Countries as money-minded libertines:

> Let Holland make discourse at large, if I have said amiss,
> Whose towns were seated in such sort, by nature framed so strong, as no assault of foreign foe might do them sudden wrong.
> No want of wealth might work their woe, no coin with them was scant, of ships great store in every port, no [pleasure] they did want.
> They lived at ease in vile excess, they sought for (lecker cost) their paunches stuffed with double beer, was that they cared for most.[8]

The image of "paunches stuffed with double beer," preceded here by the image of towns "by nature framed so strong, / as no assault of foreign foe might do them sudden wrong," establishes the moral weakness of the Dutch people—not any "foreign foe"—as the cause of their destruction. This same sentiment is expressed in a 1577 broadsheet ballad by Rafe Norris called "A Warning to London by the Fall of Antwerp," which depicts "Antwerp's plague" as self-generated from its "Devlish drunken trade"—a "rod / prepared for to scourge [its] pride."[9] Gascoigne captures this sense of Antwerp being responsible for its own doom in the *contrapasso* toward the end of the *Spoil*, where he describes "one of the richest towns in Europe" reduced to an abode of "murderers and strumpets" while the "honest trades" of its once proud Bourse, the seat of its money markets, are replaced with "as many dicing tables as might be placed round about it all the day long" (p. 597). The strumpets and dicers who take over after the fall become continuations of problems many English people had associated with Antwerp's "honest trades" all along.

The role of divine judgment in the devastation of the Low Countries by the Spanish would have been strengthened by the conviction that God dictates the outcome of military actions, which was a dimension of most professional and quasi-professional discussions about the conduct of war.[10] Rich writes in *Faultes Faults*: "War is the minister of God's justice, either for contempt of himself, of his religion, or the wicked life of worldlings, so that it is the sins of the people that unsheatheth the soldier's sword."[11] Gascoigne makes almost the same claim in his poetic essay on war, "*Dulce Bellum Inexpertis*" or "The Fruits of War," proclaiming war to be "even the scourge of God."[12]

From this context we should expect *The Spoil of Antwerp* to have no compunction about depicting the people of Antwerp as sinners who invited scourge through their embarrassment of riches, but what we find instead are people who were merely unfortunate enough to be residents of the wealthiest city in proximity of an army in need of money. "The sack and spoil of Antwerp," Gascoigne writes, "hath been . . . long pretended by the Spaniards: and that they have done nothing else but [lie] in wait continually to find any least quarrel to put the same into execution" (p. 590). The "least quarrel," for Gascoigne, came in the form of the city's decision not to "shoot at the Prince of Orange's ships, which lay within sight thereof" (p. 591). Historians would later claim that the sack followed a money shortage on the part of the Spanish army, which prompted the soldiers to find their own remunerations by sacking Antwerp.[13] In any case, Antwerp discovered, in essence, that neutrality is always a fragile position when war and all its attendant wants are swirling around one's walls, especially when one's coffers are deep.

When the attack comes, the people of Gascoigne's Antwerp do not acquit themselves like moral failures but rise to the defense of their city, constructing a massive defensive earthwork in a very short period of time: "It was a strange thing to see the willingness of the inhabitants, and how soon many hands had dispatched a very great peace of work: for before midnight they had made the trenches as high as the length of a pike" (p. 592). With the Spanish pressing the attack, the citizens do not, like their Walloon guardsmen, turn and run but stand their ground, each man before his house, prepared to defend himself even in the face of "the ruin of the city":

> So that as I came down and took my cloak and sword, to see the certainty thereof, and as I passed toward the Bourse, I met many, but I overtook none: and those which I met were no Townsmen, but soldiers: neither walked they as men which use traffic, but ran as men which are in fear: Whereat being somewhat grieved, and seeing the townsmen stand every man before his door with such weapons as they had, I demanded of one of them, what it meant. Who answered me in these words, "Alas, sir, order is utterly gone" and "behold, the ruin of the city." "Have courage, my friend," (quoth I) and so went onwards yet to the Bourse. . . . At last, a Walloon trumpeter on horseback (who seemed to be but a Boy of years) drew his sword, and laid about him crying, "Where are you people fleeing? Let's put the honor of our country to the test!" Wherewith, fifty or three score of them turned head, and went backwards towards the Bourse. (p. 594)[14]

Hardly the description of cash-fattened drunkards without pride or strength enough to defend themselves. Gascoigne is left to speculate as to what failed the citizens of Antwerp, since their personal valor clearly did not. He concludes that the problem must be the "lack of foresight in the Walloons" retained as a defensive force (p. 595) and the poor emergency management of the city fathers: "For surely the inhabitants lacked but good guides and leaders: for having none other order appointed, but to stand every man armed in readiness before his door, they died there (many of them) fighting manfully" (p. 599).

Unlike in the Old Testament, in the "scourge of God" visited on Antwerp in Gascoigne's *Spoil* the righteous suffer along with the wicked, an arrangement that troubles the conception of the doom of Antwerp as an act of divine judgment.[15] It would seem rather that the citizens who died "manfully" in Antwerp were the victims not of their own corruption but of political relations beyond their control. To complicate matters further, Gascoigne takes a soldier's delight in the efficiency and discipline of the Spanish forces, who with "good order" cleared the trenches and torched the houses of the citizen defenders in no time at all (p. 594). His praise for the Spanish becomes so fulgent at one point that he must check himself and realign the narrative with the expected moral trajectory:

> I must confess, that it was the greatest victory, and the roundliest executed, that hath been seen, read, or heard of, in our age: and that it was a thing miraculous, to consider, how trenches of such a height should be entered, passed over, and won both by footmen, and horsemen. . . . But whosoever will there most extol the Spaniards for the valor and order, must therewithall confess that it was the very ordinance of God for a just plague and scourge of the town: For otherwise it passeth all men's capacity to conceive how it should be possible. (p. 595)

As Gascoigne credits the expressly human virtues of the Spanish (their "valor and order") for the capture of Antwerp, the idea of the Spanish as mindless instruments of God's will becomes unstable. Thus, Gascoigne retrenches and reminds the reader that the miraculous victory signals God's "ordinance," without which the Spanish victory would have been impossible. But with no unambiguous indication in the narrative of how Antwerp offended God, the imposition of a contrived moral interpretation of the city's defeat calls attention to the lack of an appropriate moral interpretation. Along with the narrator we cannot help but admire the organization and energy of the Spanish and the courage of the mismanaged citizens, giving the impression that if the Spanish are a scourge, they are a particularly professional and well-organized scourge and that if the city of Antwerp sinned, its sin would seem to have been nothing worse than bad civic management.

Gascoigne insists that the reader understand the story as an allegory of divine judgment, but it is a conspicuously weak and unsupported insistence. Toward the end of the *Spoil*, this insistence becomes especially fragile when Gascoigne describes an aftermath of battle in which "17,000 men, women, and children" lay in as "many sundry shapes and forms of man's motion at time of death: as ever Michelangelo did portray in his tables of Doomsday," calling it a "pitiful massacre though God gave the victory to the Spaniards" (p. 596).

Without a clear moral coherence to the fall of Antwerp—without citizens who obviously deserve their fate, without a conqueror who is obviously mindless or acting as an instrument of divine justice, and, for that matter, without a divine intelligence that clearly directs the scourge—the political rather than the moral dimension of the situation becomes overwhelming. The trouble in Antwerp does not involve an angry god and its wayward children but two sides of a problem having to do with money and power and the people caught in the ensuing chaos. It is not insignificant in this regard that the speaker's most pronounced appeal to God in the *Spoil* comes in the form of the question "What in God's name do I here which have no interest in this action?" (p. 595). The question is natural and well known to anyone who has ever been sent to a war in which he or she has no stake, but in context the question does not simply remind the reader that war is frightening and that you don't want to be in one unless you have to but utterly strips the narrative of the moral and religious importance Gascoigne promises at the outset it will have. Where we might expect the speaker to ask in God's name why the stalwart citizens of Antwerp deserved to perish by the thousands or why the cruel but efficient Spaniards deserved to reap the spoils of the city, we get instead a question that implies that there is no moral rationale to the destruction at Antwerp at all. The Spanish army is simply very good at what it does and needed money. Antwerp simply had money, and its government was unprepared to defend against an attack. The only moral to the *Spoil* is that once the war begins, everyone who can should get far, far away from it.

ALARUM FOR LONDON would seem on its surface to be a less ambiguous work. Hale calls the play "grisly" and counts it among the "propaganda plays" encouraged by the Elizabethan state.[16]

Jorgensen, likewise, regards it as a "[dramatization] of the militarists' admonitory tracts."[17] It is, as the title suggests, alarmist. It terrorizes its English audience into believing in a looming, greedy, and irrational Spanish enemy. As Egmount says early in the play to the governors of Antwerp who are still undecided about the extent of the Spanish threat:

·Collect by this the Spaniards cruelty,
Who though occasion should not come from you,
Would pick a quarrel for occasion,
To sack your City, and to suck your blood,
To satisfy his pride and luxury. . . .
Burghers, the Spaniard waits to take your lives,
That he may spoil your town, your wealth, your wives. (p. B4)[18]

This image of the Spanish Fury was by 1602 commonplace. *An Historical Discourse, or rather a Tragical History of the City of Antwerp since the Departure of Phillip, King of Spain, out of the Netherlands, till this Present Year*, published by John Windet in 1586, reports: "Then were their daughters ravished, women abused, and of all sorts, some as well women as men, and they were of the best calling put to strange, beastly and horrible torments."[19] The culpability attributed to the sins of Antwerp in the literature of the 1570s is transferred to the perceived irrational fury of the Spanish in the decades that followed. Walter Raleigh writes to the new king in his *Discourse Touching a War with Spain* that "there are no people more industrious in all things or more provident" than the people of the Netherlands and that prosecuting war against an unappeasable Spanish king in their defense is the only way to ensure the safety of England's borders and commercial interests.[20]

Apparently, the people of Antwerp and the Low Countries underwent a retroactive moral recovery in the eyes of the English by the turn of the seventeenth century. The Burgher, who serves throughout *Alarum for London* as a spokesman for the city's penny-pinching, may reject plans to fortify Antwerp on the grounds that "twill shake our bags too much to pay so many" (p. B3). The people of Antwerp may "[spend] as much on monkeys, dogs, and parrots, / As would have kept ten soldiers all the year" (p. D). Yet there can be no doubt that the demons in this version of the sack are not those that haunt the consciences of the citizens of Antwerp, however misguided their spending habits may be. The demons are the Spanish. In the opening scenes, Alva actually rises from a coffin (p. B2) and Danila licks his lips in contemplation of the impending "slaughter" of the weak citizens of Antwerp:

Cornelius: The Citizens (were they but politick,
Careful, and studious to preserve their peace)
Might at an hour's warning fill their streets
With forty thousand well appointed soldiers.
Danila: Aye, but they are remiss and negligent,
Their bodies used to soft effeminate silks,
And their nice minds set on all dalliance;
Which makes them fat for slaughter, fit for spoil.
(p. A2)

While the play, like earlier accounts of the sack, will appeal to the *de casibus* tragic mode in which Antwerp's failings serve as a warning for other cities to avoid excesses, it is the murderous Spanish themselves who excuse their own actions according to this moral logic, rendering it suspect. Danila's claim that the people of Antwerp were "too much addicted to their private lust: / And that concludes their Martyrdom was just" (p. G) is as reductive as it is conspicuously clumsy and would seem to do little to justify earlier scenes in which Spaniards go about the streets of the city turning out every last pocket of the frightened citizens, killing children in the presence of their parents, and declaring that nothing in "war's music" pleases "[unless] it have the cheerful sound of gold" (p. E3). The Spanish, not the citizens of Antwerp, are to blame for the destruction of the city.

England was not at war with Spain when Gascoigne witnessed the destruction of Antwerp, nor was England officially supportive of the rebellion against Spanish rule in the Netherlands, although Gascoigne's personal connections to William of Orange might have made him more sympathetic to the rebel cause. It had not been so many years since England and Spain were united by the marriage of Phillip II and Mary Tudor. Elizabeth had refused to embroil her country in the Dutch Revolt, and England's reliance on ports in the Spanish Netherlands for its exports gave every encouragement to maintain stable relations with whoever controlled them. The two kingdoms had fired shots across each other's bows in Gascoigne's lifetime. Spain had captured most of John Hawkins's fleet and stolen the proceeds of his profitable slaving venture in the West Indies in 1568, and Elizabeth reciprocated by seizing Alva's pay ships later that year when they took temporary shelter in England against a storm.[21] Religious and political tensions, complicated by overseas trade competition, were certainly mounting in both kingdoms and would seem, in retrospect, to have made open war in the Netherlands inevitable, but we find Burghley still seeking peaceful resolutions to these tensions into the 1580s, and we hear in the Lord Mayor's Show of 1585 a personified London calling Elizabeth "sovereign of my peace."[22] Following the assassination of William of Orange in 1584, however, English hawks won the day and pushed England into the Dutch Revolt, formally beginning nearly twenty years of war with Spain.

During these years England and its Protestant allies initiated one of the most successful and enduring public relations campaigns in the history of the Western world, resulting in what Julián Juderías called in 1914 "*la leyenda negra*," or the Black Legend.[23] In most respects, the Black Legend differs in no significant way from any other defamation campaign launched by any country against its enemy in a time of war. During the wars of religion in France and the Low Countries, Protestant Dutch, Huguenot, and, later, English presses began circulating accounts of unspeakable cruelties committed by Spanish conquerors in the New World as a way of contextualizing the actions of Spanish forces against Protestants in Europe and, it follows, of justifying any violence used to overthrow them.[24]

The particular effectiveness of the Black Legend owes much to one way it does differ from ordinary war propaganda: it emanated from Spain itself, from Bartolome de Las Casas's *La Brevisima relacion de la destruccion de las Indias*, written in 1542 and published again along with other treatises on the Spanish conquest of America between 1552 and 1553. The publication, in context, is not as much an attack on Spanish conduct as a royalist attack on the Spanish lords of the New World, whose growing power and independence were of concern to many Spaniards, including Carlos I.[25] His son Phillip II, facing financial crisis, favored more aggressive exploitation of the New World colonies as necessary to the kingdom and so squelched any open discussion of the conduct of Spaniards toward West Indian natives. But Las Casas's work would take on new connotations among Spain's enemies.

Between 1578 and 1584, Las Casas's treatise would be published in Dutch, French, and English, and once again in German in 1599. For Protestants, the apparently self-condemnatory nature of the respected Spanish author and churchman's work served as good evidence for the corruption and indecency of Spain. This evidence provided much needed energy to the weary Protestant cause in the Netherlands. Spain had dealt the Dutch rebellion a nearly crippling blow at Antwerp, and the publication of Las Casas's *Relacion* in the Netherlands just two years after galvanized the Protestant resistance. A year later it was published in French by the Protestant Jacques de Miggrode as *Tyrranies et cruautez des Espagnols Perpetrees aux Indes Occidentales*. That same year a translation of Girolamo Benzoni's *Historia del Mondo Nuovo*, which borrows liberally from Las Casas's accounts of Spanish actions in the New World, was published in French by the Huguenot Urbain Chauveton. Five years later, in 1583, Miggrode's version of Las Casas was translated and published in England, just one year after the London publication of Christopher Plantin's account of the 1582 assassination attempt on William of Orange by the Spaniard Juan Jauregui.[26] In 1584, Richard Hakluyt cites Las Casas as his source for accounts of Spanish cruelty in the New World in a protracted argument for English colonization.[27] England's formal entry into the Dutch Revolt in 1585 was thus preceded by the emergence of pronounced anti-Spanish propaganda that has continued to color the English-speaking world's understanding of Spanish colonial practices to this day.

Las Casas is not the source of the Black Legend by any stretch. He was, rather, a convenient focal point for it. Assumptions derived from Las Casas about Spanish cruelty, however, form the first principles of most subsequent anti-Spanish propaganda and promote the idea of the Spanish as overlords so exploitative and inhumane that even fellow Spaniards could not refrain from condemning them. Surely, Spain was no more exploitative or inhumane than any other imperial overlord, and as the actions of any occupying or invading country are carried out by soldiers who, then as now, will be driven by their circumstances to commit atrocities, it is always possible to combine in one narrative (as Las Casas does) the isolated actions of individual soldiers and commanders to create an image of widespread cruelty. But military actions abroad are the aggregate of hundreds of thousands of interactions between invading forces and the people they meet, on the battlefield or in the marketplace or anywhere else. The character of this interaction can never be captured in a generalization, except perhaps that dire circumstances will provoke people to perform acts of both cruelty and kindness that are inconceivable at home.

Nevertheless, from the time of England's entry into the Dutch Revolt to the end of Elizabeth's reign, an indigenous anti-Spanish propaganda came bursting forth, building upon the assumptions derived from Las Casas but ultimately leaving his work behind. In 1585, Humphrey Mote wrote the story of the unjust Spanish assault on *The Primrose* near Bilbao and published along with it a copy of the king of Spain's order to arrest English ships.[28] The next year, Windet brought out *An Historical Discourse*, from which I quoted earlier. Following the Armada year of 1588, English anti-Spanish propaganda would become more shrill, with such titles as *The Anti-Spaniard* (1590) and *A Fig for the Spaniard* (1591).[29] It was in this context that Gascoigne's story of the Spanish Fury was adapted for the stage.

WITH SO MUCH anti-Spanish propaganda saturating the English literary marketplace in the last decades of the sixteenth century, and with *An Historical Discourse* also available, the author of *Alarum for London* need not have looked to Gascoigne's conflicted account of the sack of Antwerp for source matter, but so clearly does the play borrow from Gascoigne that, as I have said, he is very often (misleadingly) listed or cross-listed today as its author.[30] We will never know why the anonymous author of *Alarum for London* drew on the *Spoil*, but the effect of this borrowing is the release of Gascoigne's complicated observations on the sack of Antwerp into what seems in retrospect (and through the lens of the Black Legend) to be a fairly straightforward example of anti-Spanish propaganda. The play, for all its apparent propagandistic leanings, actually reintroduces to the flood of facile alarmism of its day the complicated attitudes toward war and toward the Spanish threat that were at large in the 1570s.

The hero of the drama is oddly reminiscent of Gascoigne himself. Stump, as he is called, is an old soldier whose moral and political orientation toward either the Spanish or the people of Antwerp is impossible to fix. Cynical and observant, Stump is a one-legged soldier who rouses himself to fight for a city he despises after refusing for most of the play to do anything about the Spaniards who rape women and kill children in his sight. The source of his bitter contempt for his fellow citizens is their refusal to pay him. When Champaigne implores Stump "to fight for Antwerp's liberty" (p. C2), Stump tells him flatly that he will not fight unless Antwerp is prepared to pay, adding that paying soldiers should be easy enough for city merchants and tradesmen who do not object to paying cobblers and ostlers for relatively trivial labor:

> A sweaty cobbler, whose best industry,
> Is but to clout a shoe, shall have his fee;
> But let a soldier, that hath spent his blood,
> Is lame'd, diseased, or any way distressed,
> Appeal for succor, then you look a sconce
> As if you knew him not; respecting more
> An ostler, or some drudge that rakes your kennels,
> Than one that fighteth for the common wealth. (p. C2)

Stump's willingness to let the enemy destroy his city marks him as a soldier whose sense of duty has been usurped by his own mercenary interests, which supports Jorgensen's view of the play as a dramatization of militaristic admonitions about skimping on defense spending. Stump's attitude also feeds the image of the untrustworthy and dishonorable soldier, which to some extent (as we have seen), relieves the state of its own responsibilities for the failings of military policy. This aspect of Stump becomes especially visible when we compare him to his analog in the *Spoil*, the Walloon trumpeter who mounts a horse and makes a heroic if futile call to arms against the invaders.

Although he may have been created in the context of a literary milieu saturated with propaganda, and although he is shaped by propagandistic tendencies, Stump is also the most developed character on the stage and the one with whom the structure of the drama invites the audience to develop the greatest intimacy. Thus when the Burgher challenges Stump's honor and patriotism by telling him, "It is thy Country that doth bind thee to [fight], / Not any imposition we exact," Stump's reply, "Binds me my country with no greater bonds, / Than for a groat to fight?" (pp. C2–3), reads not simply as an expression of the cliché of the corrupt soldier but as a soldier's comment on the state's self-serving and exploitative construct of honor and soldierly virtue. This is not propaganda.

In the preceding chapter, I quoted several lines from "The Steel Glass" in which Gascoigne condemns soldiers like Stump, whose sense of duty has been supplanted by corrupt mercenary interests. Gascoigne concludes this condemnation, however, with a description of "Ungrateful Princes" who are as much to blame as bad soldiers:

> Indeed I find, within this glass of mine,
> *Justinian*, that proud ungrateful prince,
> Which made to beg, bold *Belisarius*
> His trusty man, which had so stoutly fought
> in his defense, with every enemy. . . .
> Yea herewithal, most Soldiers of our time,
> Believe for truth, that proud *Justinian*
> Did never die, without good store of heirs. (pp. 158–59)

By concluding his description of the soldier who cares only for money with this description of "ungrateful princes," Gascoigne reminds the reader that the problem of the state's servants must be viewed within the framework of the state's attitude toward its servants and the predicaments it puts them in. This sentiment, which fuels "The Steel Glass" and is very much a part of the *Spoil*, finds its way, I suggest, into *Alarum for London* through Stump.

To be clear, that Antwerp's spending habits were dangerously misdirected had been a part of the story of the ruin of the city from the very first accounts, but Stump's pointed comments translate what had been a general problem of fiscal waywardness into the specific problem of exploitation and neglect of soldiers. By calling attention to the very real problem of inadequate compensation for soldiers and at the same time embodying the stereotypical avaricious soldier so often censured in Elizabethan writings, Stump steps out of his role as a figment of propaganda and becomes a ghost of Gascoigne's old narrative who tells anyone who will listen that the issues at stake in war and war policy cannot be reduced to a simple dichotomy of honor and greed. War rather sets in motion the complexities of the relationship between the state and its servants, and it is through that relationship that the actions of soldiers must be judged. Stump shows us, in simplest terms, a new problem at work in Antwerp that has less to do with money or how it used than with how the state marshals its subjects through self-serving notions of liberty and honor and discards them as useless when they are no longer needed or when they are too broken to fight on.

This function of Stump in the drama becomes particularly compelling at the moment he rouses himself to fight the Spanish. In a work of propaganda we should expect this decision to be actuated by a rediscovery of the kind of love of honor a penny-pinching state likes to instill in its soldiers, a love of honor that even certain death cannot squelch. Stump's decision emerges instead from a nearly suicidal resignation. "Die like men," he tells his followers, "what should we do, if there were any hope of safety? but there is not, there is not" (p. F2). The lines do not reverberate with the heroism of Henry's Saint Crispian's Day speech to his equally doomed men. Stump does not present battle as a means of gaining eternal fame even at the cost of certain death. Instead, he suggests that there is no hope, and so dying is as good as living. He enlarges upon this point a few lines later:

> What, but to hunt the footsteps of pale death,
> Until we rouse him in his sooty cave,
> There, will no prospect of our country's fall,
> Offend our eyesight; there no treachery
> Of haughty Spaniards tread a bloody March. (p. F4)

Death in battle has, for Stump, nothing to do with the world that will go on after the end of the war, nothing to do with patriotism or with reputation; it is merely an end to the waiting for death in a country without hope.

The idea that one is better off dead than living under the heels of "haughty Spaniards" cooperates with the propagandistic agenda of the play by encouraging its audience to accept war and death on any terms as preferable alternatives to defeat. However, one cannot with a straight face expect an audience as sophisticated as Elizabethan playgoers to read unqualified heroism into a stage soldier who scorns patriotic attachments, has no belief in a possible future, and seeks death as a means of closing his eyes one last time against a world gone desperately wrong. To understand why Stump is constructed in this way, it is helpful to look again to Gascoigne. In *"Dulce Bellum Inexpertis,"* Gascoigne describes the "Haughty Heart," who, along with the "Miser" and the "Greedy Mind," is one of the three types of people who delight in war. Of these, the Haughty Heart is the only one who serves in war, and his reward is a suffering body, a shortened life, and—in anticipation of what we know as post-traumatic stress syndrome—"broken sleeps, the dreadful dreams, the woe, / Which won with war and cannot from him go" (st. 40). The figure of the Haughty Heart is an ambiguous one in the poem that feeds war with his violent arrogance but also suffers most from war's destructive power. He is informed by a self-awareness of the problems commonly associated with soldiers, but, physically and psychologically scarred by war, he can never be anything but what war has made him. Thus for the Haughty Heart there is no end to war but death. So it is that the hero of *Alarum for London* meets the enemy not for liberty or country but for death itself.

THE QUESTION STUMP embodies is the one posed in the *Spoil*: whether for anyone there is any end to war other than death. Gascoigne's *Spoil* suggests not and admonishes the reader to stay far away from war if at all possible. This sentiment is one he develops in great detail in *"Dulce Bellum Inexpertis,"* which not only urges readers to see war for the horror it is but censures those who would seek to glorify those horrors away:

> And let us set all old sad saws aside,
> Let Poets lie, let Painters feign as fast, . . .
> But let us tell by trusty proof of truth,
> What thing is war which raiseth all this ruth. (st. 11)

While the poem rehearses many of the conventional criticisms of war and soldiers that we have seen in the preceding two chapters, it does so from a position of self-proclaimed authority by one who has found time to write, he notes in the dedicatory epistle to Lord

Grey, "at sundry times, as the Author had vacant leisures from service," and it is ever sympathetic to the "worthy Englishmen" who fought and died in war. To "them that know it best . . . war is full of woes" and "sour of taste" (st. 180). The poem concludes with a final caution to those who never served and who would represent war as anything but a dismal experience:

> I said and say that for mine own poor part,
> I may confess that *Bellum* every way,
> Is *Sweet*: but how? (bear well my words away)
> Forsooth, *to such as never did it try*. (st. 192)

While this sentiment is another kind of cliché—Gascoigne borrows the title of his poem from Erasmus's pacifistic tract of the same name—its significance to a country on the brink of war is not. It suggests that any alternative to war is better than war. In *Alarum for London*, Stump dies under the banner of just the opposite idea, that death in battle is preferable to living in a vanquished country, but the play also complicates this idea through the difficulty of judging Stump. He fights neither for money nor for country nor for honor. He dies accomplishing nothing for Antwerp, and yet his death strangely transforms the Spanish conquerors who celebrate him as a hero at the end of the play, the only one in Antwerp worthy of this recognition. Through their admiration for Stump, the hitherto demonic Spaniards gain their first traces of humanity, revealing the unthinkable possibility that even the Spanish are capable of compassion and generosity. The final image of Antwerp in *Alarum for London* is that of a city in the hands of people who are conquerors but who are also people, who recognize that once the war is over and all the money and property have changed hands, there is the dead soldier who had very little stake in the cause for which he died.

I am not suggesting here that *Alarum for London* should not be read in the context of anti-Spanish propaganda, but I am suggesting that the anti-Spanish propaganda of the later Elizabethan period should also be read in the context of works like *Alarum for London*, in which the obvious propagandistic sensibilities of the era are crosscut by discourses that were also at large in England at the time. The play's connection to Gascoigne makes this controversy easier to spot. Anti-Spanish propaganda, as I have suggested, was not rampant in Gascoigne's England but exploded onto the scene after decades in which England tried to reconcile itself to Spanish power, not rejecting the actions of Spain outright as barbaric or ungodly. Moreover, the England in which Gascoigne wrote was one that tended to regard the behaviors of the people of the Low Countries as sublimely culpable, the actions of Spain a just punishment for their wantonness, even while English people sympathized with the cause of Protestantism that was the chief source of the hostilities across the Channel. And, of course, English fortunes were intricately bound to whoever controlled the ports there. Gascoigne's writings on war and soldiers from the 1570s bear witness to the complexity of English attitudes toward Spain, European Protestantism, mercantile society, and war, a complexity that I suggest persisted in England and announced itself through the cacophony of propaganda in works like *Alarum for London* that self-consciously look back to days before relations with Spain were dangerously simplified.

The play also reaches out to soldiers' narratives to reintroduce this complexity, and this, I suggest, is the most compelling explanation for the play's otherwise puzzling reliance on Gascoigne. Throughout Gascoigne's writings on war and soldiers, we see several very strong antipropagandistic gestures. He poses soldiers' accounts of war as alternatives to stories that glorify war or stories told in the *de casibus* mode. The stories of soldiers eschew reductive moral truths of either a political or religious kind and reflect the conflicting emotions of serving in combat and witnessing death and enemy actions firsthand. In Gascoigne's work we see the soldier as a figure caught between the contradictory needs of the state, a figure who is censured by a state that aggrandizes and cleanses itself through the idea of the bad soldier, a figure who is unsupported by the state until he is needed and who is expected to make the cause of the state his own in the name of a convenient patriotism. He shows us war as a force of absolute destruction that ought to be avoided at any cost, an inevitability spawned by the cycle of accumulating wealth and the covetousness it attracts. As he writes in *"Dulce Bellum Inexpertis"*: "Plenty brings pride, pride plea, plea pine, pine peace, / Peace plenty, and so (they say) [wars] never cease" (st. 9). He shows us enemies and conquerors who may not be all that evil and life after defeat that might not be all that different from victory. He tells us about soldiers for whom there is no psychological return from the agony of combat, a point that might well be extended to include all citizens in a country so long under the shadow of war.

All of this finds its way into *Alarum for London*, and it is an old soldier who hates his country as he hates war and seeks refuge only in death who bears the message. The trouble in the fictional Antwerp of *Alarum for London* and for the England in which it was represented is that too few were listening.

5
John Donne's Emblem of War

NOT OFTEN ENOUGH do we think of John Donne's life as a soldier when evaluating his poetry and sermons. He did not call much attention to his military service, nor was his military service as extensive as Churchyard's or Gascoigne's, but a soldier he was. He is depicted in military garb in a 1591 portrait, the earliest known (figure 9).[1] He joined the thousand or so ambitious young Englishmen who followed the Earl of Essex to Cadiz in 1596 and volunteered for the expedition to the Azores the following year. Some biographers have placed him in the Low Countries in the 1580s, with Francis Drake in 1589, and in the Low Countries again in the late 1590s, perhaps even as an infantry captain in the employment of the Dutch.[2]

While there is little evidence corroborating these latter speculations, Donne's social circle included the most accomplished officers of the late Elizabethan and Jacobean periods, and his reputation among these influential people helped him secure positions of greater responsibility in church and state administration later in his life.[3] Although he did not fashion his literary persona on his career as a soldier, Donne the soldier is an essential aspect of his literary and public careers. He drew extensively on images of war in his sermons and poems, as well as in his most famous work, Holy Sonnet 14 ("Batter my heart").

For Donne, war is, on the one hand, a consummate terror that must be avoided, but, on the other hand, a focal point for a country and its citizens, a testing ground for personal valor, and a means of learning true humility not easily replaced in peacetime or even understood outside the context of war (as the speaker in "Batter my heart" makes clear). A sense emerges that in the horror of war or the lethargy of peace human beings are equally lost and

Figure 9: Engraving by William Marshall of John Donne in military garb, dated 1591. Frontispiece to the 1635 edition of *The Poems*. By permission of the Folger Shakespeare Library.

that each offers the only solution to the problems embedded in the other. In this chapter I suggest that we might better understand this paradox in the context of the emblematic tradition. In that tradition, the spiritual and intellectual enrichment that proceeds from meditation upon contradictions can be its own end. Donne's conflicted images of war thus do not provide easy answers to the questions surrounding war or peace but invite the reader to confront them and, in the process, to resist the temptation of jingoism, alarmism, pacifism, or any other moral and intellectual simplification at large during the late Elizabethan and Jacobean periods.

IN ONE SERMON read some twenty years after the end of his military career, Donne calls war an "emblem, a Hieroglyphic, of all misery."[4] By the 1620s, the long and bloody wars with Spain that burdened the last half of Elizabeth's reign were fading into memory, and Donne would seem to invoke the emblem of war to make certain his audience did not lose sight of war's grim realities and seek involvement in the religious conflicts that were raging on the continent:

> I am far from giving fire to them that desire war. *Peace* in this world, is a precious *Earnest*, and a fair and lovely *Type* of the everlasting peace of the world to come: And war in this world, is a shrewd and fearful Emblem of everlasting discord and tumult, and torment of the world to come. (6.4.182–83)

In another sermon, Donne invokes the idea of war as an emblem again, calling it an "effigy" that will make the sweetness of peace more evident by contrast:

> For the first temporal blessing of peace, we may consider the loveliness, the amiableness of that, if we look upon the horror and ghastliness of war: either in *Effigy*, in that picture of war, which is drawn in every leaf of our own Chronicles, in the blood of so many Princes, and noble families, or if we look upon war itself, at that distance where it cannot hurt us, as God had formerly kindled it amongst our neighbors, and as he hath transferred it now to remoter Nations, whilst we enjoy yet a Goshen in the midst of all those Egypts.

He goes on to bid his audience to think about the "picture of war" drawn from English history so that his listeners will "apprehend the sweetness, and pray for the continuance of peace," will be fearful of those who "make their profit of spoil" or "delight in hostility," and, above all, will be content to "till the earth, and breed up cattle, and employ their industry upon God's creatures" (2.3.81).

In both his sermons and his poetry, Donne's images of war are painted in horrible detail. He refers to ships as "wooden Sepulchers" in which one is prey to "leader's rage, to storms, to shot, to dearth."[5] He talks about the "the dread mouth of a fired gun," the "cannon bullet that comes with an inevitable, and irresistible violence," and about the wound that will "fester" and "gangrene" when the arrow is not "utterly pulled out."[6] He describes sieges wherein

> the scum, which, by needs lawless law
> ... starved men did draw
> From parboiled shoes, and boots, and all the rest
> Which were with any sovereign fatness blest.[7]

He invokes the image of "the Country that is fed upon, and wasted," to remind his audience that the consequences of war reach far beyond the soldiers who are fighting (11.4.292). He notes the effects of war on neighboring countries: it has left "Gorgeous *France*, ruin'd, ragged, and decay'd" and "mangled seventeen-headed *Belgia*."[8] Recalling England's failure to gain any traction against Spain after its victory at Cadiz, he remarks that "ill effects accompany even the most victorious war" (1.4.50).

Donne's "emblem" or "hieroglyphic" does not simply provide a graphic depiction of the horrors of war, however. Like all emblems, Donne's emblem of war is a complicated and internally conflicted image. Published in collections ranging from dozens to hundreds, emblems usually consisted of a printed image and a short poem, and they appealed to a complex of aesthetic, intellectual, and social preoccupations of early modern people. As part of the wider category of meditative verse, emblems are sites, to borrow Louis L. Martz's terms, for "thinking deliberately toward the development of certain specific emotions." Often this action involves the invocation of "sinful impulses" that are to be expelled through further meditation, through the examination of oneself and one's actions in terms of the "ultimate goal" of "conformity with the will of God."[9] The function of meditative verse is not necessarily to clarify its constituent subject matter; its constituent subject matter rather serves to invoke emotions and to prompt reflections that lead readers to contemplate a higher order of reality and their position within it.

Donne's terrifying images of war, in this light, function less to frighten English people away from seeking involvement in foreign conflict than to stimulate the dangerous emotion of fear so that it may be overcome. For this reason, the potential for war is ever lurking behind peace in Donne's descriptions:

> Let us therefore by their example, make as good use of our enemies, as our enemies have done of us. For, though we have no military enmity, no hostility with any nation, though we must all, and do, out of a true sense of our duty to God, pray ever for the continuance of peace amongst Christian Princes, and to withhold the effusion of Christian blood, yet to that intendment, and in that capacity as they were our enemies in [1588], when they provoked by the Excommunications, dangerous invasions, and in that capacity as they were enemies in 1605, when they bent their malice even against that place, where the Laws for the maintenance of our religion were enacted, so they are our enemies still, if we be still of the same religion. (4.3.124)[10]

There is nothing unusual, in terms of political rhetoric, about introducing an exhortation to maintain a defensive posture with a prayer for peace. That a country is best able to maintain a peace when it is strong enough to win a war is practical wisdom that Donne associates elsewhere with Jacob, who "neglects not the strengthening of himself, that so he might make his peace when he were able to sustain a war." For Donne, however, the relation between "love of peace and provision for war" is more than political pragmatism (7.1.268–69). He asks his audience to pray for peace while also saying that enemies have been, are, and will be everywhere present as long as England "be still of the same religion." Donne imagines a world in which two religious duties—maintaining an earnest desire for peace and a stalwart adherence to the reformed church—are in conflict; he asks his listeners to pray for a peace that cannot come and stand by a faith that provokes war.

A sense that war and peace are mutually bound emerges. Donne suggests that a country long accustomed to peace will become annealed to its benefits. "Our ancestors," he says, "who endured many years Civil and foreign wars, were more affected with their first peace, then we are with our continual enjoying thereof" (14.5.285). It follows that a country unfamiliar with war will be more traumatized by war when it does come than a country accustomed to it. For this reason, he reminds his audience that even the peace Christ promises to bring is not just the absence of war, which weakens a people: "One of Christ's principal titles was, that he was *Princeps pacis*, and yet this Prince of peace says, *Non veni mittere pacem*, I came not to bring you peace, not such a peace as should bring them security against all war. . . . If God cast a fire-brand or war, upon a State accustomed to peace, it burns the more desperately, by their former security" (2.3.84). Christ, for Donne, "comes not to settle peace, but to kindle a war" (7.3.181). There is no "security against all war." Peace is an impossibility on this earth, for "Heaven itself [has] not this peace in perfection" (1.4.46).

So what is Donne asking his listeners to think about with regard to war if to avoid it is to invite foreign invasion and lose sight of the benefits of peace? If to support the reformed church is to invite "discord and tumult and torment" that prefigures Hell (6.4.182–83)? How shall we crave peace when peace drags the spirit into lassitude? How avoid war if enemies are everywhere and war inevitable? To make these questions more vexing, the peace Christ brings, Donne argues, "is not a *pax temporis*, such a *State-peace*, as takes away honor, that secures a Nation, nor such a *Church-peace*, as takes away *zeal*, that secures a conscience" (3.2.104). Peace is not a condition of the absence of conflict either in the state or in the spirit or, rather, peace in the form of a state or a mind without conflict strips away honor and zeal. The tradition of meditative poetry helps us understand this siege of contraries. The point of a fearful image of war is not to provide the audience with an opinion on war, peace, or the relations between the two; its point is to confront the audience with an image that calls attention to human powerlessness in the face of dangerous contradictions, to remind the listener that zeal and honor are essential to spiritual strength, and to direct the audience's capacity for zeal and honor away from any earthly response to war (fear, recklessness, etc.) and toward conformity with the will of God, whatever it may be. As he writes in a sermon delivered in the early 1620s:

> We have all been either in Wars, and seen men fall at our right hand, and at our left, by the Bullet; or at Sea, and seen our Consort sunk by Tempest, or taken by Pirates.... [We] have all seen such Changes as these everywhere; but *quia non nobis*, because the Bullet, the Shipwreck, the Pirate, the Pestilence, the Judgments have not reach'd us, in our particular persons, they have not imprinted the fear of God in us.... Almighty God fill us with these fears, these reverences; that we may reverence him, who shall at last bring us, where there shall be no more changes.

Donne suggests elsewhere in this sermon that "he that fears God, fears nothing else.... For, without this fear [of God], there is no courage, no confidence, no assurance" (4.1.229–35, 233). This liberating fear does not urge the audience to crave peace, for peace is fraught with fears of its own. The image of war rather directs the audience's fear away from war or peace and toward the power of God, fear of which burns away all other fears. As Donne says by way of catechism in a sermon from April 1624: "What will this fear of the Lord teach us? *Valor*, fortitude; fear teach valor? yes; And nothing but fear? True fear" (4.6.107). This fear-consuming fear also concludes "Hymn to God the Father," which Donne wrote while coping with a grave illness.[11]

THE PROBLEM WITH reading Donne's emblem of war in terms of its meditative function is that war becomes more attractive than peace. Since peace is only knowable in terms of war, since peace in this world (i.e., "State-peace" or "Church-peace") breeds passionlessness and dishonor, and since war at least stokes zeal and honor and also burns the fear of God into those who endure it, war is less confusing morally. That is, enduring war comes with a built-in spiritual reward, whereas, with peace, one has to seek out a proper moral orientation. The ambiguous relation between peace and war in Donne's emblem shows up, indeed, in other emblems of war from this period. I turn to one from Geoffrey Whitney's *A Choice of Emblems* (1586) entitled "Ex Bello, pax" ("Out of war,

John Donne's Emblem of War   109

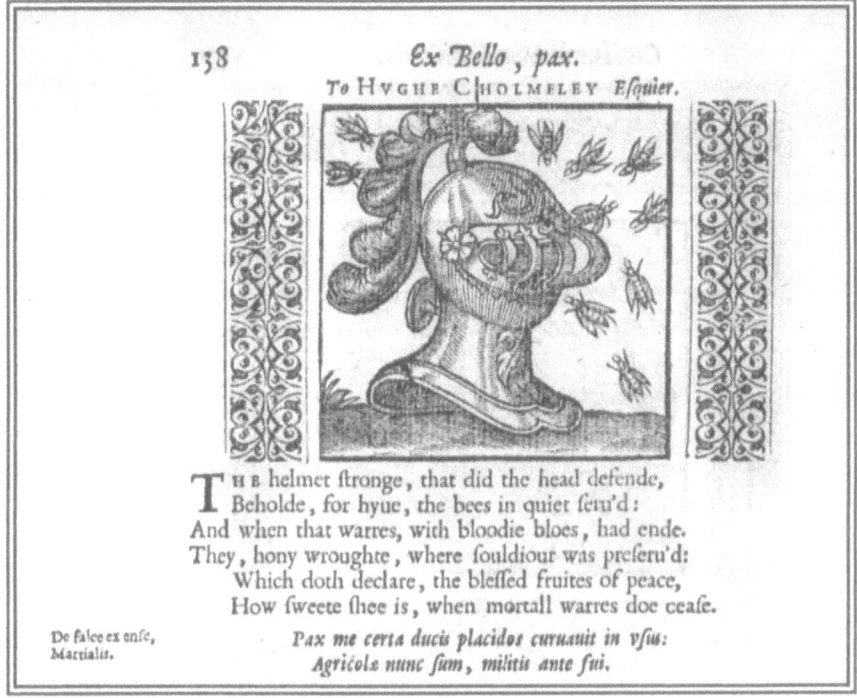

Figure 10: "Ex Bello, pax," an emblem from Geoffrey Whitney's *Choice of Emblems* (1586). By permission of the Folger Shakespeare Library.

peace," figure 10), and for the moment I would like to consider the illustration without the accompanying poem.

At a glance, the image of bees swarming around a helmet is a disturbing one, but the eglantine on the hinge of the visor gives a clue to the significance of this drawing. The helmet is empty. The bees are not harassing a human face but making their home in a discarded helmet. As the poem says:

> The helmet strong, that did the head defend,
> Behold, for hive, the bees in quiet served:
> And when that wars, with bloody blows, had end.
> They, honey wrought, where soldier was preserved:
> Which doth declare the blessed fruits of peace,
> How sweet she is, when mortal wars do cease.[12]

The poem declares the image to signify the translation of war machinery into the instruments of peace and plenty, the proverbial sword beaten into the ploughshare. The helmet that protected the soldier now yields "the blessed fruits of peace." But once translated, the image becomes disturbing. The helmet is not cast on the ground but stands upright as if still worn, shadowing forth the absent human form that once filled it. Where is that person now? Where is the face that was once there? In the poem the soldier is "preserved," but in the drawing the soldier is gone. The emblem is not just about the sweetness of peace in the aftermath of "mortal wars" but also about loss and absence.

Another ambiguous emblem touching upon the same theme is Claude Paradin's "The watchers of peace and war" from his 1591 book *Heroical Devices* (figure 11). In this emblem, a rooster stands upon a bugle, and the motto reads, "By the watching clock of the cock and the trumpet, it is easy to judge what difference there is betwixt the condition of war and peace." The ostensible meaning of the emblem is that waking up to the crowing of the rooster is more pleasant than waking up to war's trumpet, but the rooster in the drawing is not a peaceful bird. It has the hooked beak and powerful wings of an eagle. Its look is fierce and it clutches the innocuous musical instrument in claws armed with gruesome spurs. While the motto promises that judging between "the condition of war and peace" is "easy," it does not tell the reader how to make that judgment, meanwhile presenting an icon of peace that is aggressive, noisy, and warlike and an icon of war that lies beneath its feet.

Both emblems hint at the moral disorientation that comes with peace. A hostile land can be a heal-all for the philosophical and personal dilemmas that plague life at home. One reason Donne gives for volunteering for deployment was to escape his personal life.[13] On deployment, most other concerns are subordinated to the imperative to survive, and the goal of returning home gives to one's life a focus, a purpose, and a narrative clarity that has few if any equivalents in peaceful domesticity. Likewise, a national posture of war and a definite enemy such as England had throughout the late Elizabethan period provided a people with a focal point, a sense of moral purpose, tasks to be performed each day, a reason, perhaps, to understand themselves as one people at all. What are

Figure 11: "The watchers of peace and war," an emblem from Claude Paradin's *Heroical Devices of M. Claudius Paradin* (1591). By permission of the Folger Shakespeare Library.

we supposed to do when it is not a bugle but a shrieking rooster that jars us out of sleep? What does peace demand of us (for, as Paradin's emblem makes clear, it demands something)? Do farming and beekeeping furnish us with the passion or the sense of honor or accomplishment that war provides each day we survive it?

Donne anatomizes the moral disorientation of peace in Elegy 14, "A Tale of a Citizen and His Wife." The speaker encounters a couple riding toward London and asks them for news of "tradesmen's gains" (ln. 33) associated with the Virginia enterprise, the opening of the Stock Exchange, and public works projects in the areas of Aldgate in Morefield. The merchant, "as an old Courtier worn to his last suit" (ln. 30), scorns these business matters and reflects on "Lord Essex days" (ln. 40) and the long war with Spain, how England has declined from an "age of action" (ln. 41) into an age of "City trades" like tavern keeping, writing, and prostitution (lns. 45–46).

Although the speaker calls the citizen's rant "harsh talk" that is "void of reason" (lns. 52–53) and humiliates him by accepting his wife's tacit proposition in the final lines, the speaker embodies the soft degeneracy of the modern city about which the citizen complains. The speaker is a creature of an age grown fat and lecherous in the "fresh protections" (ln. 48) of the king. In this degenerate London even sexual advances are quiet, wordless, and passionless. While the old merchant and his old-fashioned ideas are presented as risible, he is nevertheless the moral center sitting between a faithless wife and a young man of base and mundane concerns. With the memory of "Lord Essex days" and the wars still fresh, the reader must imagine a time when an energetic and curious young man had nobler pursuits than those that occupy the speaker.

But if the old merchant is the moral center of the poem, he is a center that cannot hold. As Donne says often in his sermons, longing for war is a simplification. War *is* an "emblem, a Hieroglyphic, of all misery." And yet, if a righteous mind craves passion, honor, and a tempered courage, how should it not also crave war? Donne's twentieth elegy, "Love's War," proposes as a solution to bring our passion for war to bear on wooing. The battlefield of love, as the speaker presents it, has at least a clear objective, unlike foreign wars, which he suggests are pointless, costly, and unending:

> In Flanders, who can tell
> Whether the Master press; or the men rebel?
> Only we know, that which all Idiots say
> They bear most blows which come to part the fray.
> France in her lunatic giddiness did hate
> Ever our men, yea and our God of late;
> Yet she relies upon our Angels well,
> Which ne'er return; no more than they which fell.
> Sick Ireland is with a strange war possessed
> Like to an Ague; now raging, now at rest;
> Which time will cure: yet it must do her good
> If she were purged, and her dead vain let blood. (lns. 5–16)

Before advancing the elegy's central argument, the speaker reinforces the image of war as pointless and destructive in language that recalls Donne's own experiences at Cadiz and in the Azores:

> To mew me in a Ship, is to enthrall
> Me in a prison, that were like to fall;
> Or in a Cloister save that there men dwell
> In a calm heaven, here in a swaggering hell.
> Long voyages are long consumptions,
> And ships are carts for executions. (lns. 21–26)

The speaker declares that the bedroom will be his battlefield and love his objective, which is far more useful and glorious than war because it will make men and not destroy them:

> Here let me war; in these arms let me lie. . . .
> There men kill men, we'will make one by and by.
> Thou nothing; I not half so much shall do
> In these Wars, as they may which from us two
> Shall spring. Thousands we see which travail not
> To wars; But stay swords, arms, and shot
> To make at home; And shall not I do then
> More glorious service, staying to make men? (lns. 29–46)

The answer to the speaker's final question and his clichéd argument throughout is, of course, no. No, making love is not a more glorious service than fighting a war, at least as this poem sets up the comparison, for if it were the speaker would not need to invoke the language of war to give virtue to lovemaking. And therein lies the problem.

War is more than a political condition or a situation in which one finds oneself from time to time. War owns the ideas of valor and glory. The speaker is able to articulate reasons for deeming foreign wars pointless at the outset of the poem, but there is no language to describe a peaceful domesticity that is glorious or reflects valor without a comparison to war. The comparison confirms war's status as the breeding ground for the qualities that define men, whereas sex can only "make" them. The challenge for the speaker in "Love's War," as so often in the long tradition of wooing poetry, is to supply a symbolic meaning for sexual congress sufficient to authorize it. War makes no such demands on individuals, for although kingdoms and countries may err in embroiling themselves in wars and must seek out political justifications, the individuals who serve in them go and endure. War supplies its own spiritual metaphors, is itself a metaphor.

So what is the correct moral attitude toward war or, for that matter, toward peace? Should we think upon images of war in all its terror until it "[imprints] the fear of God in us"? If so, how can we avoid reviling war altogether, sacrificing in the process, like the speaker in Elegy 14, our passion for honor or, like the speaker in Elegy 20, domesticating that passion? How do we avoid becoming philistine drudges whose concerns are with "tradesmen's gains"? What do we become when we throw our passion for valor into lovemaking? Can valor be transferred from the battlefield to anyplace else at all? I do not propose there are any simple answers to these questions. Rather, I suggest the function of Donne's emblem of war is to make us fear the cooperating and contradicting energies that cause us both to crave and to revile war, to make us confront our own inability to derive a stable moral position toward war given the competing action of these energies. The result is humility, recognition of our own weakness, and, it follows, salutary fear of a power greater than ourselves.

DONNE'S TWO LONGEST war poems relate events he witnessed during his 1597 expedition to the Azores, known now as the Islands Voyage. Not long en route, the fleet was ravaged by storm and scattered. Most ships returned with Essex, their commander, to England, where the mariners and soldiers sat devouring the store of provisions and succumbing to disease. The expedition regrouped but never recovered from this initial setback, making its way to the Azores but not achieving its goal of intercepting Spanish treasure ships returning from the New World.[14] The two poems Donne wrote on this occasion are "The Storm" and "The Calm."

"The Storm" is a study in Donne's emblem of war as an image that serves to induce in the reader a spiritual struggle that derives from competing fears. In "The Storm," as in "The Calm," the spiritual nature of the struggle is emphasized by the absence of a human enemy, who remains occulted in the meager suggestion of the "foreign grave" the "sons" of England seek (ln. 10). But it is easy to cope with a foreign grave, spiritually speaking. The enemy the narrator and his comrades confront instead is an act of God, a wind, which the narrator at first likens to the gift of fertility bestowed on the aged Sara (lns. 19–22).[15] But the gift turns into a figurative enemy attack. What makes this attack frightening is that it is not directed at the narrator and his comrades. They are, rather, caught in the middle of a battle that has nothing to do with them:

> Then like two mighty Kings, which dwelling far
> Asunder, meet against a third to war,
> The South and West winds join'd, and, as they blew,
> Waves like a roiling trench before them threw.
> Sooner than you read this line, did the gale,
> Like shot, not fear'd, till felt, our sails assail. (lns. 25–30)

God does not assault them. The human victims are merely in the way of something much larger than themselves. The real enemy in "The Storm" is the gap between the power of God and the power of human beings, between the will of God and the capacity of human beings to comprehend and endure that will. Thus in "The Storm" there are no brave assaults or daring escapes; the war is fought by individuals in isolation who must wait "coffin'd in their cabins," grieving "that they are not dead, and yet must die" (lns. 45–46).

In this confusion of warring elements, human senses prove useless. The narrator wakes from a deathlike sleep to a world he cannot recognize or even describe:

> But when I waked, I saw, that I saw not.
> I, and the Sun, which should teach me, had forgot
> East, West, day, night, and I could only say,
> If th' world had lasted, now it had been day.
> Thousands our noises were, yet we 'mongst all
> Could none by his right name, but thunder call.
>   (lns. 37–42)

The humans caught in the conflict are deafened, and even if anyone "knew how to hear, there's none knows what to say" (ln. 64). Noise is everywhere, but in that noise there is nothing to be heard. The eye is beset by sights that defy comprehension and even language. Human action is futile. "Pumping hath tir'd our men, what's the gain? / Seas into seas thrown, we suck in again" (lns. 61–62). This image of war as a place where all human actions lead nowhere is one Donne uses in his epigram "The burnt ship," inspired by his firsthand experiences during the assault on Cadiz a year earlier:

> Out of a fired ship, which, by no way
> But drowning, could be rescued from the flame,
> Some men leap'd forth, and ever as they came
> Near the foe's ships, did by their shot decay;
> So all were lost, which in the ship were found,
> They in the sea being burnt, they in the burnt ship drown'd.
>   (p. 128)

In Donne's emblem of war in "The Storm," "All things are one, and that one none can be, / Since all forms [are] uniform deformity" (lns. 69–70).

The sense of utter confusion—of "uniform deformity"—governing Donne's representation of this ill-fated expedition would have been exacerbated for Elizabethan observers by the political turmoil surrounding it from beginning to end. The military success of the Cadiz expedition of the previous year was tarnished by a breakdown of command and control following the capture of the city. The all-star cast of gentleman amateurs squabbled over follow-on action and even before the fleet returned home besieged England with conflicting reports of what happened at Cadiz.[16] I cite Walter Raleigh's account at some length as an example because it gives a detailed description of the battle, reveals the tensions between the gentleman commanders, and hints at the controversies (and acts of self-congratulation) that followed:

> You shall receive many relations, but none more true than this. May it please your honor therefore to know, that on Sunday, being the 20th of June, the English came to anchor in the bay of St. Sebastian, short of [Cadiz] half a league. My lord admiral [i.e., Howard], being careful of her majesty's ships, had resolved with the earl of Essex that the town should be first attempted; ... Myself was not present at the resolution; for I was sent the day before toward the main, to stop such as might pass out from St. Lucar, or [Cadiz] along the coast. When I was arrived back again, (which was two hours after the rest,) I found the earl of Essex disembarking his soldiers; and he had put many companies into boats, purposing to make his descent on the west side of [Cadiz]; but such was the greatness of the billows . . . as the boats were ready to sink at the stern of the earl; and indeed divers did so, and in them some of the armed men: . . . All the commanders and gentlemen present besought me to dissuade the attempt; for they all perceived the danger, and were resolved that the most part could not but perish in the sea, ere they came to set foot on ground; and if any arrived on shore, yet were they sure to have their boats cast on their heads; and that twenty men in so desperate a descent would have defeated them all. The earl hereupon prayed me to persuade my lord admiral, who, finding a certain destruction by the former resolution, was content to enter the port. . . .
>
> Now, sir, may it please you to understand, that there were ranged under the wall of [Cadiz], on which the sea beateth, seventeen galleys, which lay with their prows to flank our entrance, as we passed towards galleons. There was also a fort called the Philip, which beat and commanded the harbor, There were also ordnance, which lay all along the curtain upon the wall towards the sea: there were also divers other pieces of culverin, which also scoured the channel. . . .

> I presently let slip anchor, and thrust in between my lord Thomas and the marshal, and went up further ahead all them before, and thrust myself athwart the channel.... I laid out a warp by the side of the Philip to shake hands with her: (for with the wind we could not get aboard), which when she and the rest perceived, finding also the Repulse (seeing mine) began to do the like, and the rear-admiral my lord Thomas, they all let slip, and came aground, tumbling into the sea heaps of soldiers, so thick as if coals had been poured out of a sack in many ports at once, some drowned and some sticking in mud. The Philip and the St. Thomas burnt themselves: the St. Matthew and the St. Andrew were recovered by our boats ere they could get out to fire them. The spectacle was very lamentable on their side; for many drowned themselves; many, half-burnt, leaped into the water; very many hanging by the ropes' ends by the ships' sides, under the water even to the lips; many swimming with grievous wounds, strucken under water, and put out of their pain; and withal so huge a fire, and such tearing of the ordnance in the great Philip, and the rest, when the fire came to them, as, if any man had a desire to see hell itself, it was there most lively figured.[17]

The capture of the Spanish port gave England momentum that poor logistical planning and command structure gave right back to Spain. The Islands Voyage Donne writes about in "The Storm" might be viewed as an attempt to do what was not done following the victory at Cadiz, but a year later the iron was ice cold, and controversy surrounding the reasons for this strategic error (fueled by reports such as Raleigh's) buzzed in every ear. The 1597 expedition, which was staffed by many of the same commanders, was already beset by a political storm before it ran into the gale that ravaged it on its way to the Azores. Donne acknowledges the controversies surrounding the rationale for the expedition but would seem to distance "The Storm" from them, suggesting that it is enough to know that the fleet served England, "to whom we'owe, what we be, and have" (ln. 9). "The Storm" disengages from political controversy and concerns itself instead with the vital role personal struggle plays in the strengthening of the spirit. "Honor and misery," the narrator says at the outset of the description of the assault, "have one face and way" (ln. 12).

At the height of the storm's assault, when there is no more world but the one shaped by the warring winds, the human actors step forth in all their human powerlessness. Donne likens them to dead men facing their final judgment:

> And as sin-burd'ned souls from graves will creep,
> At the last day, some forth their cabins peep:
> And tremblingly'ask what news, and do hear so,
> Like jealous husbands, what they would not know. (lns. 47–50)

This moment of suspended judgment realizes the earlier suggestion that those caught in the battle grieve "that they are not dead, and yet must die." The ships that are their last hope (and also their coffins) are transformed into sick bodies and then corpses disintegrated into rags:

> Then note they the ship's sickness, the Mast
> Shak'd with this ague, and the Hold and Wast
> With a salt dropsy clog'd, and all our tacklings
> Snapping, like too-high-stretched treble strings.
> And from our tottered sails, rags drop down so,
> As from one hang'd in chains, a year ago. (lns. 53–58)

And yet in the midst of this hieroglyphic of all misery there is a line that anticipates the function of the emblem of war articulated in the sermons: to contemplate terror until we recognize our own powerlessness before the might of God, to fear him and nothing else. The men "sitting on the hatches," the speaker says, seem "[with] hideous gazing to fear away fear" (lns. 51–52). Fearing away fear is the way to spiritual renewal. The significance of the line "Honor and misery have one face and way" (ln. 12) reveals itself in this moment when there is nothing left to hope for but death and, it follows, nothing more to fear but God. The lines that conclude the description of the battle—"so that we, except God say / Another *Fiat*, shall have no more day" (lns. 71–72)—say more than that the fleet is in God's hands. "The Storm" leads readers through consummate terror to a place where they can recognize at last the unvarying truth of these words. With or without the terror of war or storm as a reminder, there can *never* be another day unless God wills it. The warring winds in "The Storm" do not render their human victims powerless but reveal a powerlessness that is a fundamental characteristic of human existence. This powerlessness is introduced in the first line of the poem, a resonant but enigmatic parenthetical whose significance is not realized until the storm has run its course: "Thou which art I, ('tis nothing to be so)." The "I," the human actor, is nothing from the outset. "The Storm" is a poem that begins and ends in humility.

It is in this expression of sublime humility that the politics of the poem also announces itself. While "The Storm" distances itself from the controversies surrounding the military expeditions of 1596 and 1597, it nevertheless reports on the same controversial actions that were generating a great deal of print in the late 1590s, and it must be viewed to some extent in that context. Placed alongside Raleigh's account of the Cadiz expedition, what is clear about "The Storm" is that its concern with humility and universal human weakness contrasts with the vanity that fuels Raleigh's report. Donne's strong appeal to humility in "The Storm," in other words, might be viewed as a response to the literature accumulating around the Cadiz expedition, a literature aimed at celebrating and advancing its authors.

"Always I must, without glory, say for myself, that I held single in the head of all," says Raleigh of his own performance at Cadiz.[18] The other celebrity commanders—Francis Vere, Arthur Throckmorton, and Essex—all made similar claims and discredited those of their rivals.[19] Donne, who witnessed these squabbles at Cadiz and would have been well aware of their afterlife in the literature surrounding the event, begins his poetic letter from the war by saying he is "nothing." This posture of utter humility engages with the Cadiz literature and calls attention to the vainglory of the gentleman commanders responsible for it. Those commanders, moreover, remain invisible in "The Storm." The doomed mariners and soldiers serve "England"—not, by implication, Raleigh or Essex—and the force with which they contend is an expression of a power so terrible it effaces all earthly power from its presence. "The Storm" implies by omission all that those great commanders did *not* do.

As for praising individuals, Donne focuses on those who lost their lives. In "Fall of a wall," Donne memorializes a fallen captain who, with a "town for tomb," achieves a fame commensurate with the price he paid for it:

> Under an undermined, and shot-bruised wall
> A too-bold Captain perished by the fall,
> Whose brave misfortune, happiest men envied,
> That had a town for tomb, his bones to hide. (p. 128)

The contrast in the final line between a heap of broken city and a little pile of bones beneath reminds us that even the most glorious of war stories and the grandest of memorials cover over the deaths of individual persons. The living may envy the fame of those who died, as the living will, but those who avoided the captain's "brave misfortune" are the "happiest men." In the context of reports like Raleigh's, the epigram urges its readers to praise those who died, not those who envy fame while being happy enough to have survived. In Donne's epigram "Sir John Wingfield," the tension between the praise owed to the dead and the praise sought by the living is heightened by the invocation of the "Earl" (i.e., of Essex) and the question of what he did and did not dare to do:

> Beyond th'old Pillars many have travailed
> Towards the Sun's cradle, and his throne, and bed.
> A fitter Pillar our Earl did bestow
> In that late Island; for he well did know
> Farther than Wingfield no man dares to go. (p. 133)

As we have seen in Raleigh's report, the question of which nobleman rushed fastest into the fray at Cadiz was a point of great contention. "Sir John Wingfield" enters that debate reprovingly, insinuating that it is the dead who went first and farther than anyone now living dares to follow, as even Essex "well did know." The poem revises what happened after Cadiz, recasting Essex as a man who realizes his greatness through the humble erection of a monument in honor of and in the form of the late John Wingfield, a monument greater than the old Pillars of Hercules and one that demarcates the known world from the unknown and this world from the next, the field of battle from the field of wings. The historical Essex was not so selfless. Donne knew that very well.

With the subtle politics of Donne's meditative war imagery in mind, I want to explore his second poem about the Islands Voyage, "The Calm." Like "The Storm," it pits the soldiers and mariners not against a human enemy but against the power of God, which cannot be combated and so precipitates an inner struggle. In the dead calm in which the fleet is "rooted" (ln. 10), the ships and men wither in the heat. In describing this slow destruction, the narrator invokes the institutions by which humans give order to the world and represents that order (churches, courts, and plays) as all falling away:

> As water did in storms, now pitch runs out
> As lead, when a fired Church becomes one spout.
> And all our beauty, and our trim, decays,
> Like courts removing, or like ended plays. (lns. 11–14)

Later in the poem, the narrator will compare the fleet to great men humiliated: "Like Bajazet encaged, the shepherds scoff, / Or like slack sinewed Sampson, his hair off" (lns. 33–34). All the power and beauty of the human world is exposed as vainglory in a calm where "Heaven laughs" (ln. 6). Against this force, war machinery is useless and a symbol of the vanity that led the expedition to the islands:

> The fighting place now seamen's rags supply;
> And all the tackling is a frippery.
> No use of lanterns; and in one place lay
> Feathers and dust, to day and yesterday. (lns. 15–18)

While the efficacy of "The Calm," like "The Storm," lies in its capacity to create a dreadful image that prompts the reader to contemplate human weakness, the cause for terror here is not a violent force. Rather, the terror is a calm so complete it gives the human combatants nothing to do but wait. Indeed, the terror in "The Calm" is peace. The narrator describes the mariners, powerless to do anything in a world in which there is nothing to do, devouring themselves from within, giving way to morbid self-absorption, becoming each his own "priest" and "sacrifice," going mad:

> We can nor lost friends, nor sought foes recover,
> But meteorlike, save that we move not, hover,
> Only the Calenture together draws
> Dear friends, which meet dead in great fishes jaws:
> And on the hatches as on Altars lies

> each one, his own Priest, and own Sacrifice.
> Who live, that miracle do multiply
> Where walkers in hot Ovens, do not die.
> If in despite of these, we swim, that hath
> No more refreshing, then our brimstone Bath,
> But from the sea, into the ship we turn,
> Like parboiled wretches, on the coals to burn. (lns. 21–32)

Being stranded on the seas in subtropical heat is a reliable way of dying even now, and a much surer way of dying in the sixteenth century. I do not suggest that Donne is describing something other than a desperate situation here. However, in the sermons we have seen that peace confronts people with challenges that are, from a moral standpoint, as disturbing as those of war. I suggest that "The Calm," as an emblem, emphasizes those challenges by presenting the reader with a world in which there are no actions but only thoughts. It is a "bed-rid" (ln. 38) world in which "sought foes" are nowhere to be found and "lost friends" are unrecoverable. There is no thunder from which to cower and no confusion to peer through, just a stillness in which not even dust is disturbed and in which icons of domesticity in the forms of ovens, baths, and beds become instruments of death. And it is a quiet death without the prospect of honor:

> the thirst
> Of honor, or fair death, out pushed me first,
> I lose my end: for here as well as I
> A desperate may live, and a coward die. (lns. 41–44)

With no external force to combat or endure, there can be, for the speaker, no "honor" or "fair death." In the absence of these moral focal points, confusion falls ("I lose my end"), and the most terrible fear imaginable takes shape, one far worse than death by storm or shot or drowning: the fear of dying a coward.

"The Calm" concludes with a reflection on the powerlessness of human beings consistent with the poem's meditative function:

> What are we then? How little more alas
> Is man now, then before he was? he was
> Nothing; for us, we are nothing fit;

> Chance, or our selves still disproportion it.
> We have no power, no will, no sense; I lye
> I should not then thus feel this misery. (lns. 51–56)

What I want to stress, in the light of this discussion of Donne's war poetry overall, is that "The Calm" as an emblem terrifies not by showing readers images of horrible violence but by forcing them to internalize the moral confusion that accompanies peace and to recognize the vanity that drives the "thirst / of honor, or fair death"—true to the way that Donne's emblem of war "The Calm" leads readers through fear to a place where their own humility must be confronted and embraced. The object of terror, however, is not the prospect of violent death but our own vanity, which fuels our passion for war and in its turn is fueled by the moral and emotional confusion that grips us in the torpor of peace. The poem casts a subtle but searching glance at the vainglorious war literature of the late sixteenth century and at the men who wrote it and the society that welcomed it. Donne's war poetry, by contrast, requires the reader to reflect on human weakness and vanity, the agony of a mind that seeks conflict because it cannot be at peace with itself, the frailty of the human body and the machinery by which it extends itself, the frippery that is war, and the prison that is peace. It asks the reader not to praise living people and rejoice in their courage but to look upon war as the product of a complex of human flaws and despair.

6
John Harington's Journey Home

JOHN HARINGTON WRITES in his epigram "Of the wars in Ireland" that war "maketh all things sweet" (ln. 4).[1] He plays on the "dulce bellum inexpertis" theme derived from Erasmus and developed earlier, as we have seen, by Gascoigne, but for Harington the line is less moralistic than ironic. Unlike for Erasmus and Gascoigne, war for Harington is sweet because it brings into focus the sweetness of living at home in a peaceful country, something one can never take for granted again having served in war:

> At home in silken sparvers, beds of down,
> We scant can rest, but still toss up and down:
> Here I can sleep, a saddle to my pillow,
> A hedge the curtain, canopy a willow.
> There if a child but cry, oh what a spite!
> Here we can brook three larums in one night.
> There homely rooms must be perfum'd with Roses:
> Here match and powder ne're offends our noses.
> There from storm of rain we run like Pullets:
> Here we stand fast against a shower of bullets.
> Lo then how greatly their opinions err,
> That think there is no great delight in war:
> But yet for this (sweet war) I'll be thy debtor,
> I shall for ever love my home the better. (lns. 11–24)

Although this poem is in many ways a pampered court intellectual's recitation of the expected hardships of any war, it is also a war memoir by a very real soldier. Harington was a connected volunteer, as Donne was, who also followed Essex in hopes of turning his fortune and winning fame through military service. Harington nevertheless saw the worst of Elizabethan combat during his six-month deployment to Ireland in 1599, the last and bloodiest campaign of Elizabeth's war years. Unlike Donne, Harington was never able to parlay his military service into advancement as either a writer or a civil servant. Coming home would be the greatest hardship and disappointment of Harington's career as a soldier and one he could not overcome.

Like the other chapters in the book thus far, this one is about the way a man of letters represented his own experience in foreign war and used those experiences to negotiate his literary career afterward; unlike the other chapters, however, this one focuses less on the poet's representations of war than on his representations of returning from war and reintegrating into English society. The problems that attend this aspect of service in foreign war are well known to post-Vietnam generations, for whom the figure of the veteran unable to wrest normalcy from a complex of guilt, resentment, sadness, and post-traumatic stress has become iconic. We have seen in Churchyard's forgotten soldiers and in *Alarum for London*'s Stump that the Elizabethan soldier also came home from war with a sense of being owed a debt society could not repay.[2] Through Harington we can observe this problem in greater detail.

JOHN HARINGTON IS best known to posterity as the legendary inventor of the flush toilet, which supposedly bears his first name to this day. The source of this unhappy association (although I suspect Harington would find it amusing) is Harington's book *Metamorphosis of Ajax*, a Rabelaisian scatological work (a "jakes" is a toilet in Elizabethan parlance) and self-proclaimed "new discourse upon a stale subject."[3] Harington's greatest contribution to the literary Renaissance in England, however, was his translation of one of the most heroic and martial of sixteenth-century works, Ariosto's *Orlando Furioso*.

Thanks in some part to John Keats's "On First Looking into Chapman's Homer," George Chapman's translation of the *Iliad* comes up in most discussions of the great literary accomplishments of the English Renaissance. Given the privileged place of the classical inheritance in Renaissance studies, Arthur Golding's *Metamorphoses* and Thomas North's Plutarch usually find their way into such discussions as well. Less often do we place Harington's *Orlando Furioso in English Heroical Verse* in that company, and yet there are few books as important published in the English 1590s.

It gave to a society not widely fluent in Italian the complete text of one of the most admired works of the sixteenth century, which had hitherto circulated only in excerpted form in madrigals and other short poems.[4] Shakespeare likely borrowed from it in *Much Ado about Nothing*, as there is no reason to suppose he read Italian well, and the margins of Milton's copy of Harington's first edition are scrawled in with notes.[5] It was by far the most substantial translation produced by any English courtier, and it was popular not only in its own day (it underwent two editions in Harington's lifetime and another in 1634) but also in subsequent centuries.[6] It is, in every respect, one of the great poetic achievements of the Elizabethan period.

Harington gave England this translation and its constituent images of romanticized battle and courteous deeds prior to embarking on his career as a soldier, and so it provides a rare "before and after" perspective on war as a literary subject in the hands first of a poet and then of a soldier poet.

As Hans Kohn noted some time ago, Harington's *Orlando Furioso* cooperates with the growing spirit of English nationalism characteristic of the late sixteenth century.[7] It could hardly avoid doing so. Ariosto's poem is—if "nationalistic" is perhaps too much of an anachronism for some of us—unquestionably an encomium to the house of Este and must be viewed at least to some extent in terms of its function in celebrating and reinforcing the ruling hegemony of Ferrara. Harington omits much of Ariosto's encomiums as "tedious flatteries of persons what we never heard of" along with other "matters impertinent to us," and yet the poem's abiding concern with legitimizing power through and around martial exploit is everywhere present, as even a glance at the 1591 edition will tell.[8] Most of the detailed engravings that precede each book of the poem depict the principal characters in definitive combat actions (figures 12 and 13).[9]

In Harington's Ariosto, war is fundamentally allegorical.[10] In "A Brief Apology for Poetry" that serves as an introduction to the 1591 edition, Harington returns frequently to the subject of allegory by way of arguing that there is no "better and more meet study ... for a young man" than poetry, and especially "heroical" poetry "that with her sweet stateliness doth erect the mind and lift it up to the consideration of the highest matters."[11] War functions within the allegorical framework of the poem to orient read-

Figure 12: Engraving from book 1 of John Harington's *Orlando Furioso in English Heroical* Verse (1591). By permission of the Folger Shakespeare Library.

Figure 13: Engraving from book 15 of John Harington's *Orlando Furioso in English Heroical* Verse (1591). By permission of the Folger Shakespeare Library.

ers toward the "highest matters," a point to which Harington gives greater specificity in "A Brief Allegory of *Orlando Furioso*," which follows his translation. The poem's preoccupation with "arms," Harington says, serves to contrast those princes who approach war through "wisdom, learning, and religion" with those who are "rash and inexperienced," drawing attention to the larger problem of "harebrained counselors" who urge their princes to fight needlessly.[12] The meaning behind the war stories in the poem is reinforced by Harington's "Life of Ariosto," also an appendix to the 1591 edition, which depicts the Italian poet as both a counselor who had earned a "great reputation of wisdom and discretion" and a courageous volunteer who more than once "waded" through the hazards of war "for the safety and service of his country."[13] For Harington, *Orlando Furioso* is not merely a war story but a story that uses war as a site for exploring a range of moral, ethical, and political considerations, Ariosto not merely a teller of war stories but a shrewd and experienced state agent concerned less with martial prowess than with his country's safety and stability.

Appropriately, Harington strips from Ariosto's battle scenes much of the significance they may have had to contemporary Italian politics and, especially in the earlier books, scales them down—omitting general details of battle and reserving his descriptive energies for the actions of the principal characters.[14] Harington omits numerous stanzas of the description of the battle before the walls of Paris in book 14 and more than twenty stanzas on the same subject in book 16. In the latter, Harington removes Ariosto's fine and expansive details of combat in stanza 56 but includes very similar ones in book 31 when those details are not merely part of the background of the war but attributable to the sorcerer Malagigi.[15] Harington also omits or condenses the description of practical aspects of warfighting, eliminating the details of Renaldo's terrain survey, land navigation, and administrative movement in 16.31 and transforming Rodomont from an officer spurring his men up the siege ladder (an action Harington assigns to unnamed "captains" in 14.99) into a madman rushing into battle "more desperately than stoutly" (14.100). Harington meanwhile preserves Ariosto's lavish descriptions of tournament costume and ritual (e.g., Rodomont at his pavilion in 27.36–42) and the sprawling *enargeia* that comprises more than fifty stanzas of book 33, in which the future wars of France are laid out as subjects of paintings in a marvelous gallery.

Harington's *Orlando* is more mythical, ahistorical, and allegorical than Ariosto's. The characters in both are, as we would expect in a romance, isolated, laden with allegorical significance, tormented by passions, and plunged incessantly into combat, but in Ariosto they also step out of character and act like real soldiers in the middle of real battles. In Harington, less so. When, for example, an accord is reached in book 38, Ariosto's soldiers reflect inwardly and censure themselves for allowing "l'ire e i furori" (wrath and the fury) to rule their hearts (38.66), while Harington's soldiers reflect on the senselessness of war as a philosophical position, deferring to the "dulce bellum inexpertis" commonplace to do so (38.67).[16]

War does not step forward in Harington's *Orlando Furioso in English Heroical Verse* as a facet of sixteenth-century social and political reality. The poem is not, in simplest terms, a war story in the same way as are the writings we have seen of Churchyard, Gascoigne, and Donne, insofar as it does not attempt to make sense of war as something that people and countries have to endure in any real way. Nor in its own day was it mistaken for such. Harington was known as a courtier and a "merry poet," as Elizabeth called him.[17] According to legend *Orlando Furioso in English Heroical Verse* emerged from translated excerpts of some indelicate passages of Ariosto's poem that Harington had been circulating for the amusement of the ladies at court.[18] Whether or not Harington's *Orlando Furioso in English Heroical Verse* is courtly in this prurient way may be difficult to establish, but what is certain from the text itself is that it is courtly in its appeal to the tastes for romanticized war and personal heroism that, as we have seen throughout this book, were an important part of Elizabethan court performance.

WITH THESE FANCIES of war flowing from his pen, Harington's decision to follow Essex, that icon of martial valor and personal heroism, to Ireland in 1599 might be understood as an extension of an attitude toward war embodied by his translation of Ariosto. He also had more practical reasons.[19] As the son of a talented man of letters who served Henry VIII loyally and as the godson of his father's greatest pupil, Elizabeth, Harington would seem to have been well equipped to succeed in a world that honored and rewarded men who were as familiar with classical Latin as with court politics. He was educated in the best schools, taking his degrees from King's College, Cambridge, before proceeding to Lincoln's Inn, where young men from the upper middle classes were groomed for careers in law and public service. Harington's star, however, did not rise rapidly. He had little interest in public service or, apparently, in any serious business. He did not profit much from his translation of *Orlando Furioso*, however much admired it may have been, and as the 1590s wore on his writing career had taken a downward turn. He attempted without success to get into the printing business in 1592. His next project, *Metamorphosis of Ajax*, was even less successful. The playwright and satirist Thomas Nash said of the book: "What should move him to it I know not, except that he meant to bid a turd in all gentle readers' teeth."[20] The tasteless book also included sniping remarks at ranking members of the court, and so Harington, angering those he hoped to please, fled London and narrowly avoided a Star Chamber inquiry that might have earned him a prison sentence or worse. "I have spent my time, my fortune, and almost my honesty," he wrote as he lay low in his country house in Kelston waiting for the uproar to subside.[21] Three years later it did subside, or, at least, England's need for bodies to fight in Ireland encouraged forgetfulness if not precisely forgiveness. In 1599 the Earl of Essex wrote Harington personally, asking him to join his expedition as a captain under the Earl of Southampton. Harington did not refuse.

NOT ONLY BECAUSE we have the advantage of hindsight but also because we are, at the moment I am writing, involved in a protracted and costly war in the Middle East, the circumstances of 1599 are all too easy to read. The war effort rallied around and was rallied by an ambitious man who fashioned himself into a throwback to an earlier, simpler, and more manly age and who, in his zeal to enter the battle (and realize his stylized persona as a warrior prince), was perhaps too concerned with fanfare and not enough with the practical business of winning a war. Although Essex was at least an experienced soldier, he was not up to the job of commanding Elizabeth's forces in Ireland. In his personal and professional unraveling during the disastrous campaign, the myths in which he had wrapped himself were also destabilized, quickly stripping an already financially and emotionally strained country of many of the beliefs around which the war effort cohered. England invaded Ireland in the name of recovering a rebel kingdom and shoring up its defenses against Spanish encroachment in the British Isles; in practice, England was reasserting colonial domination upon a people who had for two centuries resisted English rule, a resistance that had grown more intense after England adopted what many Irish viewed as a heretical religion.[22] By the late sixteenth century English control of its recalcitrant territory depended on a relatively small garrison defending the English Pale around Dublin, on a few powerful Anglo-Irish earls whose loyalty to the crown varied, and—in what has proven to be a blueprint for disaster in theaters of war across the globe and across the centuries—on several indigenous warlords who had been unwisely promoted by successive English lord deputies to keep others in check. The most powerful of these warlords was Hugh O'Neill.

Hugh O'Neill was given the title Earl of Tyrone to bring him into the fold of the English political system, but to his people he was not an English earl but *the* O'Neill, the chieftain of his country, according to the old system of tanistry.[23] Ambitious, well educated, crafty, friendly with Spain, and hardened as many warlords of the north were by incessant skirmishing with Scots, O'Neill keenly eyed the south, where the undermanned and underfunded English struggled to maintain their control. When the lands of the renegade Earl of Desmond were disposed of in violation of the precepts of tanistry, O'Neill galvanized the warlords of the north and marched for the Pale to oust what to them had become an illegal government. The bloodiest campaign Elizabeth would ever fight was under way.[24]

IF HARINGTON'S GREATEST contribution to the literary Renaissance was his *Orlando Furioso*, his greatest contribution to English cultural history is the body of letters and other documents he produced during the war in Ireland, for it is in large part thanks to these writings that the Irish campaign comes down to us in such great detail. While other early modern chroniclers and commentators like William Camden and John Davies may have written more voluminous discussions of the Elizabethan world at war, the handful of letters Harington wrote to his friends and family from

Ireland are rare examples of a representation of war created by an Elizabethan poet from personal experience in country. As such, they are perhaps the most intimate and vivid accounts of war from this era.

Not only does Harington give us information about the way messages were sent back and forth from Ireland and itemized accounts of who in his company got paid how much and when, but also he gives us startling details of combat operations.[25] Harington witnessed Sir Conyers Clifford, governor of Connacht, march to the abbey of Boyly to meet O'Neill's ally, the Red Earl Hugh O'Donnell. Harington writes that Clifford came with "mere colors of companies" reduced by attrition, desertion, and corruption in which "sixty [stood] for a hundred and fifty."[26] The twenty-one companies Clifford led against the heavily fortified abbey should have numbered more than three thousand men, but the force that arrived at the Curlews, the narrow mountain pass outside the abbey where the rout would take place, amounted to half that number.[27] Those who marched were famished, exhausted, and expected to pay a heavy price for the abbey. Harington reports how the governor withheld food from his men until after the battle as an incentive to fight: "[the men were] weary of fasting, insomuch that they spake for meat ere they went up, but the governor promised them that they should have beef enough at night, and so drew them on: but many, God wot, lost their stomach before supper."[28] Clifford was among those who would never eat that night. He was shot in the head when his vanguard was overrun, cut off from the main body of his force and without ammunition.[29]

In the camp at Roscommon Harington witnessed the most graphic horror he would recount, and it would come in the form not of an Irish army but of filth and hunger and waiting. An English force lay in during the sultry harvest months, unable to venture forth in a country mostly under rebel control. As the men waited for reinforcements, supplies, directions, and even news, they were reduced by famine to eating raw horseflesh and drinking putrid water, aqua vitae, and even vinegar. Food stores were depleted with no means of replenishment. The men lived without a change of clothes, sleeping in their boots upon the ground or in piles of green hay for two months. Dysentery and fever tore through the company. Harington watched more than sixty of his comrades perish in the sweltering filth, "some as lusty men as any came out of England."[30] In all, the English expected to lose some two thousand soldiers a month in Ireland, most to disease and famine of the kind Harington witnessed and survived.

Through Harington we get tantalizing images of the guerilla tactics of the kerns, the Irish light infantry, who provoked and evaded battle against the invasion force, prolonging the conflict to their advantage in a way that is all too familiar to observers of modern expeditionary warfare: "[They] rather seemed a morris dance, by their tripping after their bagpipes, than any soldier-like exercise; they conveying themselves (after a while) in a ringdance into the wood."[31]

To Essex, the Irish were a frustrating enemy who refused to engage him in a standup battle, who "never showed themselves out of the wood."[32] For the Irish, like any guerilla fighters waging a defensive battle against a large expeditionary force, these hit-and-run tactics wore down their enemy's morale and supplies, eroding the English will to fight on. The closest Harington comes to expressing any recognition of the value of these tactics is to note that the English soldiers became ineffective because they feared the Irish were using black magic to conceal themselves: "I verily think the idle faith which possesses the Irishry, concerning magic and witchcraft, seized our men and lost the victory."[33] Nor does Harington ever question Essex's complaint about the Irish—the same we have heard from struggling commanders in Vietnam and the wars in the Middle East—that the enemy is somehow cowardly or otherwise to blame for refusing to fight in conditions in which its forces have no possible advantage. Harington's dedication to Essex is understandable, if difficult at times to accept. Harington had married his fortunes to Essex, and Essex had, in accordance with his romantic delusions about warfighting, dubbed Harington a knight along with some sixty others as a reward for their loyalty. Harington defends even Essex's unconscionable decision to decimate his own troops after they retreated from a battle, suggesting that Essex was merciful in executing only one in ten after condemning all to be hanged: "These which escaped by flight, or by base hiding of themselves from the force of the rebel's sword, were by a Martial Court condemned . . . to be hanged on the gallows; which sentence was mitigated by his Lordship's mercy, by which every tenth man was sentenced only to die."³⁴ When Essex himself abandoned his post, Harington remained loyal and followed his commander all the way back to England.

The English would emerge victorious in Ireland. Mountjoy, replacing Essex in command of the English forces, waged a more patient war against an enemy that was itself exhausting its resources.³⁵ After a decisive English victory at Kinsale, O'Neill eventually surrendered and signed a treaty of peace with Elizabeth's successor, James I of England and VI of Scotland. The peace was hard bought for the English. Elizabeth's ancient treasurer, William Cecil, Lord Burghley, had long managed either by creativity or chicanery to conceal the enormous cost of the wars, but Burghley had died in 1598, and his son was faced with the difficult business of replenishing an exhausted royal treasury paralyzed by debts it could not pay.³⁶ The human cost was more dispiriting. More than 10,000 Englishmen lost their lives in Ireland, a number representing about 5 percent of the population of London, or about 300,000 soldiers relative to today's population. On the Irish side, the peace was in many ways opportunistic. Ireland's rebel earls had every reason to expect acceptable terms of surrender from a king who was tolerant of Catholics and disinclined to continue his country's entanglement in foreign war. Those favorable terms did not come. As England pulled the renegade nation into the fold of the three kingdoms united, the rebels who had sought refuge in France following the truce were never allowed to return as they had hoped. The Flight of the Earls, as the exile of O'Neill and O'Donnell has come to be known, signaled the end of Irish independence, though not the end of Ireland's resistance to English rule.³⁷ In 1603 the peace with Ireland was nevertheless welcomed, as fragile, incomplete, and costly as it was.

IN A VERY literal way, the war ended for Harington before the Flight of the Earls and before O'Neill's defeat at Kinsale. He left the battlefield with Essex and had followed him to England but not, wisely, all the way to Elizabeth's bedchamber at Nonsuch, where Essex, fearing the queen's displeasure at his having met in secret with O'Neill, begged her majesty's forgiveness while she was not yet dressed and he was still in his riding clothes.³⁸ Within two years Essex would be executed as a traitor. Still, home was not the sweet refuge Harington describes in his epigram "Of the wars in Ireland." The England to which Harington returned regarded as a failure and a national shame the Essex campaign of which Harington was a publicly visible member. To make matters worse, Harington and the other newly minted knights drew fire from Elizabeth, who viewed their promotion as an expression of Essex's efforts to create a rival cult of political loyalty centered on himself. Harington wrote to his friend Sir Hugh Portman that on his return he "feared her Majesty more than the rebel Tyrone."[39] He had sunk more than three hundred pounds into the expedition, a sum that he did not likely recoup from his wages (as a captain, he received about twenty-eight shillings weekly).[40] His pocketbook, pride, and standing at court weakened by his service abroad, he returned to his country house and rededicated himself to his family, his friends, and his poetry.

In another way, the war in Ireland never ended for Harington. It occupied his thoughts and writings until his death ten years later. In the years immediately following he fashioned himself into a quiet country gentleman no longer seeking involvement in wars or matters of state, but there is nevertheless a palpable note of sadness and emptiness in his reflections on a tranquil retirement: "In December I came hither . . . but since, I hear little and do nothing but sit by a good fire, and feed my lean horses, and harken for good news, but hear none, save the certain expectation of peace." A "certain expectation of peace," rather than victory in Ireland or even some personal redemption, suffices here for "good news." He closes this letter with concern for the war in Ireland, but the tone of his writing suggests a man who doth protest too much: "Let this much suffice from a private country knight, that lives among clouted shoes, in his frieze jacket and galoshes, and who envies not the great commanders of Ireland, but hereby commends himself to them."[41]

This forlorn resignation from a model of public life epitomized in military service would become a familiar echo in Harington's writings in these last ten years. Nowhere is it more pronounced than in his discussion of Scipio in *The Praise of Private Life*. Scipio was known in the English Renaissance not merely for his military prowess and quiet retirement but also for falling victim to "untrue surmises," as George Gascoigne writes, that almost cost him his glory at home.[42] Harington describes the great Roman general as a man who turns his attention to study after fighting and winning both his country's wars and its praise, but the description comes across as a wistful and agonized revision of his own humiliating return from Ireland:

> O most noble spectacle and worthy praise, exceeding the pomp of all princes, to see a most noble Captain defender of his Country and all Italy, after he had conquered Nations and prosperously acquit the people from bondage, to leave his Soldiers in the City, and lay down the triumphal robes with all other ensigns of dignity, and that done, all alone to walk among the hills, and on the sea shore, some times to take up pretty shells, and strange stones of rare proportion.[43]

Although Harington truly was a "Captain" and a "defender of his Country," he came home not in victory but in defeat. He was met not with triumphal robes or other ensigns of dignity but with contempt, mistrust, and outrage. While he talks calmly of "setting forth for the country" and dedicating himself to "Petrarch, Ariosto, Horace, and such wise ones," he was reduced to groveling to Robert Cecil to intervene with Elizabeth, who intended to strip him and his comrades of the knighthoods they earned on the battlefield, the one "[ensign] of dignity" with which Harington did return.[44]

Harington's bitterness over the shame and ingratitude he was made to bear festered during the last three years of the war, while he was trying to forget about Ireland among his pastures and his books. His writings suggest that the source of his resentment was not the loss and suffering he personally endured for his country but the indifference of his country to the sacrifice he was asked to make. Harington was too savvy a courtier to expect to be praised for a failed campaign that nearly cost England the war, but what he could not abide was the minimization of his and his comrades' efforts, even in defeat, from people who were not there. Robert Sidney assures him in a letter from 1600 that the ranking members of court do not much discuss the misdeeds of Harington and other captains, on the grounds that subordinate commanders could not very well be held at fault for what Essex did and failed to do, but the assurance is an ambivalent one, for it implies that all the commanders were complicit in the Irish debacle, as blameless as they might have been: "Your Irish business is less talked of at her Highness's palace, for all agree that you did go and do as you were bidden; and if the great commanders went not where they ought, how should the captains do better without order?"[45] And, certainly, not being talked about is not the same as being praised, and therein lies the problem. Harington and others like him went to war because they had every reason to believe that valiant service would earn their country's praise and the rewards that came with it, but they found that the outcome of military expeditions rather than the valor of individual soldiers determines which actions are "talked of" and which are forgotten. Soldiers, as Churchyard also lamented, are not praised for losing wars.

Harington calls attention to this problem in an account of an unpleasant meeting with the queen the year before she died, in which Elizabeth seems to have forgotten that Harington was ever in Ireland in Essex's service:

> It was not many days since I was bidden to her presence. I blessed the happy moment: and found her in most pitiable state. She bade the archbishops ask me if I had seen Tyrone? I replied, with reverence, that "I had seen him with the Lord Deputy." She looked up with much choler and grief in her countenance and said, "Oh, it now mindeth me that you was *one* who saw this man *elsewhere:*"—and hereat, she dropped a tear and smote her bosom. She held in her hand a golden cup, which she often put to her lips; but, in sooth, her heart seemeth too full to lack more filling. This sight moved me to think of what passed in Ireland; and I trust she did not less think on *some* who were busier there than myself.[46]

The queen, in this stylized representation, becomes an emblem of an ungrateful country. Absorbed in her own anger over the embarrassments of the war, she forgets the service of individual soldiers because of the political legacy of the conflict. Elizabeth cannot look at the soldier in her presence without thinking about Essex's follies and alleged treacheries. A soldier and his sovereign sit across from each other remembering foreign war, each thinking about very different things.

O'Neill's return to England as an ally, which Harington mentions in the letter just quoted, prompted a rant that summarizes Harington's frustrations upon coming home:

> I was called from my home by her Majesty's command, adventured perils by sea and land, endured toil, was near starving, [ate] horse-flesh at Munster; and all to quell that man, who now smileth in peace at those that did hazard their lives to destroy him. Essex took me to Ireland; I had scant time to put on my boots; I followed with good will, and did return with the Lord Lieutenant to meet ill will; I did bear the frowns of her that sent me; and, were it not for her good liking, rather than my good deservings, I had been sore discountenanced indeed. I obeyed in coming with him to England. But what did I encounter thereon? Not his wrath, but my gracious Sovereign's ill humor. What did I advantage? Why, truly a knighthood; which had been better bestowed by her that sent me, and better spared by him that gave it. I shall never put out of remembrance her Majesty's displeasure.[47]

If the enemy can now be welcomed as a friend, should not those who fought against him now be praised for their sacrifices? Why should they have to beg not only for sustenance but also for the simple right to retain the honors they received? These are the questions Harington puts not to Elizabeth, who was dead by this time, but to England itself.

Like everyone who went to Ireland with Essex, Harington did so because England called him there in haste and with scarcely sufficient means and preparation to wage an offensive war against an enemy that outnumbered them by 50 percent. Essex's expedition was a failure, to be sure, and whether Essex even served honorably may be debated, but what Essex did or failed to do should not, for Harington, diminish the sacrifices he and others made on their country's behalf. They were called away from their lives. They "adventured perils by sea and land" and ate "horse-flesh" because England asked them to. Instead of being honored at war's end, they were at worst scorned and at best coolly found blameless. Two years later, Elizabeth having been dead and buried for three years, Harington still cannot look past the memory of his sovereign's ingratitude. "I cannot forbear remembering my dread at her frowns in the Irish affaire," he wrote, "when I followed my general (and what should a captain do better?)."[48] How could it be, Harington wondered, that those who gave so much for their country were called "knaves," while England reached out even to Ireland's rebellious earls in an effort to forge a lasting peace?[49]

The reception Harington found upon returning to England is not inexplicable. The politics surrounding a failed military expedition, then as now, are complicated and extremely painful. Even though Londoners lined the streets for four miles to exhort Essex and his followers on to victory in Ireland, few of England's empowered citizens hazarded their own lives or the lives of their children in its accomplishment.[50] With the exception of a few naive and impecunious courtiers like Harington and a few earnest soldiers like Mountjoy, most who could evade service in Ireland did so. The war, moreover, was bankrupting England and taxing beyond reasonable limits the rural parishes that supplied most of the manpower. Certainly the English people understood the threat posed by Spain and recognized the strategic importance of keeping Ireland out of Spanish hands, and yet volunteers came halting forth if they came at all. Victory in Ireland was something everybody wanted, but not so much that people were willing to fight voluntarily for it.

This in a society known as an extraordinarily patriotic and jingoistic one. As I have suggested throughout this book, there are many reasons to revise this image of Elizabethan England. Harington's ordeal is perhaps the most poignant of them. In his agonizing homecoming, the sham of Elizabethan patriotism revealed itself to Harington. Behind the cheers, behind the idealism, and behind the jingoistic literature that is synonymous with the war years was a country happy enough to commit its expendable resources to war only so long as victories came quickly. When success proved costly and the prospect of a protracted war announced itself in the growing roll call of the dead and the unceremonious return of Essex, individuals and not a kingdom's own ambivalence toward war were made to bear the blame.

In his exile, Harington imagines soldier poets as they ought to be in his fantasy. He imagines a Julius Caesar who in the respite between the "incursion of pirates, by Civil War, and at last by foreign assaults" liked to "employ his time in study." He imagines an Augustus who "oft times walked in the woods to recreate his Spirit, after long cogitation on weighty affairs."[51] And yet in the midst of this reverie the image of himself as a soldier and man of letters, which the failure of the Irish campaign prevented him from realizing on favorable terms, still asserts itself. In "Farewell to His Muse," which he sent in secret to James VI in 1602 when his succession to the throne of England seemed inevitable, Harington promises his new sovereign that he would gladly serve him with sword or pen:

> My future age to realm and king I vow,
> I may no time for wanton toys allow.
> Ever I wish, and only him to serve,
> Only his love ever I would deserve.
> If he pleased war to proclaim with Spain,
> With such a prince I'll follow wars again.
> If his great wisdom th'ancient peace renews,
> How fain of peace would I report the news.
> List he give laws to th'Irish, now well tamed.
> I could give sound advises, and unblamed.
> To build some stately house is his intention
> Ah, in this kind I had too much invention! . . .
> List he to write or study sacred writ;
> To hear, read, learn, my breeding made me fit.
> What he commands, I'll act without excuse,
> That's full resolved: farewell, sweet wanton Muse![52]

The poem is certainly a resume detailing the range of services Harington is prepared to provide to the new king, but at the same time it parodies the bitterness that characterizes Harington's writings after the war. The poem, in effect, turns the poet's sense of being nothing but a pawn of the state into a professional selling point. Rather than the words of a scorned poet become scorned soldier become forgotten soldier *and* poet, the poem assumes the voice of one who views his literary talent and military experience as nothing but resources for the king, to be used, valued, or exploited at the king's pleasure. Even the title of the poem suggests a complete forfeiture of the individual's personal stake in his own endeavors. Harington's inspiration is no longer his muse but the whims of the king. If there is war he will fight zealously. If there is peace he will forget all about war and trumpet the virtues of peace. He could provide advice. He could even be a household ornament. Set against the backdrop of the Irish campaign and the fugitive profit and glory it promised, these words serve as a eulogy upon Harington as a soldier poet, one who might have but did not achieve greatness through the pen and the sword. "Farewell to His Muse" is a farewell to the possibility of individual achievement in either endeavor and an acknowledgment, however tongue-in-cheek, that the soldier and the poet are nothing more than toys for kings.

Harington's most quoted lines come from an epigram written in the last year of his life and dedicated to Prince Henry, the stylized warrior prince. The epigram reads simply: "Treason doth never prosper;—What's the reason? / Why;—if it prosper, none dare call it treason."[53] Harington introduces the epigram by reminding Henry that his own grandfather was a "commander on the wrong side, and among the traitors, if so I may say."[54] Unlike the poem Harington wrote to Henry's father seven years earlier, with its inflated promises to ply his pen or sword as needed, this one is unreserved in its cynicism and implies that the fortunes of kings determine who is a champion or enemy of the state. Harington, like all those who followed Essex in good faith and served as they were told, became a persona non grata not because of what he did but because of his commander's political fortunes after the war. This last and sharpest comment of an embittered soldier poet asks Prince Henry to understand that Harington and those with whom he served could easily have been heroes had the war ended differently. And perhaps they were anyway.

7
Remembering Soldiers
Ben Jonson

I BEGAN THIS BOOK talking about how, for modern readers, Elizabethan England is buried under centuries of misleading assumptions about how that society was unified around its military policy. In the chapters that followed, I examined the writings of Elizabethan veterans to show that England's attitude toward its military commitments was conflicted and sensitive to the ways war and soldiers were represented by the Elizabethan state and its officials. In this final chapter I return to the writer for whom the tension between the idea of Elizabethan England as a proud and defiantly martial society and Elizabethan England as a society ambivalent about the purpose and value of its military posture is most pronounced. That writer is Ben Jonson, among the court literati of the 1620s and 1630s one of the last Elizabethan soldiers standing.

Jonson's career as a soldier began when he was nineteen or so. Having left school and abandoned his apprenticeship as a bricklayer, Jonson joined the English army in the Low Countries under the command of Francis Vere. Like Gascoigne, Harington, and Donne, Jonson was at an impasse in his life when he went to war in the early 1590s, and deployment offered if not some direction then at least a momentary respite from having none. His account of his own wartime experience in which he killed an enemy with both camps looking on, as William Drummond remembers it, reveals a mixture of pride and criticism: "In his service in the Low Countries, he had in the face of both the camps killed an enemy and taken *opima spoilia* from him, and since his coming to England being appealed to the fields he had killed his adversary, which had hurt him in the arm and whose sword was ten inches longer than his, for which he was imprisoned and almost at the gallows."[1] While Drummond describes a Jonson who delights in recounting this brave tale, the deed sounds more like a murder and a robbery than a military action, a suggestion reinforced by its placement in a narrative that includes another violent crime Jonson committed as a swaggering young man. The description thus recalls the problems associated with Elizabethan soldiers we have seen rehearsed in much of the literature of this period: their lawlessness in combat and their propensity for violence at home.

The ambivalence in his own story of his wartime experience is characteristic of Jonson's cultivated persona as an urbane critic of modern times, but it is also characteristic of his attitude toward the martial spirit of the Elizabethan age. In that age of patriotic gusto, Jonson had little sympathy for wars and soldiers. Like Donne, Jonson leaned toward Catholicism, and he was disdainful of the mysticizing and mythologizing tendencies of the late Tudor Protestantism to which Elizabethan patriotism was bound. Jonson's imagination, moreover, was perhaps more oriented toward the classical past than that of any other Elizabethan writer. He looked beyond England's vernacular traditions and cultivated instead an abiding passion for his country's Roman heritage. As a thoroughgoing Renaissance humanist he also shared that community's distrust of chivalric ideals for their tendency to promote the arts of war over the liberal arts.[2] What interested him about England was not its chivalry and its native traditions but the blemishes and contradictions, the symptoms of an anxious but unstoppable modernity that everywhere poked through the romantic veneer of fairy kingdoms and pastoral paradises of the late Elizabethan imagination.

Given Jonson's attitude toward the climate of the Elizabethan court and in particular the court's obsession with its martial ideals and chivalrous fantasies, it is that much more surprising that these energies would fuel Jonson's last contributions to English literature during the Caroline period. To understand how he would come full circle, we must better understand the cult of Elizabeth that developed in the decades following her death.

ELIZABETH'S BODY WAS not long in the ground before English writers began to fictionalize her reign. In 1604 Thomas Heywood staged *If You Know Not Me, You Know Nobody* or *The Troubles of Queen Elizabeth*, the second part of which followed in 1605. The play is more reflective than encomiastic, as is George Chapman's retrospective on Elizabeth in *Bussy D'Ambois*. In an exchange between the Guise and Henry III, the play includes criticism of Elizabethan idolatry while at the same time praising the queen's government.[3] This clear but guarded enthusiasm for the old regime reflects the mood in the months following James's accession. On the one hand, many English subjects were leery of having the king of what had long been a hostile foreign country on the throne of England, let alone one with pronounced Catholic sympathies; on the other hand, one had to be careful about extolling the woman who had sentenced the king's own mother to death. There were other reasons to qualify praise for Elizabeth. As I hope to have shown throughout this book, Elizabeth had run her kingdom ragged through two decades of wars that were a source of far more consternation than is often mentioned in popular histories. James ushered in a peace that England needed. Moreover, for English Catholics the new regime also brought with it the promise, however faint, of greater religious tolerance.[4] There was good reason for all English subjects to remember Elizabeth with some discretion in this new age of quiet uncertainty, guarded optimism, and unfamiliar peace.

Rarely can the emergence of a mass obsession like the Jacobean cult of Elizabeth be attributed to any single event, but if there were such an event the Gunpowder Plot of 1605 would be it. The facts are well known. A group of disgruntled Catholic conspirators sought to assassinate King James and the ruling Protestant hegemony by blowing up Parliament. Alternatively, a group of old guard Protestant politicians sought to reinvigorate the cause by staging this conspiracy or allowing it to develop. In either case, the plot to blow up Parliament failed, but it galvanized English Protestants into remembering the long war with Spain and the unifying image of England as a lone holdout against the forces of Catholic aggression. Thomas Dekker's *The Whore of Babylon*, which appeared soon after the Gunpowder Plot, was a celebration of Elizabeth's reign that cast the war against Spain (the play depicts the Armada attack of 1588, among other events) as a necessary response by a strong and right-thinking monarch to a real and still present Catholic threat. The play also implies a lopsided comparison between the great monarch who took arms against that sea of troubles and the new monarch whose reluctance to do so nearly brought ruin to the kingdom.[5]

Nostalgia for the clarity and bravado of England during the war years (however fanciful), with its implied criticism of the government of James, came to dominate the memory of Elizabeth in the years following the Gunpowder Plot. In 1608 Francis Bacon circulated *In Felicem Memoriam Elizabethae* (In happy memory of Elizabeth) as a direct challenge to certain Catholic writers who sought to contextualize the Gunpowder Plot within Elizabeth's bloody legacy as an oppressor of religion.[6] In this work, Bacon reinvents Elizabeth as a monarch praiseworthy for "cultivating and maintaining peace during the whole time of her reign."[7] In the decade that followed, historiographers John Speed, Robert Cotton, and William Camden began to treat Elizabethan England as a model of a virtuous society prospering under sound government.[8] To be sure, these sentiments were not created out of the Gunpowder Plot but emerged from a combination of factors. Misgivings surrounding the person of King James and the loss of a sense of shared purpose provided by the wars (which I have explored in some detail in the fifth chapter) found an outlet in the memory of Elizabeth as Gloriana, Astrea, or the Virgin Queen. It was a fifty-year propaganda effort that, as John Watkins suggests, Elizabeth finally completed "[in] dying."[9] Modern Americans can understand the apotheosis of Elizabeth in the first decade of the seventeenth century by considering the emergence of the cult of Ronald Reagan in the unstable decades following the end of the Cold War. The memory of an iconic national hero presiding over a rejuvenated society that vanquished a rival empire subsumed the records of illegal war, official corruption, onerous debt, narcotics proliferation, urban deterioration, and hate crime that also characterized those happy years. Even though the long decades of Elizabeth's reign were tormented by war and other social and economic problems, "[more] or less hagiographic accounts of Elizabeth's life and reign became," as Anne Barton has argued, "a Jacobean and Caroline feature."[10]

In an England governed by King James, an unpopular pacifist around whom swirled rumors of homosexual prurience, the martial vigor associated with the Elizabethan age became an important dimension of this "feature." English longings for Elizabeth and the great fighting noblemen of her court were transferred, under these circumstances, to Prince Henry. Born in 1594, Henry Stuart carried a name and taste for chivalry that recalled the Tudor kings and was fashioned from childhood as the ruler who would unify the two kingdoms in law and in spirit.[11] Henry's persona as an "infant warrior" was part of his appeal to his future subjects and one that his portraitists developed throughout his life (figures 14 and 15).[12] As early as 1603, John Davies was singing praises to the prince who would "take . . . us to [his] charge" and claim his place among English military heroes.[13] Henry, of course, never would fulfill this promise but instead died of typhoid in 1612, when he was only eighteen.

JONSON DID NOT embrace this myth of the Elizabethan age but remained as critical of it as he was during Elizabeth's lifetime. He remembers her to Drummond as a fraud and a debauchee so drunk on flattery she did not even know she was being flattered: "Queen Elizabeth never saw herself after she became old in a true glass. They painted her and sometimes would vermillion her nose. She had always about Christmas evenings set dice that threw sixes and fives, and she knew not they were other, to make her win and esteem herself fortunate. . . . [She] had a *membrana* on her which made her uncapable of man, though for her delight she tried many."[14] He ventured no such commentary while the queen lived, of course, but *Every Man Out of His Humor* (published in 1600 but most likely performed in 1599) registers clear concerns about the mythology with which Elizabeth surrounded herself. In the epilogue Macilente tries to atone for a scurrilous attack on just about every aspect of Elizabethan society by kneeling before a representation of the queen and begging forgiveness:

> Never till now did object greet mine eyes
> With any light content: but in her graces
> All my malicious powers have lost their stings.
> Envy is fled my soul, at sight of her,
> And she hath chas'd all black thoughts from my bosom.
>   (epilogue, lns. 1–5)

The hyperbole in the scene is difficult to bear even now. Macilente's sudden and overstated conversion turns the queen into an object of religious devotion before the eyes of an audience unaccustomed to seeing her impersonated on stage. The result is an uncomfortable

Figure 14: Engraving by William Hole of Prince Henry at the lance, from Michael Drayton's *Poly-Olbion* (1612). By permission of the Folger Shakespeare Library.

Figure 15: Portrait of Prince Henry in battledress by Isaac Oliver (ca. 1612). The Royal Collection © 2008 Her Majesty Queen Elizabeth II.

recognition of the mysticism and irrational enthusiasm at the heart of Elizabethan politics and also of its tawdriness and hollowness.

Jonson was no more seduced by the martial idealism growing up around Prince Henry, even though he welcomed his patronage. When Henry was commissioning and acquiring works that would reinforce his image as both a Tudor-style warrior prince and a thoroughly modern patron of the arts, Jonson could barely comply. In *Prince Henry's Barriers* Jonson presents a Merlin who is not the legendary enchanter but a humanistic reformed magician who gives the prince a shield depicting "not the deeds / Of antique knights" fit for "Arthur's age" but "other Acts" for "another *stage*" (lns. 168–72):

> it is not since as then:
> No giants, dwarfs, or monsters here, but men.
> His Arts must be to govern, and give laws
> To peace no less than arms. (lns. 173-76)

Jonson offers Henry a mirror that reflects the image not of a warrior prince but of a peaceful lawgiver, an image that also reflects the dim view of fighting men evident in Jonson's writings to that point. In his *Epigrams*, included in the *Works* of 1616, Jonson creates such memorable soldiers as "Cashiered Captain Surly," "Captain Hazard the Cheater," "Captain Hungry," and "Lieutenant Shift," the last of whom also appears in *Every Man Out of His Humor* as a "thread-bare Shark" who "never was Soldier, yet lives upon lendings."[15] The clown Carlo Buffoni describes this Shift as "the most strange piece of military profession that ever was discover'd" (3.5.31-32) and seeks to expose him by tempting him to sell his prized rapier. The impoverished Shift makes a longwinded refusal that rehearses the expected boasts of the braggart soldier, but in the end he is willing to part with his rapier for "some ten groats" (3.6.65-66).

So vitriolic were Jonson's Elizabethan and early Jacobean representations of soldiers that he affixed Epigram 108, "To True Soldiers," to *The Poetaster* in an apparent attempt to assuage certain officers whom he had offended.[16] The epigram is scarcely an apology, however, but a firm reminder that, a soldier himself, Jonson speaks with some authority on the conduct of captains and suggests that the only officers who ought to take offense are those, like Captain Hungry, who deserve it:

> Strength of my Country, whilst I bring to view
> Such as are mis-called Captains, and wrong you;
> And your high names: I do desire, that thence
> Be nor put on you, nor you take offence.
> I swear by your true friend, my Muse, I love
> Your great profession; which I once, did prove:
> And did not shame it with my actions, then,
> No more, then I dare now do, with my pen.
> He that not trusts me, having vow'd thus much,
> But's angry for the Captain, still: is such.[17]

The epigram takes the infuriating position that any captain who finds fault with a proven soldier's complaints against poor captains must be himself a poor captain. Jonson was an experienced enough soldier to know that the matter was not so simple. As I have suggested in the second chapter, Elizabethan military management shifted the burden of budgeting to the small unit level, forcing captains to engage in sourcing and fiscal practices that often seemed unscrupulous. Jonson is not engaging here with the complexities of military management but rather drawing uncritically on the cliché of the corrupt officer as an embodiment of a corrupt military machine, daring anyone who disagrees to do so at risk of admitting his complicity in this problem.

Jonson's criticism of military affairs is elsewhere darker and less glib. Macilente, on his knees in his mock prayer before Elizabeth in *Every Man Out of His Humor*, takes the opportunity of the queen's audience to beg for peace:

> Let foreign polity be dull as lead,
> And pale invasion come with half a heart,
> When he but looks upon her blessed soil.
> The throat of War be stopped within her land,
> And turtle-footed Peace dance fairy rings
> About her court. (epilogue, lns. 24–29)

While Jonson ostensibly praises Elizabeth for frightening off any would-be invaders (the "Invisible Armada" scare of 1599 was still fresh in everyone's mind when the play was performed), he nevertheless asks her to stop war and let peace prevail. At the moment this speech was sounded, of course, some twenty thousand Englishmen were embarking for the meat grinder that was Ireland, half of whom would never come home. Jonson will also slip the grim reality of war into his audience's mind in *The Case Is Altered*, one of his earliest works, when Nuncio says of the news of Count Ferneze's son:[18]

> 'Tis ill my Lord,
> Yet such as usual chance of war affords,
> And for which all men are prepar'd that use it,
> And those that use it not but in their friends,
> Or in their children. (3.4.6–10)

Nuncio's words are chilling and represent one of the clearest statements of the consequences of war uttered on the Elizabethan stage. The wars overseas took their toll not only on the men deployed but also on their families, their neighbors, their friends—everyone except perhaps those like Shift who trade on the patriotic spirit of the era without bearing the costs of the wars it fed and fed on. Jonson's Elizabethan plays, when they deal with the subject of war at all, do so to force its realities toward the surface of public consciousness and remind the audience that in a nearly mythical kingdom ruled by a nearly mythical queen, it would be nice if peace, too, could be part of that mythology and "dance in fairy rings / About her court." It wasn't, and it didn't. Jonson knew that as well as anybody.

IT WOULD BE easy enough to attribute Jonson's change of heart in the 1620s to the one problem that always plagued him and most other poets: he was broke. Jonson had taken leave of the stage at the height of his career in 1616 and had for a decade written masques for James's court. When James died in 1625, the mood at court changed. Charles was not much his father's son. Sanctimonious, reserved, and devoted to his wife, he was less inclined toward Jonson's keen and biting humanistic sensibilities and preferred the spectacular sceneries of Inigo Jones as a more apt display of his royal power and magnificence.[19] Of sheer necessity, the enfeebled and out-of-fashion Jonson found relief in William Cavendish, the dashing and lavish Earl of Newcastle, who was the old poet's "best patron" as well as a friend and occasional collaborator.[20] Cavendish was a cavalier in every sense, a horseman and a soldier who would fight for the Royalists in the Civil War before seeking exile in France until the Restoration, and it was toward Cavendish's taste for the old martial spirit of Elizabethan England that Jonson directed his literary efforts late in life. Cavendish's own plays *The Country Captain* and *The Variety*, published in England in 1649, feature self-styled throwbacks to Elizabethan England in the forms of Captain Sacksbury and Manly, the latter of whom likes to dress in Elizabethan costume and contemplate portraits of Leicester and Sidney while nobody is looking.[21]

Jonson's apparent revaluation of the Elizabethan fighting spirit also came at a time when England was angling for war once again. In 1618 the Thirty Years' War broke out in Bohemia when Protestant factions rejected the rule of the Hapsburg Holy Roman Emperor Ferdinand II and sought to supplant him with the Elector Palatine, Frederick V.[22] Frederick was married to James's daughter Elizabeth, but James, eager to keep England out of continental wars, sympathized with the Hapsburg cause against the deep and often vocal objections of many English Protestants.[23] James was also trying to broker the so-called Spanish Match that would marry Charles and the Infanta Maria of Spain. As the conflict in Bohemia exploded into what was to become a continentwide religious war, James appealed to Parliament in 1620 for funding to help secure the Palatinate but met a house divided between those who wanted no involvement and those who wanted to enter the war against the Catholic cause with all guns blazing. The situation became desperate when the marriage negotiations in Spain broke down after Charles had traveled there incognito with James's favorite and most trusted adviser, George Villiers, Duke of Buckingham.[24] The two came home urging a declaration of war on Spain. In 1624 they got their wish.[25] Not long after, James and the peace he had restored to England (as unpopular as it had become) had reached their end.

Charles I's career as a militaristic ruler did not go well. Buckingham's incompetence can be blamed for some of England's failed attacks on Spain and France, but so too can Charles's zealous ineptitude, which resulted in the suppression of war reporting, antagonism toward the population, the dissolution of Parliaments, rebellion, and, eventually, his own execution in 1649.[26] This familiar figure of an insecure ruler entering a war for what seem in retrospect idealistic and self-interested reasons and then hopelessly mismanaging that war reminds us that all wars are more like each other than not; what is interesting about the Caroline war years, for this book, is why Jonson, at this moment, reconnected with the patriotic fervor of the England of his youth rather than scorning this new martialism. It is not an easy question to answer, but from the more urgent of his martial writings from this period we can see that Jonson is less concerned with supporting the wars England was entering into than with the fraudulence of the would-be soldiers of the Caroline court who were overeager to drag English people onto foreign battlefields. Jonson invokes the fighting spirit of Elizabethan England, in other words, not to endorse

Caroline jingoism but to expose the hawks of his own day as hollow men.

In "A Speech according to Horace," written in the early 1630s and published posthumously in *Under-wood*, Jonson employs a mock encomium to praise the "brave Artillery yard" (ln. 23) where England's youth practices the arts of war.[27] Although these skills are never employed in actual combat, the speaker places them on par with the military exploits of their forebears. The training area is an extension of an England that

> hast not spar'd
> Powder, or paper, to bring up the youth
> Of London, in the military truth,
> These ten years' day. (lns. 24–27)

But, as the poem progresses, it is clear that paper has been more important than powder in military training. The "military truth" in which England's soldiers have for ten years been tutored comes not from practice but from the "posture book" (ln. 28). England's "Ensigns of a War" have meanwhile become "gold-chains, and pearl ... / Lent by the London dames" (lns. 11–14). This dainty and bookish army arrayed in its ladies' apparel and led by "curious" captains (ln. 29) would, in Jonson's mock encomium, cause one to "think no more of Flushing, or the Brill" (ln. 30). The ambiguous phrase suggests that the new army supplants the memory of the old but also that, with such "civil soldiery" (ln. 44), one can forget about committing the force to any serious military action abroad.

The poem shifts its criticism of military readiness from the artillery yard to the English gentry, whom Jonson compares to the fighting noblemen of old who kept "the glory of the English name, / Up among nations" (lns. 50–51). Although at first the poem gives backhanded praise to the "newer men" who keep a tamer sort of war "alive yet, in the noise" (lns. 53–56), it turns into a broadside attack on an English gentry grown luxurious and resentful of anyone who should suggest it ought be otherwise. Jonson assumes the voice of a hypothetical new gentleman and demands to know

> What's he that dare tutor us? ...
> Why are we rich, or great, except to show

> All license in our lives? What need we know,
> More than to praise a dog? or a horse? Or speak
> The hawking language? (lns. 66–72)

The voice of the dilapidated gentleman goes on to insist that industry is for the sons of "clowns and tradesmen" (ln. 73), not for men "[descended] in a rope of titles" (ln. 80). Service to the state "by councils, and by arms" (ln. 85), likewise is the responsibility of those who have yet to earn the badge of nobility, not of those who have inherited it and who "neither love the troubles, nor the harms" (ln. 86). The poem concludes with a disgusted speaker turning his back on the wreck of the English gentry, calling its constituent members "carcasses of honor" and "tailors' blocks" who tend to their pleasures while a "tottered virtue holds / Her broken arms up, to their empty moulds" (lns. 99–102).

The question of whether Jonson is saber rattling here by challenging English people to uphold the martial reputation of their Elizabethan forebears is one that must be considered. We have seen Jonson since his career began pour scorn on carpet knights, braggart soldiers, vainglorious gentlemen, and other fraudulent military men, but in the earlier works we do not find these attacks balanced by any insistence on the importance of martial prowess to the health of the kingdom. Complicating this question are poems like "An Epistle to a Friend to Persuade Him to the Wars" (written in the early 1620s), in which Jonson exhorts his unnamed friend to "seek thy peace in war" (ln. 195) as an alternative to remaining in a luxurious and effeminate England characterized by licentiousness, disingenuousness, and vanity.[28] With a new patron who fancied himself an old-fashioned cavalier and with war breaking out on the continent, Jonson's cooperation in a growing spirit of jingoism cannot be dismissed, but I would stress that while Jonson appears to be unfurling the battle standard late in his career, his praises of martial prowess focus squarely on the lassitude and moral weaknesses of Stuart society, not on the evils or dangers of an enemy. For Jonson, war as a proving ground for personal valor calls attention to England's desperate lack of valor, just as the image of fighting noblemen like the "Beauchamps, and Nevills, Cliffords, Audleys old" calls attention to the moral failure of the Stuart aristocracy.[29] Jonson's late invocations of the Elizabethan martial spirit are aimed at the problems in England, not those on the continent.

Recalling the Elizabethan martial ideal as a means of criticizing Caroline society provides cohesion in Jonson's last two completed plays, *The New Inn* (1629) and *The Magnetic Lady* (1632). In both plays, an Elizabethan-style soldier emerges as the moral center and wrestles a chaotic world into order through his courage, strength, and old-fashioned honor. *The Magnetic Lady*'s Captain Ironside is introduced in the play in hyperboles that almost beg a seasoned Jonson audience to anticipate the appearance of a braggart soldier in the mold of Lieutenant Shift. Says Ironside's friend Compass to the Lady Loadstone:

> I have brought your Ladyship a hungry guest here,
> A soldier, and my brother Captain *Ironside:*
> Who being by custom grown a sanguinary,
> The solemn, and adopted Son of slaughter:
> Is more delighted i'the chase of an enemy,
> An execution of three days, and nights,
> Then all the hope of numerous succession,
> Or happiness of issue could bring to him. (1.5.50–57)

But we do not get the impecunious and longwinded Jonsonian soldier we might expect, one short on action and content to abide any company for a free meal. Captain Ironside is a man characterized by exceptional moral clarity. He is so disgusted with the manners and mettle of the "Fiddlers, / Pragmatic Flies, Fools, Publicans, and Moths" (2.6.143–44) who congregate around Lady Loadstone's court of love (itself a shabby replica of the Elizabethan court) that he refuses to dine with them, scolding them all and storming out with his blade drawn. His scorn is directed in particular at Lady Loadstone's brother, Sir Moth Interest, who proposes that "the Prince hath need / More of one wealthy, than ten fighting Men" (2.6.66–67). Ironside is less upset by this suggestion than with the debauched and scandalous world that breeds such sentiments and such men as Moth Interest. Looking at the wreck of English society around him and sounding like a visitor from an earlier time, Ironside declares:

> [Here] are met, are all pernicious spirits,
> And men of pestilent purpose, meanly affected
> Unto the State we live in: and beget
> Himself a thanks, with the great men o' the time,
> By breeding jealousies in them of us. (2.6.125–29)

He concludes by calling Sir Moth "the common offence grown of mankind, / And worthy to be torn up from society" and declares: "I must cut his throat now: I'am bound in honor, / And by the law of arms, to see it done" (2.6.132–37).

Lady Loadstone and her parasites invoke the image of ill-bred "boisterous soldiers" (3.3.9) to condemn Ironside's action, but it is clear to the audience that they and not Ironside are the ones in need of moral correction. It is difficult, for example, to join Lady Loadstone's courtiers in censuring Ironside when the likes of Practice the attorney see in Ironside's outburst the opportunity to sue for "five thousand pound for a finger" (3.4.5) or when Sir Diaphanous Silkworm complains:

> There's nothing vexes me, but that he has stained
> My new white satin doublet; and bespatter'd
> My spick and span silk stockings, o' the day
> They were drawn on: and here's a spot i' my hose too. (3.4.7–10)

Indeed, Ironside's presence in the house of Lady Loadstone will have a restorative and even generative function, hinted at when Lady Loadstone complains that the sight of Ironside's "swaggering manners" and "weapon" has made her daughter Mistress Placentia ill (3.3.14–15). But the sight of Ironside's bravado and naked weapon is just what Mistress Placentia needs. This bold and manly act sends her into labor, and thus the drama casts Ironside as the father of a new generation of Englishmen cured of the sycophancy, degeneracy, and foppery that characterize the court of Lady Loadstone. To further this suggestion, it is Ironside himself who wins Loadstone's love at the end of the play. The time traveler from the Elizabethan age takes his place at the center of a new world reordered around the honor and manly courage of the old days.

If Ironside recalls the martial valor of the Elizabethan era, Lovel from *The New Inn*, the last play Jonson ever completed, is a spokesman for it. Cavendish modeled his character Manly on Lovel, and Jonson introduces him as a "complete gentleman, a soldier, and a scholar. . . . known to have been page to the old Lord Beaufort, follow'd him in the French wars."[30] Far more than Ironside, Lovel is a self-conscious anachronism. The drama endows him with both a sense of being from the past and a sense of that past being lost (whereas Ironside comes across, as I have suggested, as more a time traveler, quite surprised that his values are out of fashion or that anyone should object to his violent defense of them). Lovel thus does not merely embody an Elizabethan martial ideal or attempt to impose it. He is not trying to lead anyone back to the past. Rather, he functions as a commenter on the past, one who seeks to help Caroline England look beyond the glittering arms of the Elizabethan age to the more praiseworthy values that informed its fighting spirit.

This aspect of his character is especially evident in the fourth act in his lengthy treatise on valor, which he begins by castigating and dismissing the sham soldier Colonel Glorious Tiptoe and "the hostlers and the tapsters, / The under-Officers of [his] regiment" (4.4.84–85). Once this embodiment of everything contemptible and risible about soldiers has been swept away, Lovel begins his treatise in the manner of Platonic dialogue, with the host (replete with Elizabethan sensibilities of his own) and the young Lords Beaufort and Latimer as questioners. The first subject is the sort of valor that arises from anger, which Lovel distinguishes from true valor:

> For it proceeds from passion, not from judgment:
> Then brute beasts have it, wicked persons, there
> It differs in the *subject;* in the *form,*
> 'Tis carried rashly, and with violence:
> Then i' the *end,* where it respects not truth,
> Or public honesty; but mere revenge. (4.4.89–94)

Young Lord Beaufort, an eager student of this old-fashioned valor, asks Lovel to treat upon valor that emerges "t'escape the Infamy merely" (4.4.102), which Lovel calls "valor with a witness," the "worst of all" (4.4.102–4). Having laid out all that valor is not, Lovel then explains what it is:

> The things true valor is exercis'd about,
> Are poverty, restraint, captivity,

> Banishment, loss of children, long disease:
> The least is death
> 	. . . so a mind affecting,
> Or undertaking dangers, for ambition,
> Or any self pretext, not for the public,
> Deserves the name of daring, not of valor.
> And over-daring is as great a vice,
> As over-fearing. (4.4.105–21)

One thinks of Essex and Raleigh racing through a storm of bullets for the honor of landing first at Cadiz or of Jonson killing an enemy soldier in view of both camps. It is difficult to associate the sort of reserved and intellectual valor Lovel calls for with the Elizabethan character he pretends to uphold. His idea of valor is no doubt a noble one, but it does not belong to the likes of Essex or Raleigh or Drake, the bold but mercenary and self-promoting paradigms of the Elizabethan age. Jonson is revising the myth. He looks past the spectacular heroes of the Elizabethan age and taps into the sensibilities of the soldiers more like those we have encountered in this book, thoughtful soldiers who take up the burden of service because their country asked them to do so.

The revisionist nature of Lovel's Elizabethan sensibility is further revealed in his description of the education he received under old Lord Beaufort, an education not grounded on the chivalric tales that inform the construction of Elizabethan valor but on the classics:

> Did you ever know, or hear, of the Lord Beaufort,
> Who serv'd so bravely in France? I was his page,
> And ere he died, his friend! I follow'd him,
> First, i' the wars; and i' the times of peace,
> I waited on his studies; which were right.
> He had no *Arthurs*, nor no *Rosicleer's*,
> No *Knights o' the Sun*, nor *Amadis de Gaule's*,
> *Primalions*, and *Pantagruel's*, public nothings; . . .
> But great *Achilles*, *Agamemnons* acts,
> Sage *Nestors* counsels, and *Ulysses* slights,
> *Tydides* fortitude, as *Homer* wrought them
> In his immortal fant'sy, for examples
> Of the *heroic* virtue. (1.6.119–33)

The "heroic virtue" Lovel champions is of a humanistic kind, and although he presents it as an inheritance from an earlier age that "time shall not dissolve" (1.6.146), it does not recall Elizabethan personal valor expressed in the court and battlefield performances of the war years. It rather recalls humanistic oppositions to this notion of valor. Lovel dismisses the instructive value of the romances as Roger Ascham did in calling them encouragements to "slaughter and bold bawdry," celebrating instead the wise, pious, and introspective valor of Virgilian and Homeric heroes.[31] And yet, in his devotion to Lady Frampul and her mock court of love at the New Inn, in his insistence on concealing his love behind verses, in his courage in chastening the debauched men of the court, and in his ennobling melancholy, Lovel is in every respect an Elizabethan soldier, scholar, and gentleman. And like Ironside his presence is a corrective one in a world in need of moral reorientation. Also like Ironside, Lovel elicits true love from a lady to whom love had been nothing but a court performance through which she maintained her power.

That, too, is a revision of the age of Elizabeth and perhaps the deepest compliment Jonson ever paid to its soldiers.

I CLOSE THIS chapter and this book by considering Jonson's Elizabethan soldiers in the context of the question with which I began: why do we look so seldom to the works of Elizabethan soldier poets when considering the relations between the literature and the martial legend of Elizabethan England? Jonson's last plays and many of his late poems would seem to speak to this old courage and old sense of what being English meant. According to Drummond, Jonson expressed interest as early as 1620 in writing an epic poem memorializing "the worthies of his country."[32] Later, he also began work on a play called *The Sad Shepherd*, a romance about that quintessentially English hero Robin Hood, which he left unfinished when he died. While Jonson's voice as a social critic survives as one of the strongest of his time, his voice as a soldier poet speaking to the ways stories about soldiers and wars can or should cooperate in the formulation of a national character is faint. All the voices of soldier poets on this subject are faint.

And yet they are not faint at all. They were, as I have shown throughout this book, speaking loudly and copiously about the ways they were represented and exploited and about the myths and misprisions that depended on those representations and exploitations. The problem is that we have not been listening. When we examine the period's writings on war, on soldiers, on personal heroism, on writing about war, and the relations between them, we don't look to soldiers. Rather, we look to Shakespeare or, more specifically, to *Henry V*.

Shakespeare's "Harrys" have been called upon for three centuries now to help England and its former colonies understand their military commitments.[33] Hardwicke implicated *Henry V* in his apocryphal patriotic Elizabethan newspaper. Richard Steele looked to *Henry V* to praise military commanders of his day. Pope's readers saw the connection between the Achilles he translated out of the Greek and the Henrys he modernized. We have seen the inclusion of Henry in the patriotic observances leading up to the First World War. Laurence Olivier gave England his monumental film version of *Henry V* in the long dark days at the end of the Second World War.[34] Kenneth Branagh's no less monumental film version forty-five years later was accused of helping to shore up the Thatcher regime and rekindle the memory of the Falklands campaign.[35] From my own experience, I can remember discussing Branagh's *Henry V* in a graduate seminar in 1991, when the Gulf War concluded with a reckoning of coalition dead so low that only the Battle of Agincourt scene could provide sufficient context. And when our wars in the Middle East resumed a decade later, I was teaching *Henry V* to soldiers in an expeditionary camp in which the sergeant major had affixed to his door Henry's Saint Crispian's Day speech. Whenever the English-speaking world goes to war, it seems, it brings *Henry V* with it. Or, at least, it brings those excerpts that support and give particular meaning to military actions.

Jonson never gave us a Harry. He gave us, as did all the soldier poets I have presented in this book, people whose experiences in war stripped from them its romance and whose experiences with a government at war stripped from them the possibility of unqualified patriotism. Toward the end of his career and his life, Jonson turned to soldiers' stories and not war stories to express his own concerns with England's character during a time of military escalation in order to emphasize that a strong country begins not with rousing speeches and bold actions but with morally strong people. It is easy to go to war. It is easy to cry, "God for Harry, England, and Saint George," to name an enemy, to send men on ships to fight the enemy. Far easier than it is to abide by one's own convictions and to act with moral courage in everyday life.

Of course, Shakespeare did not give us a Harry either, at least not the Harry that subsequent generations have been keen to conjure up whenever war looms. He too gave us soldiers with distinct and critical voices. Although barely audible above the noise of the chorus and the declarations of a king, they are there, those English Mercuries.

They are lost in their own memories. They derive an often inflexible moral code from those memories. As often, their moral code develops clarity in response to confusing quotidian pressures. They speak back to those pressures in a language others do not understand, or understand incorrectly. They never leave the wars they fought, but, for the same reasons, neither do they mistake the fleeting obsessions of their social worlds for matters on which the stability of a country depends. They are not stooges of the state or servants of its whims, although they do serve with a sometimes inconvenient and self-destructive idea of virtue fixed in their minds. Their loyalties are difficult for the outside observer to gauge, difficult to understand in terms of patriotism or its opposite.

They are, above all, products of political violence and witnesses to how people come to terms with political violence not as an idea but as an action they must commit or endure. The stories they left us about their own experiences tell us more about the Elizabethan world at war, as I think Shakespeare also knew, than any Harry ever could.

Notes

INTRODUCTION

1. Shakespeare, *Henry V* (4.3.109). All parenthetical citations of Shakespeare refer to the *Riverside Shakespeare*, 2nd ed., listed in the bibliography.
2. This paragraph is adapted from McKeown, "Soldiers Seek an Elusive Escape."
3. Shakespeare, *Love's Labour's Lost* (1.1.13–14).
4. The well-known argument derives from the tenth book of Plato's *Republic*.
5. Shapiro, *A Year in the Life*, p. 180.
6. Murrin, *History and Warfare*, p. 15.
7. Baldo, "Wars of Memory," p. 132.
8. Marx, "Shakespeare's Pacifism," p. 55. Although Marx's use of the term "pacifism" in no way (to my mind) renders his argument anachronistic or unclear, it is worth noting that Musto ("Just Wars and Evil Empires") suggests that "peacemaking," with its biblical connotations, rather than the twentieth-century concept of pacifism, is more appropriate to sixteenth-century attitudes toward war and peace.
9. Green, *A Short History*, pp. 421–22.
10. Einstein, *Tudor Ideals*, pp. 190, 189.
11. Pollard, *Factors in Modern History*, pp. 127, 11.
12. Greenfeld, *Nationalism*, p. 67. See also Kumar, *Making of English National Identity*, pp. 114–21.
13. Helgerson, *Forms of Nationhood*, pp. 299, 13.
14. Cahill, *Unto the Breech*, pp. 10, 11.
15. Dollimore, *Radical Tragedy*, pp. 218–20.
16. Fussell, *Great War and Modern Memory*, p. 63.
17. Althusser, "*Lenin and Philosophy*," p. 162.
18. Fussell, *Great War and Modern Memory*, p. 241.
19. Shepard, "Endless Sacks," p. 743.
20. Sinfield, *Faultlines*, p. 10.
21. Ibid., p. 26.
22. Murrin, *History and Warfare*, p. 241. On the dramaturgical development of the single combat motif see also Snyder, "Ourselves Alone." The popularity of romanticized individual combat as courtly entertainment must also be considered as an influencing factor. See Yates, "Elizabethan Chivalry," and Strong, *Cult*. Consider also West's

comments in "Spenser's Art of War" on the "mock-heroic sensibility" in Elizabethan literature.
23. Harvey, *A Muse of Fire*, p. 5.
24. On military manuals and memoirs, see Webb, *Elizabethan Military Science*; Taunton, *1590s Drama and Militarism*; and Harari, *Renaissance Military Memoirs*.
25. Sidney, *A Defence of Poetry*, p. 66.
26. Ibid., p. 26.
27. Ibid., p. 1.
28. Interestingly, the term "mercurist" was first employed (1602) in contrast to the far more familiar term "martialist." *Oxford English Dictionary*, s.v. "mercurist."

CHAPTER 1

1. Andrews, *History of British Journalism*, vol. 1, pp. 19–25. The hoax was formally exposed by Thomas Watts, as he recounts in his letter to the *Gentleman's Magazine* in 1850 (see Watts, "Authorship").
2. Warner, *The People for Whom Shakespeare Wrote*, p. 181.
3. For the Huntington Library list, see Gabler, "Check List of English Newspapers," pp. 12, 51. On the use of the document by Web pages maintained by universities, see www.fordham.edu/halsall/mod/modsbook06.html, www.boisestate.edu/courses/reformation/visitors/references.shtml, djvued.libs.uga.edu/text/otstxt.txt, and eudocs.lib.byu.edu/index.php/History_of_Spain:_Primary_Documents.
4. Foucault, *The Archeology of Knowledge*, p. 25.
5. Anderson, *Imagined Communities*, pp. 37–46. See also K. Wilson, "Citizenship, Empire," pp. 70–71.
6. K. Wilson, "Citizenship, Empire," p. 73.
7. Ibid., p. 76. See also Sichert, "Functionalizing Cultural Memory."
8. Stone, "Shakespeare in the Periodicals," p. 221.
9. *Tatler* 137, qtd. in ibid., p. 225. See also Williams, *Poetry*, p. 149.
10. Williams, *Poetry*, pp. 135–72.
11. The "national poet" label is from Aspden, "Ballads and Britons," p. 38. See also Dobson, *Making of the National Poet*.
12. Joseph Warton, *Essay on the Genius and Writing of Pope* (1756), qtd. in Mitchell, "Benjamin West's 'Death,'" p. 28.
13. Feibel, "Vortigern," p. 3.
14. Levine, *Highbrow/Lowbrow*, p. 16.
15. For an excellent summary of Shakespeare in the Victorian and Edwardian eras, see Kahn, "Remembering Shakespeare Imperially," pp. 458–67.
16. See prefatory note to Nash, *Mansions*.
17. On Poel and the Elizabethans and the Reading Society, see Moore, "William Poel," pp. 22–24. On the foundation of the Stage Society, see Kennedy, *Looking at Shakespeare*, p. 40.
18. Hodges, "Van Buchel's Swan," p. 489.

19. Glick, "William Poel," p. 15. On the evidence supporting Elizabethan stage conventions, see also Mullin, "Observation."
20. See Kahn, "Remembering Shakespeare Imperially," and Engler, "Shakespeare in the Trenches."
21. Qtd. in Kahn, "Remembering Shakespeare Imperially," p. 456. See also Sinfield, "Royal Shakespeare."
22. Engler, "Shakespeare in the Trenches," p. 107.
23. Qtd. in E. G. R. Taylor, "Francis Drake," p. 360. Roberts's poem, it should be noted, predates the Armada victory.
24. The reference is to Lope de Vega's epic *La Dragontea*, published in 1598.
25. See Fitter, whose central claim is that 2 *Henry VI*'s adaptation and revision of chronicle sources reveals a Shakespeare whose "primary concern was political engagement of his contemporary moment, rather than reconstruction of the mid-fifteenth century" ("Emergent Shakespeare," p. 133).
26. John Upton writes in the Variorum edition of *The Faerie Queene* that the references to the wars in the Low Countries in book 5 are "so very apparent, that the most superficial readers of Spenser never could mistake them." Spenser, *The Works*, 5:300n. Spenser does not name the countries but gives near approximations like "Belge" for Belgium, "Bourbon" for Navarre, and "Irene" for Ireland.
27. Matheson, "Hamlet," p. 383.
28. Howard-Hill, "Buc and the Censorship," p. 53.
29. I am indebted in this discussion of censorship to Clegg, *Press Censorship*, and Dutton, *Licensing*.
30. On Elizabethan censorship apparatuses and their interrelations, see Clegg, *Press Censorship*, pp. 30–76.
31. Whetstone, *Sidney*, pp. b4–c2.
32. Rodriguez-Salgado, *Armada*, p. 53.
33. C. Wilson, *Queen Elizabeth*, pp. 1–2, 21–62. A sermon would have fallen under the authority not of the Stationers Company but of the English Church.
34. Nolan, "Muster," p. 394.
35. Clegg, *Press Censorship*, p. 222.
36. Jonson, *The Poetaster*, 4.7.1536.
37. Whetstone, *Sidney*, from the title page. Naunton, in his entry for "Sir Philip Sidney" in *Fragmenta Regalia*, writes: "They have a very quaint conceit of him, that Mars, and Mercury, fell at variance, whose servant he should be" (p. 20).
38. Rich, *Mercury*, pp. B3, B4.
39. Ibid., p. A3.
40. Naunton, *Fragmenta Regalia*, p. 15.
41. John Florio, *Florios second frutes* (London: 1591), qtd. in Fox, "Rumour," p. 601.
42. See Fox, "Rumour," especially pp. 601–12.
43. *Timon of Athens*, 4.3.161.

44. See Hammer, "Myth-Making," for an excellent and thorough examination of what the author calls the "myth-making" that followed the Cadiz expedition.
45. See *Deceit unmask'd* and Scoufos, "Harvey," pp. 305–8.
46. Frank, *Beginnings*, p. 2. The Donne quote is from "Mercurius Gallo-Belgicus," *Poems*, p. 131, ln. 8.
47. See *Downfall of temporizing poets*.
48. "Ideology is a 'representation' of the imaginary relationship of individuals to the real conditions of their existence." Althusser, "*Lenin and Philosophy*," p. 162.
49. Foucault, *The Archeology of Knowledge*, p. 25.
50. All citations of Christopher Marlowe's *Edward II* appear in parentheses in the text.
51. Nolan, "Militarization," pp. 417–18.
52. I am not considering in this reckoning of soldiers the militias that could have been mobilized in tens of thousands, as they were in 1587 and 1588 (see Nolan, "Muster").
53. On the legal concept of the king's "two bodies," see Kantorowicz, *The King's Two Bodies*.

CHAPTER 2

1. *True Copy*, p. 40. No author is given in the 1589 edition, but the author is supposed to be Sir Anthony Wingfield. Throughout the text I attribute the quotes to Wingfield as appropriate.
2. Churchyard, *Flaunders*, p. 11.
3. Hale, *War and Society*, p. 193.
4. The term "military revolution" is associated with Michael Roberts's lecture of that same name, given in 1956 and often reprinted. See also Parker, *Military Revolution*; Rogers, *Military Revolution Debate*; and Downing, *Military Revolution*.
5. Troops attempting to gain control of the marketplace in Cadiz "were shot at from loopholes and windows, and sometimes encountered by the enemy's pikes in places of advantage." Slyngisbie, "Relations of the Voyage," p. 76.
6. Styward, *Pathwaie*, p. 150.
7. On the emergence of the military memoir, see Harari, *Renaissance Military Memoirs*, especially his introduction and first chapter. For a comprehensive discussion of the place of the military manual in the sixteenth century see Taunton, *1590s Drama and Militarism*, pp. 1–22. An invaluable overview of Elizabethan military manuals can be found in Webb, *Elizabethan Military Science*, pp. 3–50.
8. Machiavelli's *Dell' arte della guerra* was first translated into English by Peter Whitehorne in 1560. Castiglione's *Il Libro del Cortegiano*, which dedicates much of the first book to the courtier as a man of war, was first published in English translation by Thomas Hoby in 1561.

9. Roger Williams, *A Briefe Discourse of Warre* (1590), qtd. in Webb, *Elizabethan Military Science*, p. 64.
10. For an excellent study of the pressure on the males of the Elizabethan aristocracy to present themselves as men of personal valor and daring, see Rebhorn, "Crisis of Aristocracy."
11. I owe a particular debt to Wayne Lee, who was willing not only to help me revise and substantiate this chapter but also to share with me much of his unpublished and forthcoming work.
12. On modern operational maps, the movements of friendly forces are designated by blue arrows (of the enemy, by red), hence, the strategic and tactical aspects of warfighting are referred to collectively as "the big blue arrow."
13. Nolan, "Militarization," p. 418.
14. C. S. L. Davies, "Provisions for Armies," p. 234.
15. Pearce, "Elizabethan Food Policy," p. 40.
16. See C. S. L. Davies, "Provisions for Armies," p. 239.
17. On the strategic objectives of Elizabethan expeditionary warfare, see Nolan, "Militarization," and Wernham, *After the Armada*. For a thorough examination of the military and diplomatic policies upholding Tudor border country in the north of England as well as the pales in Ireland and France, see Ellis, *Tudor Frontiers*, especially pp. 1–77, 207–32.
18. *True Copy*, pp. 49, 52.
19. Ibid., p. 10.
20. Styward, *Pathwaie*, p. 61.
21. Ibid., p. 149.
22. *True Copy*, p. 53.
23. On the militia, see Boynton, *Elizabethan Militia*; Stearns, "Conscription"; and Nolan, "Muster."
24. For this entire discussion on muster rolls, see Rich, "Population of Elizabethan England."
25. Ibid., p. 251.
26. Nolan, "Militarization," p. 418.
27. *True Copy*, p. 11.
28. Knyvett, *Defense of the Realm*, pp. 40–50, identifies profiteering as a significant problem on all levels of military operation and urges better compensation for generals, county officials, and even soldiers and spies. See also Styward, *Pathwaie*, pp. 164–65, on the value of having an experienced soldier oversee the muster in order to reduce frictions.
29. Jonathan Davies, *English Companies of Foot*, pp. 8–9, gives the figure of six days as a typical training period for firearms, with each trainee allocated enough powder to fire off twenty to fifty practice rounds. These figures may reflect an accelerated training schedule caused by the fear of a Spanish invasion. Nolan, *Sir John Norreys*, pp. 183–84, notes that the soldiers were sometimes allowed only two practice shots. A modern marine will fire off hundreds of live rounds before leaving initial training.

30. On the problem of acquiring enough carts, see C. S. L. Davies, "Provisions for Armies," p. 245.
31. Gainsford, *Earle of Tirone*, p. 30.
32. Slyngisbie, "Relations of the Voyage," pp. 58–60, 92.
33. *True Copy*, p. 44.
34. Ibid., pp. 6–7.
35. Slyngisbie, "Relations of the Voyage," pp. 56–57, describes a perilous movement on a foggy night where ships kept a safe distance apart by beating drums. Bytharne, *Booke of War*, pp. 13–15, describes a night movement in which ships pulled in close together and followed the admiral's flagship to avoid getting lost.
36. Slyngisbie, "Relations of the Voyage," p. 57, reports that striking an officer was a capital offense during the expedition to Cadiz. Another veteran of that campaign describes how certain soldiers were executed for mutiny "in a very fair and pleasant green" ("Honorable Voyage," p. 285).
37. Styward, *Pathwaie*, p. 62, explains and justifies the practice of decimation. Borrowed from the Romans, it was enacted at least once during the Elizabethan period, by Essex in the ill-fated Irish expedition.
38. Ibid., p. 149.
39. Churchyard, *Flaunders*, p. 43.
40. Ibid., pp. 38–47.
41. Gainsford, *Earle of Tirone*, p. 24.
42. "Letter from a Soldier," pp. 357–58.
43. For a detailed description of the practice of acquiring food in country, see *True Copy*, pp. 26–30.
44. Gruffydd, *1544 "Enterprises,"* p. 21.
45. See Jonathan Davies's appendix 3, ibid., pp. 47–52, and also C. S. L. Davies, "Provisions for Armies."
46. *True Copy*, p. 45.
47. For example, violence against the people of Cadiz was forbidden but pillaging was allowed for a certain period (see "Honorable Voyage," p. 298).
48. Gruffydd, *1544 "Enterprises,"* p. 18, notes that during the French campaign the commanders could have relieved the hunger of the force had they only been willing to pay the going rate for grain: "Indeed, if the wheat had been ground and baked, there would have been no shortage of bread and also there would have been no lack of wheat to grind, if the King's Purveyors had given sixpence and eight-pence for every peck of wheat.... But they refused to do this because they set more store by their advantage than by doing a hapworth of good to the common soldiers."
49. Ibid., pp. 17–18.
50. Churchyard, *Churchyardes choise*, p. a.iii.
51. "Letter from a Soldier," p. 346.
52. Styward, *Pathwaie*, pp. 125–29.
53. John Smythe, recalling his service in the Low Countries, mentions

soldiers sleeping hundreds together on the bare floor of a church. *Certaine Discourses Concerning the Formes and Effects of Divers Sorts of Weapons* (1590), qtd. in Webb, *Elizabethan Military Science*, p. 151.
54. *CSP, Ireland* (November 1600–July 1601), p. 113. Cited in ibid., pp. 153, 214n21.
55. For this discussion of Elizabethan medical and field medical practices, I am indebted to Webb, "English Military Surgery during the Age of Elizabeth." Webb summarizes much of this article in *Elizabethan Military Science*, pp. 148–68, but the article is essential reading for anyone interested in this subject.
56. Gruffydd, *1544 "Enterprises,"* p. 25.
57. Churchyard, "Siege of Leeth," in Churchyard, *Chippes*, p. 4.
58. Gruffydd, *1544 "Enterprises,"* p. 28.
59. "Honorable Voyage," p. 200.
60. Ibid., p. 296.
61. Churchyard, *Flaunders*, p. 41.
62. Styward, *Pathwaie*, p. 136.
63. Harington, *Nugae Antiquae*, 1:p. 273.
64. Styward, *Pathwaie*, p. 136.
65. Churchyard, "Siege of Leeth," p. 10.
66. Styward, *Pathwaie*, p. 149.
67. *True Copy*, p. 20.
68. Ibid., p. 21.
69. Gruffydd, *1544 "Enterprises,"* p. 25.
70. Lodging might be demanded in cities and towns, and the burden of supplying lodging might be distributed fairly with the help of city officials. Lichefield, *Compendious Treatise*, pp. 5–6.
71. *True Copy*, p. 9.
72. Knyvett, *Defense of the Realm*, p. 58–59.
73. *True Copy*, p. 17.
74. "Letter from a Soldier," p. 351.
75. Gruffydd, *1544 "Enterprises,"* p. 34.
76. That Styward, *Pathwaie*, p. 142, sees fit to insist upon the burial of the dead on the grounds that "unwillingness in the minds of the soldiers to adventure their lives, knowing that if they happen to fight for their country and be slain, they are not like to be buried," suggests this basic decency was often overlooked.
77. *True Copy*, p. 47.
78. Gruffydd, *1544 "Enterprises,"* p. 20.
79. Styward, *Pathwaie*, pp. 49–50.
80. Webb, *Elizabethan Military Science*, p. 126. Webb's source is Garrard, *The Arte of Warre*, p. 278.
81. Gascoigne, "Dulce Bellum Inexpertis," st. 131.
82. Knyvett, *Defense of the Realm*, p. 58.
83. Blandie, *Castle*, p. 20.
84. *True Copy*, p. 48.

CHAPTER 3

1. Churchyard, *Churchyardes choise*, preface.
2. Maria M. Scott, *Re-Presenting*, p. 22.
3. For Churchyard's bibliographical information, see Adnitt, *Thomas Churchyard*; Chalmers, *Churchyard's Chips*; and Goldwyn, "Notes on the Biography." Goldwyn lists among Churchyard's brushes with authority an indictment or "true bill" for not attending church services for over six months (p. 4).
4. The discussion of "Davy Dycars Dreame" that follows is indebted to Lucas, "Diggon Davie."
5. All references to "Davy Dycars Dreame" are drawn from Churchyard, *Contention*. "Davy Dycars Dreame" appears on pp. A.i.–A.ii.
6. King, *English Reformation Literature*, p. 106.
7. George Gascoigne mentions the Davy Dycar controversy in his own politically critical work, "The Steel Glass." Spenser may have been entering the controversy with the invention of Diggon Davie, a character in the "September eclogue" of *The Shepheardes Calender*. The debate was famous enough to warrant two republications of the poem. For a critical commentary on this poetic exchange see Lucus, "Diggon Davie," pp. 152–53.
8. "Small soldier" is from Churchyard, *Churchyardes choise*, preface; the "sword and pen" quote is from a letter from Churchyard to Christopher Hatton in Nicolas, *Memoirs*, p. 176.
9. Spenser, "Colin Clout's Come Home Again," lns. 396–99, *The Shorter Poems*.
10. Thomas Nash, *Strange News*, p. 7; Meres, *Palladis Tamia*, p. 24.
11. Goldwyn, "Notes on the Biography," pp. 3–12.
12. Churchyard, "The Siege of Leeth," p. 1; subsequent cites of this work are noted by page number in the text.
13. My primary source for this discussion of the Siege of Leith and the end of the regency of Marie de Guise is Camden, *Anno Domini 1560, Annales*. I am indebted also to Marshall, *Mary of Guise*, especially pp. 199–256; and Dunn, *Elizabeth and Mary*.
14. Marshall, *Mary of Guise*, p. 212.
15. See Edington, *Court and Culture*; Keller, *Scotland*; and Cowan and Shaw, *Renaissance and Reformation*.
16. Camden, *Anno Domini 1560*, section 2, *Annales*.
17. Fissel, *English Warfare*, p. 120.
18. Marling and Silberman, "Statue," pp. 9–10.
19. From the booklet "Vietnam Memorial Fund Competition" (1980), qtd. in ibid., p. 10.
20. Baldo, "Wars of Memory," p. 141.
21. I am deeply indebted in this discussion of *The Lepanto* to Appelbaum, "War and Peace," from whom I quote James (pp. 340–43).
22. Polemon, *Booke of Battailes*, title page.
23. Alford, *Early Elizabethan Polity*, pp. 85–90.
24. Worden, *Sound of Virtue*, pp. 172–83.

25. Camden, *Anno Domini* 1560, section 6, *Annales*, lists "The fort at Aymouth in Scotland shall be razed" among the articles of the peace treaty.
26. Alford, *Early Elizabethan Polity*, pp. 85–86.
27. For a more complete summary see Jorgensen, *Shakespeare's Military World*, pp. 208–314.
28. Burghley, "Certain Precepts," p. 11.
29. Osborne, "*Advice*," pp. 94–95.
30. Churchyard, *Feastfull*, pp. 85, 13.
31. Styward, *Pathwaie*, p. 161.
32. On the "Trained Bands," see Nolan, "Militarization."
33. See Cruickshank, "Pensioner Reserve," p. 638. Sir Henry Sidney evidently tried to expand the pensioner reserve system in Ireland but received pressure to reduce its numbers.
34. Churchyard, *Churchyardes Chippes*, p. 58.
35. Ibid., p. 59.
36. Ibid., p. 95.
37. More, "Richard the Third," pp. 54–57.
38. See Steible, "Jane Shore," pp. 4–7.
39. For excellent overviews of the representation of Mistress Shore in Elizabethan literature, see Maria M. Scott, *Re-Presenting*; Rowan, "Shore's Wife"; and B. Brown, "Sir Thomas More."
40. "A New Sonnet, Containing the Lamentation of Shore's Wife" (ln. 19), qtd. in Maria M. Scott, *Re-Presenting*, p. 29.
41. For a similar interpretation of Churchyard's Mistress Shore, see R. D. Brown, "'A Talkative Wench.'"
42. All selections quoted in this section are from Churchyard, "Shores Wife." Parenthetical cites refer to page numbers in the edition listed in the bibliography.
43. *Henry V* (4.1.134–85).
44. As the subtitle of Maria M. Scott's *Re-Presenting "Jane" Shore* indicates, Shore was a heroine but she was also a harlot. In the stanza immediately following the one I just discussed, Shore speaks about the pleasure she took in having power over a king and in enjoying his money, sounding somewhat like the Wife of Bath as she invokes her weakness almost as an excuse: "What need I more to clear myself so much? /A king me won and had me at his call: / His royal state, his princely grace was such, / The hope of will that women seek of all; / The ease and wealth, the gifts which were not small, / Besieged me so strongly round about, / My power was weak: I could not hold him out" (p. 132).
45. Steible argues for an even more subversive reading of Churchyard's Shore, which stands on the fact that in Churchyard's version of the story Shore curses Richard III. Richard may have been, for Tudor readers, a villain, but Steible's argument is that in cursing a king Shore "denounces monarchal tyranny" in general (p. 4). Her claim that Churchyard's

Shore is defiant rather than lamenting (p. 7) and "powerful in [her] subversiveness" (p. 4) is a subtle and persuasive one.
46. Churchyard letter to Hatton (undated), reprinted in Adnitt, *Thomas Churchyard*, pp. 40–41.

CHAPTER 4

1. *Calendar of State Papers*, p. 444. For notes on the biography and poetic career of Gascoigne, I am indebted to Prouty, *George Gascoigne*.
2. Gascoigne traded on his checkered personal history in developing his persona as a rough-and-ready soldier. See Shannon, who calls him "the most successful alleged failure in Elizabethan letters" ("Poetic Companies," p. 453).
3. See Lodge and Gascoigne, *A Larum for London*; also see *Larum for London* (no author).
4. See Hughes, "Gascoigne's Poses," p. 7; and Quinn, *Elizabethans*. On the controversy attracted by his influential prose fiction, see Gascoigne, *Adventures of Master F. J.*
5. Cunningham, "Renaissance Execution," p. 212.
6. Gascoigne, *Spoil*, p. 590. All parenthetical citations of *Spoil* refer to this edition. It should be noted that some authorship questions have arisen in the past surrounding *The Spoil of Antwerp*; see Stage, "Spoyle."
7. On the Antwerp money market, see Outhwaite, "Trials of Foreign Borrowing." On the Jewish community in Antwerp and England's relations to the larger European Jewish community, see Metzger, "'Now by My Hood.'"
8. Rich, *Allarme*, "The Author to the Reader," n.p.
9. Norris, "Warning to London," n.p.
10. See, for instance, John Norden's *The Mirror of Honour* (1596). See also Rothschild, "Conqueror Hero," and Jorgensen, "Formative Shakespearean Legacy."
11. Rich, *Faultes*, p. O.
12. Gascoigne, "*Dulce Bellum Inexpertis*," st. 12; subsequent cites of this work are noted by stanza number in the text.
13. See Parker, *Spanish Road*, pp. 48–60, and "Mutiny and Discontent" throughout.
14. The dialogue in Gascoigne's description is written in French, which I have translated in the citation. The original reads: "Helas mounsieur, il ne a point de ordre, & voila la ruine de ceste ville. Aiez courage mon amy (quoth I)"; and "Ou est que vous eufuiez canaille? faisons teste pour le honeur de la patrie."
15. See Genesis 18:23, where Abraham asks God with regard to Sodom and Gomorrah, "Wilt thou also destroy the righteous with the wicked?" (King James translation).
16. Hale, "War and Opinion," p. 25.
17. Jorgensen, "War and Peace," p. 321.
18. Parenthetical citations of *A Larum for London* refer to the page

numbers in the 1602 edition. The drama plays fast and loose with historical accuracy. The character Egmount is certainly Lamoral, Count of Egmont, who was executed in 1568, along with Count van Hoorn, who also appears in *A Larum for London*. The most notable liberty involves the Duke of Alva, who was recalled from the Netherlands three years prior to the sack of Antwerp. Other characters, like Danila—Don Sancho D'Avila—are simply spelled oddly. In this chapter I have left the names of the characters as they were printed in 1602; these are, after all, characters in a play and not the real people to whom those characters correspond.

19. *Historical Discourse*, chapter 4, p. eiii.
20. Raleigh, *The Works*, vol. 8, p. 300.
21. See Read, "Queen Elizabeth's Seizure."
22. Qtd. in Bergeron, "Elizabethan Lord Mayor's Show," p. 276. The Lord Mayor's Show of 1585 was written by George Peele, and its appeals to peace are frequent.
23. Calvo, "Politics of Print," p. 282, and Keen, "Black Legend Revisited," p. 706.
24. Sandberg, "Beyond Encounters," p. 20; Schmidt, *Innocence Abroad*, p. 98; and Mackenthum, *Metaphors of Dispossession*, p. 66. See also Hillgarth, *Mirror of Spain*.
25. For the following discussion of Las Casas, I am deeply indebted to Keen, "Black Legend Revisited."
26. Las Casas's Relacion first appeared in English as *The Spanish colonie, or Briefe chronicle of the acts and gestes of the Spaniardes in the West Indies, called the newe world* (London: 1583). Plantin was published as *A true discourse of the assault committed vpon the person of the most noble prince, William Prince of Orange* (London: 1582).
27. Hakluyt, *Discourse Concerning Western Planting*, pp. 71–82 (chapter 11). See also commentary by Hart, *Representing the New World*, pp. 125–29.
28. Humphrey Mote, *The Primrose of London* (London: 1585).
29. Both these titles were published by John Wolfe, who is famous for propaganda of this sort.
30. There is a tradition, stemming from a suggestion in Lowndes, *Bibliographer's Guide* (vol. 1, p. 24), that *A Larum for London* is adapted from *An Historical Discourse* and not *The Spoil*. A comparison of the two prose accounts—particularly the former's omission of any character reminiscent of Stump—makes this claim difficult to support.

CHAPTER 5

1. Gosse, *John Donne*, 1:23. Post also suggests the portrait is evidence of Donne's "military aspirations" (*English Lyric Poetry*, p. 3). See also Creswell, "Giving a Face."
2. See Bald, *John Donne*, pp. 55–100, and Flynn, *John Donne*, pp. 136–72.
3. For Donne's personal associations with Elizabethan military men, see

Sellin, "Souldiers." That Donne might have gone to war with Essex to prove his loyalty to the kingdom has been proposed by Carey, *John Donne*, p. 18.
4. Donne, *Sermons*, Sermon 1, vol. 4, p. 48; subsequent cites of *Sermons* are noted in the text by sermon, volume, and page numbers (e.g., 1.4.48).
5. Satire 3, lns. 18–19; all references to Donne's poetry are to Donne, *The Complete English Poems*.
6. Donne, Elegy 8, ln. 39 ; Sermon 9, vol. 1, p. 312; Sermon 1, vol. 2, p. 65.
7. Donne, Elegy 8, lns. 9–12.
8. Donne, Elegy 11, "The Bracelet," lns. 40–42. Donne is speaking particularly about the war as the effect of greed.
9. Martz, *Poetry of Meditation*, pp. 14, 132. The relation of emblems to the wider tradition of meditative poetry has been discussed extensively by Lewalski, *Protestant Poetics*.
10. Also cf. Donne, *Sermons*, Sermon 16, vol. 2, p. 328; Sermon 11, vol. 2, p. 238; Sermon 4, vol. 4, p. 139; and Sermon 12, vol. 4, p. 306.
11. Cf. lns. 13–18.
12. Whitney, *A Choice of Emblems*, p. 138.
13. Gosse, vol. 1, introduction.
14. MacCaffrey, *Elizabeth I*, pp. 126–30.
15. See Genesis 21:6–7.
16. Hammer, "Myth-Making," and MacCaffrey, *Elizabeth I*, pp. 116–23.
17. From "A Relation of Cadiz Action," Raleigh, *The Works*, vol. 8, pp. 667–72. Although his account was published some years after the expedition, Raleigh, like many of the gentleman commanders, circulated letters describing his version of the assault even while the fleet was returning to England. For a thorough study of these reports, see Hammer, "Myth-Making."
18. Raleigh, *The Works*, vol. 8, p. 671.
19. Hammer, "Myth-Making," pp. 622–26.

CHAPTER 6

1. Numbers in the parenthetical citations of Harington's epigrams refer to the line numbers in Harington, *Letters and Epigrams*, unless otherwise stated.
2. See Harari, "Martial Illusions," on the disgruntlement of early modern veterans. Harari contends that the depression and resentment suffered by returning soldiers has too frequently been identified with twentieth-century warfare, and he argues throughout that the phenomenon is traceable in early modern veterans' experiences as well.
3. From Harington, *Ajax*, title page.
4. On English translations of the *Orlando Furioso*, see Ainsworth, "Stanzas," and Mary Augusta Scott, "Elizabethan Translations."
5. On Shakespeare's knowledge of Italian, see Shaheen, "Shakespeare's

Knowledge of Italian." On Milton's notes in his copy of Harington's translation, see Sims, "*Orlando Furioso*," p. 132.
6. On Harington's Ariosto and courtier poetry, see Scott-Warren, *Sir John Harington*, p. 35. On the reception of the book in the seventeenth and eighteenth centuries, see Morini, *Tudor Translation*, p. 102.
7. Kohn, "English Nationalism," p. 77n11.
8. These remarks are in the concluding paragraph of the "Apology." The page is unnumbered in the 1591 edition. For Harington's other alterations, see Trotter, "Harington's Fountain."
9. The engravings are nearly identical to the ones by Girolamo Porro used in an Italian edition of 1584. See McNulty, introduction to *Ludovico Ariosto's "Orlando Furioso."*
10. Plett and Heath observe that Harington "continually allegorizes the epic he has translated" ("Aesthetic Constituents," p. 608).
11. Harington, *Orlando*, "A Brief Apology for Poetry," p. iii. On Harington and allegory, see also Caldwell, "Allegory."
12. Harington, *Orlando*, "A Brief Allegory of Orlando Furioso," p. 412.
13. Ibid., "The life of Ariosto," p. 417.
14. Harington does leave almost the entire scene of the battle for Biserta intact in book 40. Throughout this comparison of the two versions, the parenthetical citations refer to book or canto followed by stanza numbers in Ariosto and Harington, *Orlando Furioso*.
15. Regarding the details in stanza 56: "L'alto rumor de le sonore trombe, / Di timpani e di barbari strumenti, / Giunti al continuo suon d'archi, di frombe, / Di machine, di ruote e di tormenti, / E quel di che piu par che 'l ciel ribombe, / Gridi, tumulti, gemiti e lamenti; / Rendeno un' alto suon, ch'a quel s'accorda, / Con che i uicin, cadeno, il Nilo assorda" (16.56). On the details attributable to Malagigi, compare Harington, *Orlando*, 31.73, with Ariosto, 31.86–87.
16. Unless otherwise specified, all translations from Ariosto are my own.
17. Harington, *Nugae Antiquae*, vol. 1, pp. 239–40.
18. See McLure's introduction to Harington, *Letters and Epigrams*, p. 13.
19. For Harington's biography I am indebted to McClure's introduction to Harington, *Letters and Epigrams*, which provides a very coherent summary of *Nugae Antiquae*, from which most of what we know about Harington's life is taken.
20. Nash writes this in a letter to William Cotton, qtd. in Anspaugh, "Ulysses upon Ajax," p. 14.
21. Harington, *Nugae Antiquae*, vol. 1, p. 168.
22. For the background and history of English dealings with Ireland, see Quinn, *Elizabethans*, pp. 1–19. For the Irish movement toward rebellion, see Falls, *Elizabeth's Irish Wars*, pp. 168–201, and MacCaffrey, *Elizabeth I*, pp. 372–403.
23. For a good summary of the principles of tanistry, see Echeruo, "Tanistry."
24. See Falls, *Elizabeth's Irish Wars*, pp. 202–52.
25. See Harington, *Letters and Epigrams*, pp. 74–75, 79.

26. Harington, "To Sir Anthony Standen: Athlone, in Ireland, 1599," *Nugae Antiquae*, vol. 1, p. 264.
27. Harington, "To Master Thomas Combe: Ireland, August 31, 1599," *Nugae Antiquae*, vol. 1, p. 256: "the Governor [of Connacht] would needs undertake a journey to Sligo, with twenty-one weak companies, that were not 1400 strong; and less of horse than hath been requisite for such a purpose."
28. Harington to Standen, 1599, *Nugae Antiquae*, vol. 1, p. 265.
29. Falls, *Elizabeth's Irish Wars*, pp. 242–45.
30. Harington to Combe, *Nugae Antiquae*, vol. 1, p. 258.
31. Harington, report of May 10th through July 3rd, 1599, *Nugae Antiquae*, vol. 1, p. 279.
32. From the *Journall of the L. Lieutenants procedinges from the xxviijth Aug. tyll the viijth of Sept. 1599*, in Harington, *Nugae Antiquae*, 1:pp. 293–302.
33. Harington to Standen, 1599, *Nugae Antiquae*, vol. 1, p. 267.
34. Harington, report of May 10th through July 3rd, *Nugae Antiquae*, vol. 1, p. 292.
35. See Falls, *Elizabeth's Irish Wars*, pp. 253–340.
36. Shapiro, *Life*, pp. 43–47.
37. Falls, *Elizabeth's Irish Wars*, p. 339.
38. Shapiro, *Life*, pp. 267–70.
39. Harington, "To Sir Hugh Portman: Kelston, October 9, 1601," *Nugae Antiquae*, vol. 1, p. 317.
40. Harington to Combe, *Nugae Antiquae*, vol. 1, pp. 260–61.
41. Harington, "To Sir Anthony Standen: Kelston, February 20, 1600," *Nugae Antiquae*, vol. 1, pp. 310–11.
42. Gascoigne, "The Steel Glass," introduction.
43. Harington, *Letters and Epigrams*, p. 373.
44. See Harington, "To Sir Robert Cecil: Greenwich, June 25, 1600," *Letters and Epigrams*, pp. 81–83.
45. Robert Sydney to Sir John Harington, 1600, in Harington, *Nugae Antiquae*, vol. 1, p. 312.
46. Harington, "To Lady Mary Harington: December 27, 1602," *Letters and Epigrams*, p. 97.
47. Harington, "To Dr. John Still, Bishop of Bath and Wells: Bath or Kelston, October, 1603," *Letters and Epigrams*, pp. 107–8.
48. Harington, "To Lord Thomas Howard: April, 1603," *Letters and Epigrams*, p. 99.
49. Harington, "To Robert Markham: 1606," *Letters and Epigrams*, p. 122.
50. On the fanfare preceding Essex's departure for Ireland, see Shapiro, *Life*, pp. 102–3.
51. Harington, *Letters and Epigrams*, vol. 1, pp. 370–71.
52. "Farewell to His Muse" is part of a missive sent as a New Year's gift to James VI in 1602, when the queen's death seemed immanent. I cite from

Harington, *Nugae Antiquae*, vol. 1, pp. 325–35, in which it is entitled a "*laterna secreta.*"
53. Harington, "To Prince Henry: 1609," *Letters and Epigrams*, p. 136.
54. Ibid., p. 155.

CHAPTER 7

1. Jonson, *Conversations with Drummond*, p. 139. Jonson, *Ben Jonson*, is the source for all the Jonson works I quote in this chapter. For plays, parenthetical references are to act, scene, and line number; for poems, line number; and for prose works, page number.
2. For an excellent summary of the tension between humanistic and chivalric ideals in the sixteenth century, see Council, "Ben Jonson," pp. 261–68.
3. Chapman, *Bussy D'Ambois*, 1.2.12–33. I am indebted in my discussion of this play to Barton, "Harking," p. 712.
4. On attitudes of English Catholics toward Elizabeth and James, see Watkins, *Representing Elizabeth*, pp. 19–25.
5. On *The Whore of Babylon* and the Gunpowder Plot, see Watkins, *Representing Elizabeth*, p. 25, and Perry, *Jacobean Culture*, pp. 179–81.
6. Watkins, *Representing Elizabeth*, pp. 23–24.
7. Qtd. in Perry, *Jacobean Culture*, p. 160.
8. See Barton's excellent summary of these historians' efforts in "Harking," pp. 714–15.
9. Watkins, *Representing Elizabeth*, p. 17. The development of Elizabeth's royal image according to these ideals has been well documented, but Strong, *Cult*, and Yates, *Astrea*, are still the seminal texts.
10. Barton, "Harking," p. 714.
11. On Henry and the revival of chivalry, see Council, "Ben Jonson," and Strong, "Inigo Jones."
12. See also Orgel's comment on Henry's image in "Idols."
13. John Davies, "Cambria," p. 19. On Henry as an "infant warrior," see Badenhausen, "Disarming."
14. Jonson, *Conversations with Drummond*, pp. 141–42.
15. The soldiers' names appear in Epigrams 82, 87, 107, and 12, respectively. The description of Shift is from character descriptions in Jonson, *Every Man Out*, p. 426.
16. See Jonson, *The Poems, The Prose Works*, p. 69, note cviii.
17. All citations of shorter poems refer to Jonson, *The Poems, The Prose Works*.
18. On the difficulty in dating *The Case Is Altered*, see Jonson, *Ben Jonson*, 1:305–27 and 3:94–102. Although it is not published until 1609, its title is mentioned as early as 1599, in Nash's *Lenten Stuff*.
19. See Lewalski, "Milton's *Comus*," and also Orgel, *Jonsonian Masque*.
20. On the collaboration of Jonson and Cavendish see Fitzmaurice, "William Cavendish." Jonson calls Cavendish his "best patron" in a letter from Westminster dated 20 December 1631 (Jonson, *Ben*

Jonson, 1:212). See also commentary in Harp and Stewart, *Cambridge Companion*, p. 11.
21. See Barton, "Harking," pp. 706–8.
22. This discussion of the complex and controversial set of military actions we now call the Thirty Years' War is obviously a simplification. For a fine recent summary of the politics and progress of the wars, see Sutherland, "Origins."
23. See Wright, "Propaganda."
24. On the Spanish Match, see Pursell, "End."
25. Sutherland, "Origins," p. 619.
26. On Charles's suppression of war reporting see Cogswell, "Politics of Propaganda." On the proliferation of news from the wars, see also Beller, "Contemporary," p. 276, and Wright, "Propaganda."
27. "A speech according to Horace" is in Jonson, *The Poems, The Prose Works*, pp. 213–16. All parenthetical citations of Jonson's verse refer to the line numbers in the editions listed in the bibliography.
28. "An Epistle to a Friend, to perswade him to the Warres" is in ibid., pp. 162–68.
29. Jonson, "A speech according to Horace" (ln. 52). On the significance of these names, see Jonson, *Commentary*, p. 84.
30. This description of Lovel is from "The Persons of the Play," Jonson, *New Inne*, p. 402.
31. Ascham, *Scholemaster*, p. 27. For a comprehensive study of humanistic objections to chivalry see also Herman "Is This Winning?" and Baker-Smith, "Inglorious Glory." The idea that the Tudor dynasty drew heavily on models of nobility borrowed from romances is well known, but for analyses of the evolution of this modeling as well as its economic and ideological functions, see McCoy, *Rites*, and Siegel, "English Humanism."
32. Drummond gives *Herologia* as the proposed title. Jonson, *Conversations with Drummond*, p. 132.
33. Joseph Warton, *Essay on the Genius and Writing of Pope* (1756), qtd. in Mitchell, "Benjamin West's 'Death,'" p. 28.
34. Pierpont, "Onward."
35. François Rigolot, "Henry Comes to Aid Margaret Thatcher," *New York Times*, 18 February 1990.

Works Cited

PRIMARY

Ariosto, Lodovico. *Orlando Furioso*. Venice: 1560.
Ascham, Roger. *The Scholemaster*. London: 1570.
Blandie, William. *Castle, or a picture of pollicy*. London: 1581.
Burghley, William Cecil, Lord. "Certain Precepts of the Well Ordering of a Man's Life" (1584). *Advice to a Son*. Ed. Louis Wright. Ithaca: Cornell University Press, 1962. Pp. 7–13.
Bytharne, Jehan. *Booke of War by Sea and Land* (1543). *The Naval Miscellany*. Ed. Julian S. Corbett. London: Naval Records Society, 1902. 1:1–21.
Calendar of State Papers, Domestic Series, of the Reigns of Edward VI, Mary, and Elizabeth I, 1547–1580. Ed. Robert Lemon. London, 1856.
Camden, William. *Annales*. London: 1625.
Chapman, George. *Bussy D'Ambois*. London: 1607.
Churchyard, Thomas. *The Contention betwyxte Churchyard and Camell, vpon Dauid Dycers Dreame*. London: 1560.
———. *A Feastfull of sad cheere*. London: 1592.
———. *The First Parte of Churchyardes Chippes*. London: 1575.
———. *A Generall rehearsall of warres, called Churchyardes choise*. London: 1579.
———. *A Lamentable, and pitifull Description of the woefull warres in Flaunders, since the last yeares of the Emperor Charles the fifth, his raigne*. London: 1578.
———. "Shores Wife." *Churchyards Challenge*. London: 1593.
Clowes, William. *A Prooved practise for all young chirurgians*. London: 1591.
Davies, John. "Cambria" or "Wales to Her Prince." *Microcosmos*. London: 1603. Pp. 19–22.
Deceit unmask'd: being a letter from a Flemish merchant to Don Diego de Mondragon concerning the false reports of a great victory claimed by the Spanish Armada (c. 1588). Cambridge, Mass.: CLXXXVI Press, 1951.
Digges, Thomas. *Arithmetical warlike treatise named Stratioticos*. London: 1579.
Donne, John. *The Complete English Poems*. New York: Knopf, 1991.
———. *The Sermons of John Donne*. 10 vols. Ed. George R. Potter and Evelyn M. Simpson. Berkeley: University of California Press, 1953.

The Downfall of temporizing poets, unlicenst printers, upstart booksellers, trotting mercuries, and bawling hawkers. London: 1641.

Drayton, Michael. *Poly-Olbion.* London: 1612.

Gainsford, Thomas [T. G.]. *The True Exemplary and Remarkable History of the Earle of Tirone.* London: 1619.

Gale, Thomas. *Certaine works of chirurgerie.* London: c. 1563.

Garrard, William. *The Arte of Warre.* London: 1591.

Gascoigne, George. "The Adventures of Master F. J." *The Complete Works of George Gascoigne.* Ed. John W. Cunliffe. Cambridge: Cambridge University Press, 1907. 1:383–453.

———. "*Dulce Bellum Inexpertis*" or "The Fruits of War." *The Complete Works of George Gascoigne.* Ed. John W. Cunliffe. Cambridge: Cambridge University Press, 1907. 1:139–84.

———. *The Spoil of Antwerp. The Complete Works of George Gascoigne.* Ed. John W. Cunliffe. Cambridge: Cambridge University Press, 1910. 2:587–99.

———. *The Steel Glass. The Complete Works of George Gascoigne.* Ed. John W. Cunliffe. Cambridge: Cambridge University Press, 1910. 2:133–74.

Gruffydd, Elis. *Elis Gruffydd and the 1544 "Enterprises" of Paris and Boulogne.* Ed. Jonathan Davies. Trans. M. Bryn Davies. Surrey: Pike and Shot Society, 2003.

Hakluyt, Richard. *Discourse Concerning Western Planting.* Ed. Charles Deane. Cambridge, Mass.: 1877.

Hall, Joseph. *The Discovery of a New World or A Description of the South Indies Hetherto Unknowne, by an English Mercury.* London: 1609.

Harington, John. *A Brief Apology for Poetry* (1591). *Elizabethan Critical Essays.* 2 vols. Ed. Gregory M. Smith. Oxford: Clarendon Press, 1904. 2:194–222.

———. *The Letters and Epigrams of Sir John Harington, together with The prayse of private life.* Ed. Norman E. McClure. New York: Octagon Books, 1977.

———. *A New Discourse of a Stale Subject, Called the Metamorphosis of Ajax.* London: 1596.

———. *Nugae Antiquae: Being A Miscellaneous Collection of Original Papers in Prose and Verse; written during the reigns of Henry VIII, Edward VI, Queen Mary, Elizabeth, and King James.* 2 vols. London: 1804.

———. *Orlando Furioso in English Heroical Verse.* London: 1591.

An Historical Discourse, or rather a Tragicall Historie of the Citie of Antwerpe, since the Departure of Phillip King of Spain out of the Netherlands, till this Present Year. London: 1586.

The Honorable Voyage unto Cadiz (1596). Arthur F. Kinney, ed. *Elizabethan Backgrounds: Historical Documents of the Age of Elizabeth I.* Hamden, Conn.: Archon Books, 1975. Pp. 276–309.

Jonson, Ben. *Ben Jonson.* 11 vols. Ed. C. H. Herford, Percy Simpson, and Evelyn Simpson. Oxford: Clarendon Press, 1925–1952.

———. *The Case Is Altered* (before 1599). *Ben Jonson*, vol. 3.
———. *Commentary, Literary Record, Notes, Index. Ben Jonson*, vol. 11.
———. *Conversations with Drummond* (1619). *Ben Jonson*, 1:128–78.
———. *Every Man Out of His Humor* (c. 1599). *Ben Jonson*, vol. 3.
———. *The Magnetick Lady* (1632). *Ben Jonson*, vol. 6.
———. *The New Inne* (1629). *Ben Jonson*, vol. 6.
———. *The Poems, The Prose Works. Ben Jonson*, vol. 8.
———. *The Poetaster* (1601). *Ben Jonson*, vol. 4.
———. "Prince Henries Barriers." *Ben Jonson*, vol. 7.
Knyvett, Sir Henry. *The Defense of the Realm* (1596). Oxford: Clarendon Press, 1906.
A Larum for London or The Siedge of Antwerp. London: 1602.
Larum for London, or, The Siege of Antwerp, together with The Spoyle of Antwerp, by George Gascoigne. London: 1872.
"A Letter from a Soldier of good place in Ireland." Ed. Arthur F. Kinney. *Elizabethan Backgrounds: Historical Documents of the Age of Elizabeth I*. Hamden, Conn.: Archon Books, 1975. Pp. 336–60.
Lichefield, Nicholas. *A Compendious Treatise entitled De re militari, containing principall orders to be observed in Martiall affaires*. London: 1582.
Lodge, Thomas, and George Gascoigne. *A Larum for London*. New York: AMS Press, 1970.
Marlowe, Christopher. *Edward the Second*. Ed. W. Moelwyn Merchant. New York: Norton, 1975.
Meres, Francis. *Palladis Tamia*. London: 1598.
More, Thomas. "The History of King Richard the Third." *The Yale Edition of the Complete Works of St. Thomas More*. Vol. 2. Ed. Richard Sylvester. New Haven: Yale University Press, 1963.
Nash, Thomas. *Lenten Stuff*. London: 1599.
———. *Strange News, of the Intercepting of Certain Letters*. London: 1593.
———. *The Unfortunate Traveler or The Life of Jack Wilton*. London: 1594.
Naunton, Robert. *Fragmenta Regalia*. London: 1641.
Norden, John. *The Mirror of Honour*. London: 1597.
Norris, Rafe. "A Warning to London by the Fall of Antwerp (to the tune of 'Row Well, Ye Mariners')." London: 1577.
Osborne, Francis. *"Advice to a Son or Directions for Your Better Conduct" (1648)*. *Advice to a Son*. Ed. Louis Wright. Ithaca: Cornell University Press, 1962. Pp. 33–114.
Paradin, Claude. *Heroicall Devises of M. Claudius Paradin*. London: 1591.
Polemon, John. *Second Part of the Booke of Battailes*. London: 1587.
Raleigh, Walter. *The Works*. 8 vols. Oxford: Oxford University Press, 1829.
Rich, Barnabe. *Allarme to England*. London: 1578.
———. *Faultes Faults* (1606). Ed. Melvin H. Wolf. Gainesville: Scholars' Facsimiles and Reprints, 1965.
———. *A Path-Way to Military Practice*. London: 1587.
———. *A Right Excellent and Pleasant Dialogue Between Mercury and an English Soldier*. London: 1574.

Segar, William. *The Book of Honor and Arms*. London: 1590.
Shakespeare, William. *The Riverside Shakespeare*, 2nd ed. Ed. Herschel Baker, Anne Barton, Frank Kermode, Harry Levin, Hallett Smith, and Marie Edel. Boston: Houghton Mifflin, 1997.
Sidney, Philip. *A Defence of Poetry*. Ed. Jan A. Van Dorsten. Oxford: Oxford University Press, 1971.
Slyngisbie, Sir William. "Relations of the Voyage to Cadiz" (1596). *The Naval Miscellany*. Ed. Julian S. Corbett. London: Naval Records Society, 1902. 1:23–92.
Spenser, Edmund. *The Shorter Poems*. Ed. William A. Oram, Einar Bjorvand, Ronald Bond, Thomas H. Cain, Alexander Dunlop, and Richard Schell. New Haven and London: Yale University Press, 1989.
———. *The Works of Edmund Spenser: A Variorum Edition*. 10 vols. Ed. Edwin Greenlaw, C. G. Osgood, and F. M. Padelford. Baltimore: Johns Hopkins University Press, 1932–1957.
Styward, Thomas. *The Pathwaie to Martial Discipline*. London: 1581.
A True Copy of a Discourse written by a gentleman employed in the late Voyages of Spaine and Portingale. London: 1589.
A True Discourse of the Armie which the king of Spain caused to be assembled in the haven of Lisbon in the kingdom of Portungall in the yeare 1588, against England. The which began to go out of the said haven on the 29 and 30 of May. Trans. from French to English by Daniel Archdeacon. London: 1588.
Whetstone, George. *Sir Phillip Sidney, his honorable life, his valient death, and true vertues*. London: 1587.
———. *The Honorable Reputation of a Soldier*. London: 1585.
Whitney, Geffrey. *Choice of Emblemes*. London: 1586.

SECONDARY

Adnitt, Henry W. *Thomas Churchyard, 1520–1604*. Shropshire: Shropshire Archeological and Natural History Society, ca. 1880.
Ainsworth, Edward G. "Stanzas of the *Orlando Furioso* in English Collections of Madrigals." *Review of English Studies* 7:27 (1931), pp. 327–30.
Alford, Stephen. *The Early Elizabethan Polity: William Cecil and the English Succession Crisis, 1558–1569*. Cambridge: Cambridge University Press, 1998.
Althusser, Louis. *"Lenin and Philosophy" and Other Essays*. Trans. Ben Brewster. New York: Monthly Review Press, 1971.
Altman, Joel. *The Tudor Play of Mind: Rhetorical Inquiry and the Development of Elizabethan Drama*. Berkeley: University of California Press, 1978.
Anderson, Benedict. *Imagined Communities: Reflections on the Origins and Spread of Nationalism*. London: Verso, 1983.
Andrews, Alexander. *The History of British Journalism, from the*

foundation of the newspaper press in England, to the repeal of the Stamp Act in 1855. 2 vols. London: 1859.
Anglo, Sidney. "The British History in Early Tudor Propaganda." *Bulletin of the John Rylands Library* 44 (1961), pp. 17–48.
Anspaugh, Kelly. "Ulysses upon Ajax: Joyce, Harington, and the Question of Cloacal Imperialism." *South Atlantic Review* 60:2 (1995), pp. 11–29.
Appelbaum, Robert. "War and Peace in *The Lepanto* of James VI and I." *Modern Philology* 97:3 (2000), pp. 333–63.
Archer, Ian W. "The Burden of Taxation on Sixteenth-Century London." *Historical Journal* 44:3 (2001), pp. 599–627.
Aspden, Suzanne. "Ballads and Britons: Imagined Community and the Continuity of 'English' Opera." *Journal of the Royal Musical Association* 122:1 (1997), pp. 24–51.
Badenhausen, Richard. "Disarming the Infant Warrior: Prince Henry, King James, and the Chivalric Revival." *Papers on Language and Literature* 31 (1995), pp. 20–37.
Baker-Smith, Dominic. "'Inglorious Glory': 1513 and the Humanist Attack on Chivalry." *Chivalry in the Renaissance*. Ed. Sidney Anglo. Woodbridge (UK): Boydell, 1990. Pp. 129–44.
Bald, R. C. *John Donne: A Life*. New York: Oxford University Press, 1970.
Baldo, Jonathan. "Wars of Memory in *Henry V*." *Shakespeare Quarterly* 47:2 (1996), pp. 132–59.
Barton, Anne. "Harking Back to Elizabeth: Ben Jonson and Caroline Nostalgia." *English Literary History* 48:4 (1981), pp. 706–31.
Beaud, Michel. *A History of Capitalism, 1500–1980*. Trans. Tom Dickman and Amy Lefebvre. New York: Monthly Review Press, 1983.
Beller, Elmer. "Contemporary English Printed Sources for the Thirty Years' War." *American Historical Review* 32 (1927), pp. 276–82.
Bergeron, David M. "The Elizabethan Lord Mayor's Show." *Studies in English Literature* 10:2 (1970), pp. 269–85.
Boynton, Lindsay. *The Elizabethan Militia, 1588–1638*. London: Routledge and Kegan Paul, 1967.
Brown, Barbara. "Sir Thomas More and Churchyard's 'Shore's Wife.'" *Yearbook of English Studies* 2 (1972), pp.41–48.
Brown, R. Danson "'A Talkative Wench (Whose Words a World Hath Delighted In)': Mistress Shore and Elizabethan Complaint." *Review of English Studies* 49:196 (1998), pp. 395–415.
Cahill, Patricia A. *Unto the Breech: Martial Formations, Historical Trauma, and the Early Modern Stage*. Oxford: Oxford University Press, 2008.
Caldwell, Mark L. "Allegory: The Renaissance Mode." *English Literary History* 44:4 (1977), pp. 580–600.
Calvo, Hortensia. "The Politics of Print: The Historiography of the Book in Early Spanish America." *Book History* 6 (2003), pp. 277–305.
Campbell, John Lord. *Life of Sir Christopher Hatton*. London: 1851.
Carey, John. *John Donne: Life, Mind, Art*. New York: Oxford University Press, 1981.
Catalano, Michele. *Vita di Ludovico Ariosto*. 2 vols. Geneva: Olschki, 1930.

Chalmers, George. *Churchyard's Chips Concerning Scottland: Being a Collection of his Pieces Relative to that Country, and Life of the Author.* London: 1818.

Clegg, Cyndia Susan. *Press Censorship in Elizabethan England.* Cambridge: Cambridge University Press, 1997.

Clough, Shepard B., and Richard T. Rapp. *European Economic History: The Economic Development of Western Civilization.* 3rd ed. New York: McGraw-Hill, 1975.

Cogswell, Thomas. "The Politics of Propaganda: Charles I and the People in the 1620s." *Journal of British Studies* 29 (1990), pp. 187–215.

Council, Norman. "Ben Jonson, Inigo Jones, and the Transformation of Tudor Chivalry." *English Literary History* 47:2 (1980), pp. 259–75.

Cowan, Ian, and Duncan Shaw, eds. *The Renaissance and Reformation in Scotland: Essays in Honour of Gordon Donaldson.* Edinburgh: Scottish Academic Press, 1983.

Cranfill, Thomas M., and Dorothy Hart Bruce. *Barnaby Rich: A Short Bibliography.* Austin: University of Texas Press, 1953.

Creswell, Catherine. "Giving a Face to an Author: Reading Donne's Portraits and the 1635 Edition." *Texas Studies in Literature and Language* 37 (1995), pp. 1–15.

Cruickshank, C. G. *Army Royal.* Oxford: Oxford University Press, 1969.

———. "An Elizabethan Pensioner Reserve." *English Historical Review* 56:224 (1941), pp. 637–39.

Cunliffe, John W., ed. *The Complete Works of George Gascoigne.* 2 vols. Cambridge: Cambridge University Press, 1907–1910.

Cunningham, Karen. "Renaissance Execution and Marlovian Elocution: The Drama of Death." *PMLA* 105:2 (1990), pp. 209–22.

Davies, C. S. L. "Provisions for Armies, 1509–50." *Economic History Review,* 2nd series, 17 (1964), pp. 234–48.

Davies, Jonathan. *The English Companies of Foot in 1588.* Surrey: Pike and Shot Society, 2000.

De Somogyi, Nick. *Shakespeare's Theatre of War.* Burlington, Vt.: Ashgate, 1998.

Dobson, Michael. *The Making of the National Poet: Shakespeare, Adaptation, and Authorship, 1660–1769.* Oxford: Oxford University Press, 1992.

Dollimore, Jonathan. *Radical Tragedy: Religion, Ideology, and Power in the Drama of Shakespeare and His Contemporaries.* 2nd ed. Durham, N.C.: Duke University Press, 1993.

Donagan, Barbara. "Halcyon Days and the Literature of the War: England's Military Education before 1642." *Past and Present* 147 (1995), pp. 65–100.

Downing, Brian. *The Military Revolution and Political Change in Early Modern England.* Princeton: Princeton University Press, 1992.

Dunn, Jane. *Elizabeth and Mary: Cousins, Rivals, Queens.* New York: Knopf, 2004.

Dutton, Richard. *Licensing, Censorship, and Authorship in Early Modern England: Buggeswords*. New York: Palgrave, 2000.
Dymkowski, Christine. *Harley Granville Barker: A Preface to Modern Shakespeare*. Cranberry, N.J.: Folger Books, 1986.
Echeruo, Michael J. "Tanistry, the 'Due of Birth' and Macbeth's Sin." *Shakespeare Quarterly* 23:4 (1972), pp. 444–50.
Edington, Carol. *Court and Culture in Renaissance Scotland*. Amherst: University of Massachusetts Press, 1994.
Einstein, Lewis. *Tudor Ideals*. London: Bell, 1921.
Ellis, Steven G. *Tudor Frontiers and Noble Power*. Oxford: Clarendon Press, 1995.
Engler, Balz. "Shakespeare in the Trenches." *Shakespeare Survey* 44 (1991), pp. 105–11.
Falls, Cyril. *Elizabeth's Irish Wars*. New York: Barnes and Noble, 1950.
Feibel, Juliet. "Vortigern, Rowena, and the Ancient Britons: Historical Art and the Anglicization of National Origins." *Eighteenth-Century Life* 24:1 (2000), pp. 1–21.
Fissel, Mark Charles. *English Warfare, 1511–1642*. New York: Routledge, 2001.
Fitter, Chris. "Emergent Shakespeare and the Politics of Protest: 2 *Henry VI* in Historical Contexts." *English Literary History* 72:1 (2005), pp. 129–58.
Fitzmaurice, James. "William Cavendish and Two Entertainments by Ben Jonson." *Ben Jonson Journal* 5 (1998), pp. 63–80.
Flynn, Dennis. "Donne the Survivor." *The Eagle and the Dove: Reassessing John Donne*. Ed. Claude J. Summers and Ted-Larry Pebworth. Columbia: University of Missouri Press, 1986. Pp. 15–24.
———. *John Donne and the Ancient Catholic Nobility*. Bloomington: Indiana University Press, 1995.
Foucault, Michel. *The Archeology of Knowledge and The Discourse on Language*. Trans. A. M. Sheridan Smith. New York: Pantheon, 1972.
Fox, Adam. "Rumour, News and Popular Political Opinion in Elizabethan and Early Stuart England." *Historical Journal* 40:3 (1997), pp. 597–620.
Frank, Joseph. *The Beginnings of the English Newspaper, 1620–1660*. Cambridge: Harvard University Press, 1961.
Frye, Susan. "The Myth of Elizabeth at Tilbury." *Sixteenth Century Journal* 23 (1992), pp. 95–114.
Fuchs, Barbara. "Spanish Lessons: Spenser and the Irish Moriscos." *Studies in English Literature* 42:1 (Winter 2002), pp. 43–62.
Fussell, Paul. *The Great War and Modern Memory* (1975). Oxford: Oxford University Press, 2000.
Gabler, Anthony. "Check List of English Newspapers and Periodicals before 1801 in the Huntington Library." *Huntington Library Bulletin* 2 (1931), pp. 1–66.
Gallagher, P., and D. W. Cruickshank. "The Armada of 1588 Reflected in the Serious and Popular Literature of the Period." *God's Obvious*

Design. Ed. P. Gallagher and D. W. Cruickshank. London: Tamesis Books, 1990. Pp. 167–86.
Glick, Claris. "William Poel: His Theories and Influence." *Shakespeare Quarterly* 15:1 (1964), pp. 15–25.
Goldwyn, Merrill Harvey. "Notes on the Biography of Thomas Churchyard." *Review of English Studies*, New Series, 17:65 (1966), pp. 1–15.
Gosse, Edmund. *The Life and Letters of John Donne*. 2 vols. London: 1899.
Green, John Richard. *A Short History of the English People* (1878). London: Macmillan, 1907.
Greenfeld, Liah. *Nationalism: Five Roads to Modernity*. Cambridge, Mass.: Harvard University Press, 1992.
Hadfield, Andrew. *Literature, Politics, and Public Opinion: Reformation to Renaissance*. Cambridge: Cambridge University Press, 1994.
Hale, J. R. "War and Opinion: War and Public Opinion in the Fifteenth and Sixteenth Centuries." *Past and Present* 22 (1962), pp. 18–35.
———. *War and Society in Renaissance Europe, 1450–1620* (1985). Montreal: McGill-Queens University Press, 1998.
Hammer, Paul E. J. "Myth-Making: Politics, Propaganda and the Capture of Cadiz in 1596." *Historical Journal* 40:3 (1997), pp. 621–42.
Harari, Yuval Noah. "Martial Illusions: War and Disillusionment in Twentieth-Century and Renaissance Memoirs." *Journal of Military History* 69:1 (2005), pp. 43–72.
———. *Renaissance Military Memoirs: War, History, and Identity, 1450–1600*. Suffolk: Boydell Press, 2004.
Harp, Richard, and Stanley Stewart, eds. *The Cambridge Companion to Ben Jonson*. Cambridge: Cambridge University Press, 2000.
Hart, Jonathan. "Las Casas in French and Other Languages." *Approaches to Teaching the Writing of Bartoleme de Las Casas*, ed. Santa Arias and Eyda M. Merediz. New York: Modern Language Association, 2008.
———. *Representing the New World: The English and French Uses of the Example of Spain*. New York: Palgrave, 2001.
Harvey, A. D. *A Muse of Fire: Literature, Art, and War*. London: Hambledon Press, 1998.
Helgerson, Richard. *Forms of Nationhood: The Elizabethan Writing of England*. Chicago: University of Chicago Press, 1992.
Herman, Peter C. "'Is This Winning?' Prince Henry's Death and the Problem of Chivalry in *The Two Noble Kinsmen*." *South Atlantic Review* 62:1 (1997), pp. 1–31.
Hillgarth, J. N. *The Mirror of Spain, 1500–1700: The Formation of a Myth*. Ann Arbor: University of Michigan Press, 2000.
Hodges, C. Walter. "Van Buchel's Swan." *Shakespeare Quarterly* 39:4 (1988), pp. 489–94.
Howard-Hill, T. H. "Buc and the Censorship of Sir John Van Olden Barnavelt in 1619." *Review of English Studies* 39:153 (1988), pp. 39–63.
Hughes, Felicity A. "Gascoigne's Poses." *Studies in English Literature* 37 (1997), pp. 1–19.

Jorgensen, Paul A. "A Formative Shakespearean Legacy: Elizabethan Views of God, Fortune, and War." *PMLA* 90:2 (1975), pp. 222–33.
———. "Moral Guidance and Religious Encouragement for the Elizabethan Soldier." *Huntington Library Quarterly* 13:2 (1950), pp. 241–59.
———. *Shakespeare's Military World*. Berkeley: University of California Press, 1956.
———. "Shakespeare's Use of War and Peace." *Huntington Library Quarterly* 16:4 (1953), pp. 319–52.
Kahn, Coppélia. "Remembering Shakespeare Imperially: The 1916 Tercentenary." *Shakespeare Quarterly* 52:4 (2001), pp. 456–78.
Kantorowicz, Ernst. *The King's Two Bodies: A Study in Medieval Political Theology*. Princeton: Princeton University Press, 1957.
Keen, Benjamin. "The Black Legend Revisited: Assumptions and Realities." *Hispanic American Historical Review* 49:4 (1969), pp. 703–19.
Keightley, Ron. "An Armada Veteran Celebrates the Death of Drake: Lope de Vega's *La Dragontea* (1598)." *England and the Spanish Armada*. Ed. Jeff Doyle and Bruce Moore. Canberra: Australian Defense Force Academy, 1990. Pp. 79–112.
Keller, Clare. *Scotland, England, and the Reformation, 1534–1561*. Oxford: Oxford University Press, 2004.
Kennedy, Dennis. *Looking at Shakespeare: A Visual History of the Twentieth-Century Performance*. 2nd ed. Cambridge: Cambridge University Press, 2001.
King, John N. *English Reformation Literature*. Princeton: Princeton University Press, 1982.
Kinney, Arthur F., ed. *Elizabethan Backgrounds: Historical Documents of the Age of Elizabeth I*. Hamden, Conn.: Archon Books, 1975.
Kohn, Hans. "The Genesis and Character of English Nationalism." *Journal of the History of Ideas* 1:1 (1940), pp. 69–94.
Kumar, Krishan. *The Making of English National Identity*. Cambridge: Cambridge University Press, 2003.
Levine, Lawrence W. *Highbrow/Lowbrow: The Emergence of a Cultural Hierarchy in America*. Cambridge, Mass.: Harvard University Press, 1990.
Lewalski, Barbara Kiefer. "Milton's *Comus* and the Politics of Masquing." *The Politics of the Stuart Court Masque*. Ed. David Bevington and Peter Holbrook. Cambridge: Cambridge University Press, 1998. Pp. 296–320.
———. *Protestant Poetics and the Seventeenth-Century Religious Lyric*. Princeton: Princeton University Press, 1979.
Lowndes, William Thomas. *The Bibliographer's Guide to English Literature*. 4 vols. London: 1864.
Lucas, Scott. "Diggon Davie and Davy Dicar: Edmund Spenser, Thomas Churchyard, and the Poetics of Public Protest." *Spenser Studies* 26 (2002), pp. 151–65.
MacCaffrey, Wallace T. *Elizabeth I: War and Politics, 1588–1603*. Princeton: Princeton University Press, 1992.
Mackenthun, Gesa. *Metaphors of Dispossession: American Beginnings*

    and the Translation of Empire, 1492–1637. Norman: University of Oklahoma Press, 1997.
Maltby, William S. *The Black Legend in England: The Development of Anti-Spanish Sentiment, 1558–1660.* Durham, N.C.: Duke University Press, 1971.
Manning, Roger B. *An Apprenticeship in Arms: Origins of the British Army, 1585–1702.* Oxford: Oxford University Press, 2006.
Marling, Karal Ann, and Robert Silberman. "The Statue Near the Wall: The Vietnam Veterans Memorial and the Art of Remembering." *Smithsonian Studies in American Art* 1:1 (1987), pp. 5–29.
Marshall, Rosalind K. *Mary of Guise.* London: Collins, 1977.
Martz, Louis L. *The Poetry of Meditation: A Study in English Religious Literature of the Seventeenth Century.* New Haven: Yale University Press, 1954.
Marx, Steven. "Shakespeare's Pacifism." *Renaissance Quarterly* 45:1 (1992), pp. 49–95.
Matheson, Mark. "Hamlet and 'A Matter Tender and Dangerous.'" *Shakespeare Quarterly* 46:4 (1995), pp. 383–97.
McCoy, Richard C. *The Rites of Knighthood: The Literature and Politics of Elizabethan Chivalry.* Berkeley: University of California Press, 1989.
McEachern, Claire. *The Poetics of English Nationhood, 1590–1612.* Cambridge: Cambridge University Press, 1996.
McKeown, Adam N. "Soldiers Seek an Elusive Escape in Shakespeare." *All Things Considered.* National Public Radio, 4 April 2006.
McNulty, Robert, ed. *Ludovico Ariosto's "Orlando Furioso": Translated into English Heroical Verse by Sir John Harington (1591).* Oxford: Clarendon Press, 1972.
Metzger, Mary Janell. "'Now by My Hood, a Gentle and No Jew': Jessica, *The Merchant of Venice*, and the Discourse of Early Modern English Identity." *PMLA* 113:1 (1998), pp. 52–63.
Miskimin, Harry A. *The Economy of Early Renaissance Europe: 1300–1460.* New York: Cambridge University Press, 1975.
Mitchell, Charles. "Benjamin West's 'Death of General Wolfe' and the Popular History Piece." *Journal of the Warburg and Courtauld Institutes* 7 (1944), pp. 20–33.
Moore, Edward M. "William Poel." *Shakespeare Quarterly* 23:1 (1972), pp. 21–36.
Morini, Massimiliano. *Tudor Translation in Theory and Practice.* Burlington, Vt.: Ashgate, 2006.
Mullin, Donald C. "An Observation on the Origins of the Elizabethan Theatre." *Educational Theatre Journal* 19:3 (1967), pp. 322–26.
Mulryne, J. R., and Margaret Shewring, eds. *War, Literature, and the Arts in Sixteenth-Century Europe.* New York: St. Martin's Press, 1989.
Murrin, Michael. *History and Warfare in Renaissance Epic.* Chicago: University of Chicago Press, 1994.
Musto, Ronald G. "Just Wars and Evil Empires: Erasmus and the Turks." *Renaissance Society and Culture: Essays in Honor of Eugene F. Rice,*

Jr. Ed. John Monfasani and Robert G. Musto. New York: Italica Press, 1991, pp. 197–216.
Nash, Joseph. *The Mansions of England in the Olden Time.* Ed. Charles Holme. London: 1906.
Nicolas, Harris. *Memoirs of the Life and Times of Sir Christopher Hatton.* London: 1847.
Nolan, John S. "The Militarization of the Elizabethan State." *Journal of Military History* 58 (1994), pp. 391–420.
———. "The Muster of 1588." *Albion* 23 (1991), pp. 387–407.
———. *Sir John Norreys and the Elizabethan Military World.* Exeter: University of Exeter Press, 1997.
Onega, Susana. "The Impact of the Spanish Armada on Elizabethan Literature." *England and the Spanish Armada.* Ed. Jeff Doyle and Bruce Moore. Canberra: Australian Defense Force Academy, 1990. Pp. 177–95.
Orgel, Stephen. "Idols of the Gallery: Becoming a Connoisseur in Renaissance England." *Early Modern Visual Culture.* Ed. Peter Erickson and Clark Hulse. Philadelphia: University of Pennsylvania Press, 2000. Pp. 251–83.
———. *The Jonsonian Masque.* New York: Columbia University Press, 1981.
Outhwaite, R. B. "The Trials of Foreign Borrowing: The English Crown and the Antwerp Money Market in the Mid-Sixteenth Century." *Economic History Review,* New Series, 19:2 (1966), pp. 289–305.
Papazian, Mary Arshagouni, ed. *John Donne and the Protestant Reformation.* Detroit: Wayne State University Press, 2003.
Parker, Geoffrey. *The Army of Flanders and the Spanish Road, 1567–1659.* Cambridge: Cambridge University Press, 1972.
———. *The Dutch Revolt.* Ithaca: Cornell University Press, 1977.
———. *The Military Revolution.* Cambridge: Cambridge University Press, 1988.
———. "Mutiny and Discontent in the Spanish Army of Flanders, 1572–1607." *Past and Present* 58 (1973), pp. 38–52.
Pearce, Brian. "Elizabethan Food Policy and the Armed Forces." *Economic History Review* 12 (1942), pp. 39–46.
Perry, Curtis. *The Making of Jacobean Culture: James I and the Renegotiation of Elizabethan Literary Practice.* Cambridge: Cambridge University Press, 1997.
Pierpont, Claudia Roth. "Onward and Upward with the Arts: The Player Kings." *New Yorker,* 19 November 2007, p. 70.
Plett, Heinrich F., and Peter Heath. "Aesthetic Constituents in the Courtly Culture of Renaissance England." *New Literary History* 14:3 (1983), pp. 597–621.
Pollard, A. F. *Factors in Modern History.* New York: G. P. Putnam's Sons, 1907.
Post, Jonathan F. S. *English Lyric Poetry: The Early Seventeenth Century.* New York: Routledge, 1999.

Prouty, Charles Tyler. *George Gascoigne: Elizabethan Soldier, Courtier, and Poet.* New York: Columbia University Press, 1942.

Pursell, Brennan C. "The End of the Spanish Match." *Historical Journal* 45 (2002), pp. 699–726.

Quinn, David Beers. *The Elizabethans and the Irish.* Ithaca: Cornell University Press, 1966.

Read, Conyers. "Queen Elizabeth's Seizure of the Duke of Alva's Pay-Ships." *Journal of Modern History* 5:4 (1933), pp. 443–64.

Rebhorn, Wayne. "The Crisis of Aristocracy in *Julius Caesar.*" *Renaissance Quarterly* 43:1 (1990), pp. 75–111.

Rich, E. E. "The Population of Elizabethan England." *Economic History Review* 2:3 (1950), pp. 247–65.

Roberts, Michael. "The Military Revolution, 1560–1660: An Inaugural Lecture Delivered before the Queen's University of Belfast" (1956). *The Military Revolution Debate: Readings on the Transformation of Early Modern Europe.* Ed. Clifford J. Rogers. Boulder, Colo.: Westview Press, 1995.

Rodriguez-Salgado, Mia J. *Armada: The Official Catalog of the National Maritime Museum Exhibition.* London and New York: Penguin, 1988.

Rogers, Clifford J., ed. *The Military Revolution Debate: Readings on the Transformation of Early Modern Europe.* Boulder, Colo.: Westview Press, 1995.

Rothschild, Herbert B., Jr. "The Conqueror Hero, the Besieged City, and the Development of an Elizabethan Protagonist." *South Central Review* 3:4 (1986), pp. 54–77.

Rowan, D. F. "Shore's Wife." *Studies in English Literature* 6:3 (1966), pp. 447–64.

Rowe, Nick. "'My Best Patron': William Cavendish and Jonson's Caroline Drama." *Seventeenth Century* 9:2 (1994), pp. 197–212.

Rugoff, Milton Allan. *Donne's Imagery: A Study in Literary Sources.* New York: Russell and Russell, 1962.

Sandberg, Brian. "Beyond Encounters: Religion, Ethnicity, and Violence in the Early Modern Atlantic World, 1492–1700." *Journal of World History* 17:1 (2006), pp. 1–25.

Schmidt, Benjamin. *Innocence Abroad: The Dutch Imagination and the New World, 1570–1670.* New York: Cambridge University Press, 2001.

Scott, Maria M., *Re-Presenting "Jane" Shore: Harlot and Heroine.* Burlington, Vt.: Ashgate, 2005.

Scott, Mary Augusta. "Elizabethan Translations from the Italian." *PMLA* 11:4 (1896), pp. 377–484.

Scott-Warren, Jason. *Sir John Harington and the Book as a Gift.* Oxford: Oxford University Press, 2001.

Scoufos, Alice Lyle. "Harvey: A Name-Change in *Henry IV.*" *English Literary History* 36:2 (1969), pp. 397–418.

Sellin, Paul R. "'Souldiers of one Army': John Donne and the Army of the States General as an International Protestant Crossroads." *John Donne and the Protestant Reformation.* Ed. Mary Arshagouni Papazian. Detroit: Wayne State University Press, 2003. Pp. 143–92.

Shaheen, N. "Shakespeare's Knowledge of Italian." *Shakespeare Survey* 47 (1994), pp. 161–69.

Shannon, Laurie. "Poetic Companies: Musters of Agency in George Gascoigne's 'Friendly Verse.'" *Journal of Lesbian and Gay Studies* 10:3 (2004), pp. 453–83.

Shapiro, James. *A Year in the Life of William Shakespeare.* New York: Harper Collins, 2005.

Shepard, Alan. "Endless Sacks: Soldiers' Desire in Tamburlaine." *Renaissance Quarterly* 46:4 (1993), pp. 734–53.

———. *Marlowe's Soldiers: Rhetorics of Masculinity in the Age of the Armada.* Burlington, Vt.: Ashgate, 2002.

Sichert, Margit. "Functionalizing Cultural Memory: Foundational British Literary History and the Construction of National Identity." *Modern Language Quarterly* 64:2 (2003), pp. 199–217.

Siegel, Peter N. "English Humanism and the New Tudor Aristocracy." *Journal of the History of Ideas* 13:4 (1952), pp. 450–68.

Simpson, Evelyn M. *A Study of the Prose Works of John Donne.* 2nd ed. Oxford: Clarendon Press, 1948.

Sims, James H. "*Orlando Furioso* in Milton: Heroic Flights and True Heroines." *Comparative Literature* 49:2 (1997), pp. 128–50.

Sinfield, Alan. *Faultlines: Cultural Materialism and the Politics of Dissident Reading.* Berkeley: University of California Press, 1992.

———. "Royal Shakespeare: Theatre and the Making of Ideology." *Political Shakespeare: Essays in Cultural Materialism.* Ed. Jonathan Dollimore and Alan Sinfield. 2nd ed. Manchester: Manchester University Press, 1994. Pp. 182–205.

Snyder, Susan. "Ourselves Alone: The Challenge to Single Combat in Shakespeare." *Studies in English Literature* 20 (1980), pp. 201–16.

Stage, John W. "'The Spoyle of Antwerpe' (1576)." *Modern Language Review* 6:1 (1911), pp. 88–92.

Stearns, Stephen. "Conscription and English Society in the 1620s." *Journal of British Studies* 11 (1972), pp. 1–23.

Steible, Mary. "Jane Shore and the Politics of Cursing." *Studies in English Literature* 43:1 (2003), pp. 1–17.

Stone, George Winchester, Jr. "Shakespeare in the Periodicals, 1700–1740." *Shakespeare Quarterly* 2:3 (1951), pp. 220–32.

Strong, Roy. *The Cult of Elizabeth: Elizabethan Portraiture and Pageantry.* London: Thames and Hudson, 1977.

———. "Inigo Jones and the Revival of Chivalry." *Appollo* 86 (August 1967), pp. 102–7.

Sutherland, N. M. "The Origins of the Thirty Years War and the Structure of European Politics." *English Historical Review* 107 (1992), pp. 587–625.

Taunton, Nina. *1590s Drama and Militarism: Portrayals of War in*

  Marlowe, Chapman, and Shakespeare's "Henry V." Burlington, Vt.: Ashgate, 2001.
Taylor, E. G. R. "Francis Drake and the Pacific: Two Fragments." *Pacific Historical Review* 1:3 (1932), pp. 360–69.
Taylor, Gary. *Reinventing Shakespeare: A Cultural History from the Restoration to the Present.* New York: Weidenfeld and Nicolson, 1989.
Trotter, Margaret. "Harington's Fountain." *Modern Language Notes* 58:8 (1943), pp. 614–16.
Wallerstein, Immanuel. *The Modern World-System Capitalist Agriculture and the Origins of the European World Economy in the Sixteenth Century.* New York: Academic Press, 1974.
Warner, Charles Dudley. *The People for Whom Shakespeare Wrote.* New York: Harper and Brothers, 1897.
Watkins, John. *Representing Elizabeth in Stuart England: Literature, History, Sovereignty.* Cambridge: Cambridge University Press, 2002.
Watteville, H. de. *The British Soldier: His Daily Life from Tudor to Modern Times.* London: Dent, 1954.
Watts, Thomas. "Authorship of the Fabricated 'Earliest English Newspaper' perpetrated by the Second Earl of Hardwicke." *Gentleman's Magazine*, New Series, 33 (May 1850), pp. 485–91.
Webb, Henry J. *Elizabethan Military Science: The Books and the Practice.* Madison: University of Wisconsin Press, 1965.
———. "English Military Surgery during the Age of Elizabeth." *Bulletin of the History of Medicine* 15 (1944), pp. 261–75.
Wernham, R. B. *After the Armada.* Oxford: Oxford University Press, 1984.
West, Michael. "Spenser's Art of War: Chivalric Allegory, Military Technology, and the Elizabethan Mock-Heroic Sensibility." *Renaissance Quarterly* 41:3 (1988), pp. 654–704.
Whitehead, Bertrand T. *Brags and Boasts: Propaganda in the Year of the Armada.* Dover, N.H.: Alan Sutton, 1994.
Williams, Abigail. *Poetry and the Creation of a Whig Literary Culture, 1681–1714.* New York: Oxford University Press, 2005.
Wilson, Charles. *Queen Elizabeth and the Revolt of the Netherlands.* Berkeley: University of California Press, 1970.
Wilson, Kathleen. "Citizenship, Empire, and Modernity in the English Provinces, c. 1720–1790." *Eighteenth-Century Studies* 29:1 (1996), pp. 69–96.
Worden, Blair. *The Sound of Virtue: Philip Sidney's Arcadia and Elizabethan Politics.* New Haven: Yale University Press, 1996.
Wright, Louis B. "Propaganda against James I's 'Appeasement' of Spain." *Huntington Library Quarterly* 6 (1943), pp. 149–72.
Yates, Frances. *Astrea: The Imperial Theme in the Sixteenth Century.* London: Routledge, 1975.
———. "Elizabethan Chivalry: The Romance of the Accession Day Tilts." *Journal of the Warburg and Courtauld Institutes* 20 (1957), pp. 4–25.

Index

Alarum for London (Lodge/
 Gascoigne), 18–19, 174–75n18
 as propaganda play, 89–91, 94–98,
  99–100, 101
 The Spoil of Antwerp as source for,
  83–84, 94, 99–100
Alarum to England (Rich), 85–86
Althusser, Louis, 10, 37
Alva, "Iron Duke" of (Fernando
 Alvarez de Toledo), 52–53, 92,
 175n18
Anderson, Benedict, 24
Andrews, Alexander, 21
Antwerp
 devastation of, 84–89
 See also *Alarum for London*; *Spoil
  of Antwerp, The*
Ariosto, Lodovico, 19, 126
 Harington's translation of, 126–31
Ascham, Roger, 161
Athenian Mercury, 23
Azores expedition (Islands Voyage),
 102, 114–15
 Donne's poems relating to, 115–16,
  118–21

Bacon, Francis, 147
Baldo, Jonathan, 68
Barton, Anne, 147
Benzoni, Girolamo, 93
Black Legend, 18, 92–94
Blount, Charles. *See* Mountjoy, Lord
Branagh, Kenneth, 162
Bryce, Lord, 28
Buckingham, Duke of (George
 Villiers), 154

Burghley, Lord (William Cecil), 18,
 21, 73, 74, 136
 and the Treaty of Edinburgh, 67,
  71–72

Cadiz expedition, 35, 51, 58, 168n5
 Donne as soldier in, 102, 113,
  116–17
 Raleigh's account of, 117–18, 120
Cahill, Patricia A., 9
"Calm, The" (Donne), 19, 115, 121–24
Camden, William, 67, 133, 147
Camel, Thomas, 63
Case Is Altered, The (Jonson), 152–53
Castiglione, Baldassare, 44, 168n8
Catholicism, 146
Cavendish, William, 153, 158–59
Cecil, Robert, 138
Cecil, William. *See* Burghley, Lord
Chalmers, George, 21
Chapman, George, 17, 126, 145–46
Charles I, King, 153–54
Charles V, Holy Roman Emperor, 65
chivalry, 44, 180n31
Choice of Emblems, A (Whitney),
 108–10
Churchill, John. *See* Marlborough,
 Duke of
Churchyard, Thomas, 11, 16–17, 139
 contemporary perception of, 63–64
 "Davy Dycar's Dream," 63–64
 poetry of as memorial to soldiers,
  67–68, 69–72, 74
 "The Praises of Our Soldiers," 77
 "Shore's Wife," 18, 78–81,
  173–74n45

195

Churchyard, Thomas *cont.*
  "The Siege of Leith," 18, 66–68, 69–72, 74, 77
  as soldier, 17–18, 52, 53, 54, 57, 58, 59, 65–68
  "A Tragical Discourse of the Unhappy Man's Life," 76–77
  on treatment of discharged soldiers, 74–77
  "The Unhappy Man's Dear Adieu," 74–75
  war as viewed by, 64–65
Churchyard's Chips (Churchyard), 65, 77
Churchyard's Choice (Churchyard), 63, 64
Clegg, Cyndia Susan, 31
Clifford, George, 21
Clifford, Sir Conyers, 134
Clowes, William, 56
Cotton, Robert, 147

Davies, John, 133, 148, 169n29
"Davy Dycar's Dream" (Churchyard), 63–64, 172n7
Dekker, Thomas, 146
Deloney, Thomas, 79
Desmond, Earl of, 133
De Somogyi, Nick, 9
Devereux, Robert. *See* Essex, Earl of
de Witt, Johannes, 27–28, 29
Digges, Thomas, 15, 44
Discourse Touching a War with Spain (Raleigh), 90
Djibouti, 1, 12
Dollimore, Jonathan, 9
Donne, John, 11, 16–17, 35
  "The Calm," 19, 115, 121–24
  Elegy 14, 112, 114
  Elegy 20, 112–14
  Holy Sonnet 14, 19, 102
  religious evocations of, 106–8, 119–20
  as soldier, 102, 113, 114–17, 175–76n3
  "The Storm," 19, 115–16, 118–21
  war as emblem for, 19, 104–8, 115–24
  war as viewed by, 102–4
  war imagery in writings of, 102, 105, 106
Drake, Francis, 21, 28, 30, 102
Drayton, Michael, 17, 149
Drummond, William, 144–45, 161
Drury, William, 43
"Dulce Bellum Inexpertis" (Gascoigne), 86, 98–99, 100
Dutch Revolt, 91, 93

early modern literature
  war as aspect of, 6–7
  See also Elizabethan literature
Ecole Lemonier, 1–3
Edinburgh, Treaty of, 67, 70, 71–72
Edward II (Marlowe), 38–40
Edward IV, King, 78
Edward VI, King, 63
Einstein, Lewis, 8
Elegy 14, "A Tale of a Citizen and His Wife" (Donne), 112, 114
Elegy 20, "Love's War" (Donne), 112–14
Elizabeth I, Queen
  and John Harington, 139–40
  idolatry of following her death, 145–48
  as military leader, 73
  military victories of, 7–8
  as recollected by Jonson, 148–50
Elizabethan England
  anti-Spanish propaganda in, 84, 92–94, 99–100
  attitudes toward war in, 40, 41–42, 46–48, 144
  censorship in, 30–31, 64, 84
  mythology of, 20, 148–50
  nationalism of, 127
  relationship with Spain, 91–92
  stage conventions of, 28
Elizabethan literature
  Mars as symbol in, 34
  Mercury as symbol in, 32–34
  soldiers' credibility in, 35
  war as depicted in, 6–12, 13–14, 15–20, 30–31, 38–40
  See also names of individual authors and works
Elizabethan Stage Society, 27

England. *See* Elizabethan England
English Mercurie, The
　credibility of, 35
　as hoax, 14, 21–24, 25
　as supplement to documentary record, 29–30, 42
English Mercuries
　Shakespeare's use of term, 14, 23, 31–32, 34, 35, 36, 41–42
English Renaissance. *See* Elizabethan England; Elizabethan literature
Erasmus, 99, 125
Essex, Earl of (Robert Devereux), 30, 43–44, 45, 102, 120
　failures of in Irish campaign, 136–37, 139, 140
　as leader of Irish campaign, 19, 132–33, 135–36
　relationship with Harington, 135–36
　See also Cadiz expedition
Every Man Out of His Humor (Jonson), 148–50, 151, 152

Faerie Queene, The (Spenser), 167n26
"Farewell to His Muse" (Harington), 142–43
Faultes Faults (Rich), 86
Ferdinand II, Holy Roman Emperor, 154
Fitter, Chris, 167n25
Florio, John, 34
forlorn hope, 58
Foucault, Michel, 22
Frederick V, Elector Palatine, 154
Frobisher, Martin, 21
Fussell, Paul, 9, 10, 13

Gaedertz, Karl Theodore, 28
Gainsford, Thomas, 51, 53
Gale, Thomas, 56
Gascoigne, George, 11, 16–17, 18–19, 32, 33, 137
　"*Dulce Bellum Inexpertis*," 86, 98–99, 100
　as soldier, 60, 83
　soldier stereotypes described by, 72–73

　as source for *Alarum for London*, 83–84, 94, 99–100
　The Spoil of Antwerp, 18, 84–89, 94
　"The Steel Glass," 72–73, 96, 172n7
　war as viewed by, 100–101
　See also Alarum for London
gentleman commanders, 44–45
Golding, Arthur, 126
Gollancz, Israel, 28, 38
Green, John Richard, 7, 8
Greenfeld, Liah, 8
Gruffydd, Elis, 53–54, 57, 59, 60, 170n48
Gunpowder Plot, 146, 147

Hadfield, Andrew, 8
Hakluyt, Richard, 93
Hale, J. R., 89
Hall, Joseph, 23
Hamlet (Shakespeare), 2
Harari, Yuval Noah, 176n2
Hardwicke, second Earl of (Philip Yorke), 21, 23, 162
Harington, John, 11, 16–17
　and the Earl of Essex, 135–36
　education of, 132
　Metamorphosis of Ajax, 19, 126, 132
　Orlando Furioso in English Heroical Verse, 19, 126–31
　and return to England following war with Ireland, 19–20, 126, 136–43
　as soldier in Ireland, 19, 59, 125–26, 133–35
　war as viewed by, 125, 127–31
Harvey, A. D., 11
Hastings, Lord, 78
Hatton, Sir Christopher, 82
Hawkins, John, 21, 92
Helgerson, Richard, 8
Henry, Prince, 143, 147–48, 149
　Jonson's depiction of, 150–51
Henry IV, Part 1 (Shakespeare), 39
Henry IV, Part 2 (Shakespeare), 35, 39

Henry V (Shakespeare), 7, 30, 79–80
  chorus in, 36–38
  "English Mercuries" referred to in, 14, 23–24, 34, 35, 36, 41–42
  and memories of war, 68
  as representation of war, 2, 162–63
Henry VI, Part 2 (Shakespeare), 167n25
Henry VIII, King, 17–18
Heroical Devices (Paradin), 110, 111
Hertford, Earl of (Edward Seymour), 63
Heywood, Thomas, 145–46
History of Richard III (More), 78
Hole, William, 149
Holy Sonnet 14, "Batter my heart" (Donne), 19, 102
Howard, Charles, 21
Howard, Henry. *See* Surrey, Earl of
"Hymn to God the Father" (Donne), 108

ideology, 10
Iliad (Homer), 126
Ireland, expedition to, 126, 152
  Essex as leader of, 131, 132–33
  Harington as soldier in, 125–26, 133–35
Ireland, William-Henry, 25
Islands Voyage. *See* Azores expedition

James VI of Scotland/James I of England, 68, 136, 142, 154
  unpopularity of, 146, 147
Jauregui, Juan, 93
John of Austria, Don, 68–69
Jones, Inigo, 153
Jonson, Ben, 16–17, 20, 32
  The Case Is Altered, 152–53
  on Elizabeth, 148–50, 152
  Epigrams, 151
  "An Epistle to a Friend to Persuade Him to the Wars," 156–57
  Every Man Out of His Humor, 148–50, 151, 152
  The Magnetic Lady, 20, 157–58
  The New Inn, 20, 157, 158–61
  The Poetaster, 32, 151–52
  Prince Henry's Barriers, 150–51
  as soldier, 17, 144–45
  "A Speech according to Horace," 155–56
  war as viewed by, 148–61
Jorgensen, Paul A., 6, 90, 95
Juderías, Julián, 92
Julius Caesar (Shakespeare), 10

Keats, John, 126
King, Tom, 25
Knox, John, 67
Knyvett, Henry, 50–51, 60, 61, 169n28
Kohn, Hans, 127
Kumar, Krishan, 8

Las Casas, Bartolome de, 92–94
leaders, responsibility of, 79–80
Leicester, Earl of, 31, 34
Leith campaign, 66–67. *See also* "Siege of Leith, The"
Lepanto, battle of, 68–69
Lepanto, The (James VI of Scotland), 68–69
literary criticism
  and author's experience, 3–4
  and military history, 6–7
Lodge, Thomas, 83. *See also Alarum for London*
Lope de Vega, 30
Low Countries, wars in, 167n26
  Jonson as soldier in, 144–45
  See also Antwerp

Machiavelli, Niccolò, 44, 168n8
Magnetic Lady, The (Jonson), 20, 157–58
Mansions of England in the Olden Time, The (Nash), 25, 26, 27
Marie de Guise, 66–67
Marlborough, Duke of (John Churchill), 24
Marlowe, Christopher, 10, 17, 30, 38–40
Mars
  in Elizabethan literature, 32
  See also Mercury
Marshall, William, 103
Martz, Louis L., 105

Marx, Steven, 7, 8, 165n8
Mary, Queen of Scots, 67, 70
Mary Tudor, 91
Massacre at Paris (Marlowe), 30
Matheson, Mark, 30
McEachern, Claire, 8
Mercure François, 23
mercurist, 17, 166n28
Mercury
   and role of soldiers as messengers, 34–36
   symbolism of in Shakespeare's time, 32–34
   as term used for news pamphlets, 23, 31, 35
   See also *English Mercurie, The*; English Mercuries
Meres, Francis, 64
Metamorphoses (Ovid), 126
Metamorphosis of Ajax (Harington), 19, 126, 132
Miggrode, Jacques de, 93
military camps, conditions in, 53–57
military strategy and organization, 169n17
   Jonson's criticism of, 151–52
   in the sixteenth century, 43–44, 59–60
militia, 49
Milton, John, 127
More, Thomas, 78
Mote, Humphrey, 94
Mountjoy, Lord (Charles Blount), 53, 136, 141
Much Ado about Nothing (Shakespeare), 127
Mundus alter et idem, 23
Murrin, Michael, 6, 11

Nash, Joseph, 25–27, 35
Nash, Thomas, 64
Naunton, Robert, 32, 34
Neoplatonism, 16
New Inn, The (Jonson), 20, 157, 158–61
Norris, Rafe, 86
North, Thomas, 126

O'Donnell, Hugh, 134, 136
old historicism, 6
Oliver, Isaac, 150
Olivier, Laurence, 162
O'Neill, Hugh, 133, 136–37, 139–40
O'Neill rebellion, 53, 58
"On First Looking into Chapman's Homer" (Keats), 126
Operation Enduring Freedom, 12
Operation Iraqi Freedom, 12
Orlando Furioso (Ariosto), 19
   Harington's translation of, 126–31
Orlando Furioso in English Heroical Verse (Ariosto/Harington), 126–31
Osborne, Francis, 73–74

pacifism, 7, 165n8
Paradin, Claude, 110, 111
peace
   Donne's view of, 106–7, 108–14
   moral ambiguity associated with, 108–14, 124
Philip II, 91, 92–93
Plantin, Christopher, 93
Plato, 3
Plutarch, 126
Poel, William, 27, 28
Poetaster, The (Jonson), 32, 151–52
poetry
   Sidney's theory of, 16
   See also soldier poets
Polemon, John, 69
Pollard, A. F., 8
Pope, Alexander, 24, 162
Portman, Sir Hugh, 136
Praise of Private Life, The (Harington), 137–38
"Praises of Our Soldiers" (Churchyard), 77
Prince Henry's Barriers (Jonson), 150–51
print-capitalism, 24
Protestantism, 93, 100, 146

Raleigh, Walter, 17, 32, 33, 90
   at Cadiz, 117–18, 120

Reagan, Ronald, 147
Renaissance
    pacifism in, 7
    See also Elizabethan England; Elizabethan literature
Rich, Barnabe, 11, 16–17
    Alarum to England, 85–86
    Faultes Faults, 86
    Mercury in works of, 32–34
Richard III, King, 78, 173n45
Right Excellent and Pleasant Dialogue Between Mercury and an English Soldier (Rich), 32–34
Roberts, Henry, 30

Sad Shepherd, The, 161
Scipio, 137–38
Scott, Maria M., 173n44
seasonal campaigning, 54
Seymour, Edward. *See* Hertford, Earl of
Shakespeare, William, 127, 167n25
    idolatry of in the eighteenth century, 24–25
    military experience of, 2–5
    as taught in a war zone, 12–14
    See also *Henry IV, Part 2*; *Henry V*
Shapiro, James, 5
Shepard, Alan, 9, 10
Shepheardes Calender, The (Spenser), 172n7
Shore, Jane (Mistress Shore), 78–81, 173n44, 173–74n45
"Shore's Wife" (Churchyard), 18, 78–81
Sidney, Henry, 65
Sidney, Philip, 15, 16, 17, 30, 31, 32
    war experience of, 45
Sidney, Robert, 138
"Siege of Leith, The" (Churchyard), 18, 66–68, 69–72, 74, 77
Sinfield, Alan, 10
soldier poets
    deployment experiences of, 45–46, 59, 60, 65–68, 83, 102, 113, 114–17, 125–26, 133–35, 144–45
    voices of, 161–63
    See also Churchyard, Thomas; Donne, John; Gascoigne, George; Harington, John; Jonson, Ben
soldiers, Elizabethan
    in combat, 57–60, 66–67
    and dangers of deployment, 48, 52–56, 134–36
    deployment experience of, 42, 44–46, 48–49, 61–62
    discipline of, 52
    expeditionary camps of, 53–57
    hunger as experienced by, 52–53, 170n48
    medical care for, 56
    memoirs by, 15–16
    mustering of, 48–49, 50–51, 75
    pride of, 62
    as purveyors of news, 34–36
    remuneration of, 60–61, 74
    and the state, 73–74, 77–81, 82, 96–97
    stereotypes of, 72–73, 96
    supplies for, 51–52
    as veterans, 74–77, 126
    See also war
soldiers, modern
    drafting of, 50
    reserve activation of, 49–50
Spain
    England's relationship with, 91–92
    English propaganda directed at, 84, 92–94, 99–100
    See also *Spoil of Antwerp, The*
Spanish Armada, English victory over, 7–8, 9, 47, 146
Spanish Fury, 84, 90, 94
"Speech according to Horace, A" (Jonson), 155–56
Speed, John, 147
Spenser, Edmund, 17, 30, 64, 167n26, 172n7
Spoil of Antwerp, The (Gascoigne), 18
    as commentary on war, 84–89
    divine judgment in, 84–85, 88–89
    as source for *Alarum for London*, 83–84, 94
    See also *Alarum for London*

state, the
    and the treatment of soldiers,
        73–74, 77–81, 82, 96–97,
        136–43
Steele, Richard, 24, 162
"Steel Glass, The" (Gascoigne),
    72–73, 96
Steible, Mary, 173–74n45
"Storm, The" (Donne), 19, 115–16,
    118–21
Stow, John, 30
Stratioticos (Digges), 15
Styward, Thomas, 44, 48, 52, 55, 58,
    59, 169n28, 171n76
Surrey, Earl of (Henry Howard),
    17–18, 65
Swan theater, 27–28, 29

Tatler, The, 24
Taunton, Nina, 9
Thatcher, Margaret, 162
Thirty Years' War, 153–54
Throckmorton, Arthur, 120
Throckmorton, Job, 31
"Tragical Discourse of the Unhappy
    Man's Life, A" (Churchyard),
    76–77
Tyrone, Earl of. See O'Neill, Hugh

Under-wood (Jonson), 155
"Unhappy Man's Dear Adieu, The"
    (Churchyard), 74–75
Upton, John, 167n26

van Buchel, Arend, 27
Vere, Francis, 120, 144
veterans, treatment of, 176n2
    Churchyard's descriptions of,
        74–77
    Harington's descriptions of,
        19–20, 126, 136–43
    Vietnam Veterans Memorial, 67,
        68, 69
Villiers, George. See Buckingham,
    Duke of

Waller, Edmund, 11
Walloons. See *Spoil of Antwerp, The*
Walsingham, Francis, 21
war
    as adventure, 62
    as allegory, 127–31
    as backdrop for teaching
        Shakespeare, 12–14
    Churchyard's view of, 64–65
    death as inevitable in, 97–98, 99
    Donne's view of, 102–4
    Elizabethan attitudes toward, 40,
        41–42, 46–48, 144, 154–55
    as emblem for Donne, 104–8,
        115–24
    emblems of, 108–14
    Gascoigne's view of, 100–101
    Harington's view of, 125, 127–31
    Jonson's view of, 148–61
    memorials of as creator and
        preserver of narrative, 66–69
    as represented in Elizabethan
        literature, 6–12, 13–14, 15–20,
        38–40
    as spiritual struggle, 115–24
    See also soldiers, Elizabethan
Warner, Charles Dudley, 21
Warton, Joseph, 25
Watkins, John, 147
weaponry, 43, 169n29
Webb, Henry J., 6
Whetstone, George, 31, 32
Whitney, Geoffrey, 108–10
Whore of Babylon, The (Dekker), 146
William of Orange, 66, 83, 86, 91, 92
Williams, Abigail, 24
Windet, John, 90, 94
Wingfield, Anthony, 47, 48, 50, 52, 57,
    60, 62
Wingfield, Sir John, 121
Wolfe, John, 31
women, Elizabethan, 78–79
World War I, reporting of, 9–10

Yorke, Philip. See Hardwicke, second
    Earl of

www.ingramcontent.com/pod-product-compliance
Lightning Source LLC
Chambersburg PA
CBHW030111010526
44116CB00005B/197